Split Personalities
Arklow 1885-1892

By

Jim Rees

Dee-Jay Publications

First published in 2012 by
DEE-JAY PUBLICATIONS
3 Meadows Lane,
Arklow,
Co. Wicklow,
Ireland.
www.dee-jay.ie

Typeset by DEE-JAY PUBLICATIONS

Printed by Naas Printing Ltd.
Main Street, Naas, Co. Kildare.
Tel: 8972092
Email: naasprinting@gmail.com

ISBN: 978-0-9519239-6-2 (hardback)
      978-0-9519239-7-9 (paperback)

CONTENTS

ACKNOWLEDGEMEMNTS

This book has taken far longer than I ever imagined. As always, I must thank the staffs of Wicklow County Library, both at Ballywaltrim (especially Robert Butler and Cíara O'Brien) and all in the Arklow branch library without whom no local history is possible. The staffs of the National Library of Ireland, the National Archives (especially Brian Donnelly), Margaret White Mulligan of Irish Midlands Ancestry, the Tipperary Family History Office, Rathdowney branch library (Laois), Edward Sterling and Peter Queally of Rockwell College, Blackrock College, Catríona Mulcahy of UCC, Paul Raven of the Royal Navy Museum Library, Robert Mills of the Royal College of Physicians of Ireland, Steven Kerr of the Royal College of Physicians Edinburgh, the Registry of Deeds and the Valuation Office. I must especially thank Noelle Dowling of the Dublin Diocesan Archive and Catherine Wright of County Wicklow Archives. Keith Troy of New South Wales was also unstinting in supplying information about his family after they left Arklow.

Others who deserve mention are Pat Power, whose encyclopaedic knowledge of the county is unrivalled; Eva Ó Cathaoir; Stan O'Reilly; Tomás Halpin; Billy Lee, Denis O'Rourke and John and Stephanie O'Toole. This is not a complete list, far from it. There are just too many who have helped me in the last nine years to mention. You know who you are and I thank you all.

Those of us who knew Mae Greene will understand why I regard this book as hers. She loved every aspect of Arklow's history and this story particularly was one that could raise her hackles. I hope that I have gone some way to easing her ire when the Dunphy-Molony affair is mentioned.

Finally, I must thank my wife Dorothy, without whom I might never have touched a keyboard – so blame her.

For Mae Greene

INTRODUCTION

Two decades ago the outline of the story which follows was brought to my attention by Mae Greene. It was cut away to its barest details of a mutual antagonism between two leading men in the small town of Arklow in the 1880s. Over the next few years Mae would intermittently ask: 'Have you looked into that yet?' Each time I would have to admit that I hadn't, although it was kicking about the recesses of my mind as something I should do. Finally, after about six or seven years and several embarrassing admissions of not having 'started yet', I made my first tentative explorations into the story which follows. It was to take far longer than expected, as these things usually do, as it was soon obvious that many strands had to be investigated and pulled together in the hope (probably forlorn) that some semblance of Arklow at that time might be recreated.

What would bring a young Tipperary-born doctor, with a career taking off in London, to a backwater like Arklow? This was a town in the south-east corner of County Wicklow with a population of just 4,777. It was poor, fishing being its primary economic source, and it was riven with social, political and religious division. Perhaps he simply wanted to return to Ireland. He was a member of the National League, his uncle was parish priest in Barndarrig, the neighbouring parish to the north of Arklow, he had a commitment to ministering to the poor, and it would seem that because of the control of the Arklow parish priest, Fr James Dunphy, he was almost certain of getting the job. Given all this, why did his relationship with Dunphy fall apart so suddenly and irrevocably? What drove the two men to mutual animosity?

In following this story I would have to use a variety of sources such as original letters in the collections of the National Library of Ireland, the Dublin Diocesan Archives, and the National Archives of Ireland, diaries, contemporary newspapers, government reports, census returns, Rathdrum Board of

Guardian records, trade directories, folklore, epitaphs on head-stones, baptismal and marriage records, and college registers. Secondary sources such as books by leading historians dealing with home rule, Land League, National League, the emergence of nationalist representation in the network of poor law unions, biographies of Charles Stewart Parnell, Michael Davitt, as well as local histories have all contributed to the compilation of the story. They, and other sources, are all listed in the appropriate places in footnotes and bibliography.

I can only hope that I have answered the questions put to me by Mae all those years ago. Unfortunately, I will never know, as I took too long in completing the task.

Jim Rees
Arklow,
September 2012

PROLOGUE

At three o'clock on the morning of Tuesday, 26 March 1889, several members of the R.I.C. in the barracks in Wicklow town were roused from their beds by their senior officer and told to dress in plain clothes. Eleven constables and four drivers, under the command of district inspector Shaw from Bray, travelled in four horse-drawn police cars towards Arklow. Their route was a roundabout one, taking in Rathnew and Redcross; at each place more constables joined the party. The route became even more indirect when, instead of travelling straight to Arklow via Barniskey or the Dublin road, they passed through Avoca, Woodenbridge, Thomastown and Ballyduff to enter Arklow from the west, on the Coolgreaney road near the cemetery. Their destination was Lamberton Cottage, a house about two hundred yards nearer the town - the home of the local Catholic curate, Fr Laurence Farrelly.

Farrelly had been expecting their arrival for some time and had taken several measures to make their task an awkward one. Head constable Martin knocked on the door and demanded admittance. The voice which responded was that of Farrelly's servant, Mary Merna, who asked what he wanted. When Martin replied that he had a warrant for Farrelly's arrest she asked him to read it to her through the door. This he did, but still she refused to admit him. While Martin urged her to co-operate, some of his constables made their way to the rear of the house and forced their way in through a broken window and within minutes had the front door opened. A search of the small house was made, but it was immediately obvious that Farrelly had gone into hiding.

It was at this point that the parish priest, Fr Dunphy, came by, saw what was happening and quickly returned to the town centre. Within minutes the chapel bell could be heard and an estimated crowd of 2,000 people assembled outside Fr Farrelly's house. They surrounded the police, shouting and hooting. Stone-throwing followed and several of the constables were injured in the first few volleys. Still the stones flew and the injuries grew more numerous and more serious. The policemen were armed, but their officer refused to issue the command to produce their weapons. Some of the crowd managed to curb the stone-throwers long enough to allow the police to flee towards the safety of the barracks at Parade Ground, by which time all had received injuries to a greater or lesser degree.

News of the debacle was telegraphed to other R.I.C. centres and 150 reinforcements were despatched to Arklow by train. These received the same stone-throwing welcome as the earlier arrivals and also made haste towards the protection of the barracks, although in the scuffles did manage to arrest two women. The large crowd remained outside the barracks all day, their shouting and threatening behaviour complemented by the continuous ringing of the chapel bell directly across the road. At one point, the large force of armed R.I.C. officers sent a servant girl from the barracks to the shop for refreshments. A group of men in the crowd outside called her names and threatened her with physical violence. The situation calmed as the day progressed and by three o'clock in the afternoon it was deemed safe for fifty police officers who had travelled from Wexford to return there. They were again stoned as they made their way from the barracks to the railway station. They drew their batons and a street battle took place with severe injuries on both sides. That, however, was the end of the day's events and all the drafted-in police returned to their home bases. They would have to return another day to complete their task – the arrest of Fr Laurence Farrelly.

Just how could such things have taken place in this small town. Why were the police so determined to take a Roman Catholic priest into custody? Why were the parishioners so well primed that the sound of the church bell could rally 2,000 of them to Farrelly's house at short notice? How implicit was the parish priest, Fr James Dunphy? Who were Dunphy, Farrelly, and the other main players in Arklow at that time of great social and political unrest?

CHAPTER 1:
Fr James Dunphy, PP

By the time of the opening of this story in early 1885, Fr James Dunphy had been in Arklow for almost thirty years. Over those three decades he had developed a remarkable empathy with the people of the town, and seemed to have a particular affinity with the fishermen and their families. He had learned their ways, knew their peculiarities which had evolved from their relationship with the sea, and understood the strange manner in which their year was structured, so different to the agricultural cycle of seasons into which he had been born and with which he had grown up.[1]

Although there is some confusion as to exactly where he was born, as will be seen shortly, it can be stated that his native place lay about four miles west of the landlocked village of Durrow and roughly three miles east of Rathdowney in what was then Queen's County, now County Laois – about as far from the sea as it is possible to be in Ireland. The confusion surrounding the precise location is the fact that his brother John was born in 1825 in the townland of Ballyboodin,[2] his brothers William (1832) and Philip (1834) were born in the nearby townland of Cannonswood, both places are in the Catholic parish of Durrow, and brothers Peter (1836) and Patt (1838) were born in the townland of Kilnaseer, adjoining Cannonswood but in the Catholic parish of Aghaboe.[3] Unfortunately no record of James' baptism has been found, but according to his headstone in Arklow cemetery he was born in 1828. As his parents, William and Anne (née Bowe or Bowes), were married in the parish of Durrow (townland unspecified) on 1 September 1822 and their first recorded child, John, was baptised in 1825 and the second, William, was baptised in 1832 it is highly probable that James' baptism simply was not recorded, 'not an uncommon occurrence of the period'.[4] In fact two other siblings, an unnamed sister who became a nun in the Poor

Clare order[5] and Joseph who was born in 1829,[6] also seem to have slipped the registrar's memory.

The Dunphy family

William Dunphy m. Anne Bowe(s)							
m. 1 Sept 1822							
Daughter	John	James	Joseph	William	Philip	Peter	Patt
1823/4	1825	1828	1829	1832	1834	1836	1838

The unnamed daughter joined the Order of the Poor Clares. Her conjectured position here as first-born is based on the dates of birth of her siblings. She could have been the second child.
John became parish priest of Kilmanagh, Co. Kilkenny
James became parish priest of Arklow
Joseph became parish priest of Mooncoin, Co. Kilkenny
William became parish priest of Naul, Co. Dublin and Barndarrig, Co. Wicklow.

This being the case, it can be taken that James was born in either Ballyboodin or Cannonswood, depending on when the family changed address. It is of little significance for two reasons; one, even if he were born in Ballyboodin, he would have been an infant at the time of the move, and two, there is less than a mile separating the two townlands, so it was the same area with the same hinterland, the same type of farming, the same weather, the same neighbours. It is also possible that in those pre-ordnance survey days no actual relocation took place. Townland boundaries were fluid generalities before surveyors and attendant antiquarians committed them to paper with obsessive exactness in the late 1830s. A farm might be said to be in one townland one year and a neighbouring one the next. According to the Tithe Applotment Books, compiled for the area in 1830, a William and a James Dunphy jointly held eighty-eight acres at an annual rent of £10-19-8³/₄ in the townland of Canningswood [sic]. There was also a William Dunphy who held nineteen acres in Newtown, adjoining Ballyboodin, and a William Dunphy holding fifty-four acres with Laurence Broderick in nearby Cullahill.[7] Whether these were all different William Dunphys or the same person is difficult to determine. What can be said is that James Dunphy was born to tenant farmer William and his wife Anne in 1828 in the very rural western part of the parish of Durrow, with the village of Rathdowney two or three miles to the west and the village of Durrow four or five miles to the east.

As centres of population, neither had much to offer. Rathdowney boasted 211 houses which gave shelter to 1,214 inhabitants. These dwellings and other buildings were indifferently built, and the village's ill-paved streets had a neglected look, with few 'indications of prosperity'.[8] At the heart of the village was the Protestant parish church, erected in 1815 in the later English style of architecture with a well proportioned spire. There was also the Catholic parish church, 'a plain sparse building', and two outlying chapels, one at Grogan and the other at Killismista. The local congregation of Wesley Methodists also had a place of worship. The area's economic base was the countryside of excellent agricultural land virtually unmarked by scrub or bog. Durrow was a little better. It was marginally larger with 1,298 inhabitants in 236 houses. Many of these buildings were slated. It had a market house which was opened for business on Fridays, and petty sessions were held on alternate Fridays. The Protestant church stood at one side of the square and was modern and large with a tower. The Catholic chapel, too, was worthy of note, 'a remarkably fine structure, very spacious, interior magnificently fitted up'.[9]

Durrow had an air of past importance about it. There had been an abbey which fell to the general dissolution of the monasteries in the sixteenth century. Although little is known of it, there is a surviving artefact that has ensured its place in history. *The Book of Durrow* is a seventh century illuminated manuscript containing the four gospels, believed to be the oldest in Ireland and Britain. During the seventeenth century 'the book was dipped into a trough for sick cattle to drink out of, as it was believed to possess curative powers'.[10] The Dunphys probably knew of the book's existence and of the former importance of the long-gone abbey. An obituary of William junior, born 1832, stated that 'his youthful mind was impressed with the traditions of the ancient monastery and at an early age he realised he had a vocation for the priesthood.'[11] As a committed Catholic, William senior would have taken pride in the manuscript's historical and religious importance. As a farmer, perhaps he would also have appreciated its beneficial powers for under-the-weather cattle.

It is likely that when it came to observing their religious duties William and Anne would have opted to attend the Catholic church nearest to them, the small, functional chapel in Ballynevin. There can be no doubt of their commitment to their Catholicism, because their first five children would later take holy orders. The unnamed sister, who might have been the first- or second-born child, that is born either before or after John (the gap in dates would allow either possibility) became a nun,[12] John became parish priest of Kilmanagh, Co Kilkenny,[13] James parish priest of Arklow, Joseph parish priest of Mooncoin,

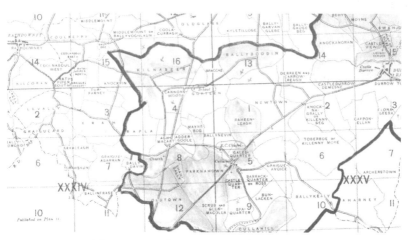

Durrow-Rathdowney area where James Dunphy was born and grew up.

Co Kilkenny,[14] and William parish priest of Naul, Co Dublin and other parishes in the Dublin diocese.[15] This remarkable dedication suggests that not only were William and Anne devout but also that there were adequate finances available to enable them to have their children suitably educated. It is possible that the beginnings of that education took place in the school in the townland of Gorteen, between Cannonswood and Ballyboodin, before going on to more ambitious establishments.

In 1829, the year after James' birth, the Catholic Emancipation Act was passed,[16] bringing an end to an era in which Catholics were second class citizens. With the last of the legislative restrictions abolished, the 1830s were a time of great expectations. The role of the church in education and politics could be voiced and planned with new confidence, but there were a number of vexed questions still to be resolved. The greatest of these was tithes, a tax everyone, including Catholics, had to contribute for the upkeep of the Protestant church. This amounted to nominally one-tenth of earnings, although that sum was seldom achieved in Ireland. Originally tithes were paid in kind, that is livestock or produce, but cash payments were substituted in the seventeenth and eighteenth centuries.[17] Throughout Ireland, the growing dissatisfaction with tithes, and other issues which were deemed socially unjust and politically abhorrent, led to an increase in agrarian tension and outbreaks of sectarian violence. By the 1820s self-described anti-tithe and tenant protection organisations such as Ribbonmen and Whiteboys had been active for some time. In Dunphy's own Queen's County in 1822, the parish priest of Maryborough (now Portlaoise) extracted promises from twenty-two of his parishioners to give up ribbonism. In 1827, just one year before James' birth, James Delany, parish priest of Ballynakill in the same county, 'got rid of two travelling masons who were said to be administering oaths to inhabitants of his parish by denouncing them from the altar.'[18] Other priests around Ireland were doing likewise, anxious that nothing should rock the Catholic emancipation boat.

After 1829, however, a new dynamic was introduced.

With emancipation safely achieved, the clergy began to assume leadership of a non-violent campaign to remove the statutory imposition of tithes. They were supported in this by urban and middle-class Catholics as well as Catholic farmers. Between 1831 and 1833 changes in the system were introduced, including the government's decision not to pursue defaulters.[19] In 1838, tithes were replaced by a supplementary rent-charge. Although the Protestant Established Church still indirectly benefitted from these increased rents made by Catholics to their landlords, this development was seen as something of a moral victory.

Because of the increasing level of violence used by some factions in the campaign, the Catholic church had disassociated itself from the movement in 1835, yet its role was not forgotten and it was increasingly seen as a protector of the people, an image it carefully fostered and refined, bringing it to an astonishing level in the 1880s. Catholics, both as individuals and as members of a church growing in confidence, saw what could be achieved by peaceful solidarity. With strong leadership and the vast majority of the population being members of that church, what might not be achieved?

This was the social and political milieu into which James Dunphy was born. His most formative years were spent in a world of blurred boundaries, a place where religion and politics were inextricably linked. It was epitomised by Daniel O'Connell who straddled the land as a cross between political icon and walking saint. In his maxim, which every Irish child of a certain age has learned, 'my body to Ireland and my heart to Rome',[20] O'Connell summed up the twin identities of many Irish Catholics at that time. With emancipation a reality, and the qualified success of the tithe reforms, if the same forces were brought to bear upon the government, could not some measure of political as well as religious independence be achieved for a Catholic people in a Catholic country?

The first half of the 1840s was marked by O'Connell's campaign to do just that by attempting to force the government to repeal the Act of Union (1801) and to establish a more representative government in Dublin. That campaign came to nothing, mainly because the British government knew that O'Connell and the Catholic church would never adopt violent means to achieve their aims. But the 'monster meeting' at the Hill of Tara in August 1843 amply displayed the power of a mass movement when motivated by a charismatic leader and controlled by the church. Catholicism and nationalism became interchangeable as labels of affiliation. To be Catholic in Ireland was no longer to be downtrodden, it was a badge of opportunity, it was to ride the crest of a swelling wave. But in the second half of the decade that wave came crashing against the rocks of a catastrophe which history has dubbed the Great Famine. All new-found confidence and the flexing of young muscles were cast off as the population scrambled to survive repeated potato crop failures. As the 1840s came to a dispirited end, the country was socially and economically devastated.

Many landlords and their agents looked on the mayhem as an opportunity to restructure their estates, and there were those in the Catholic hierarchy who looked on it as an opportunity to restructure society, a society which could be more closely controlled by their priests and bishops. The clergy had always been found in the hovels of the poor, but now they were increasingly found in the mercantile establishments of a rising Catholic middle class as well. Most importantly, the church was establishing itself in the corridors of power. It was involved in the structuring of national education, in formulating law, and in the very fabric of a society re-inventing itself.

As a boy and young man James Dunphy had witnessed all these changes. In 1850, when he was twenty-two, the 'first national synod of the Irish church for almost seven hundred years'[21] was held in Thurles. Its purpose was to assess how the church should prepare to meet the challenges and opportunities that would be faced in post-Famine Ireland. A raft of new ecclesiastical legislation was introduced to place the clergy on a different social footing to the laity. The harsh penal times of the eighteenth century had eroded the distinction between priests and people. Church services and practices had been carried out clandestinely, and this inevitably led to a fraternal aspect entering the relationship between cleric and congregation, there was a communal sense of 'being in it together'. In the absence of iconic buildings, the modest houses of the faithful or rocks large enough to be used as makeshift altars in isolated places became the centres of Catholic worship. The church had, to a certain extent, become democratised. Even after emancipation, customs such as 'stations' - the saying of mass in chosen houses - continued. It was this dispersal of activity, this absence of centrality, that had allowed the church to survive in times of persecution. It had allowed it to escape the control and punishment of a hostile secular authority. But, by 1850, times had changed. Survival was no longer the issue; it was time to reestablish centralised control. The Synod of Thurles was primarily aimed at consolidating episcopal authority, and the separation of clergy and laity was vital to bringing this about. Priests were forbidden to attend dances, race meetings and other social gatherings. They were obliged to read and study approved religious tracts and attend theological retreats. In short, a distancing between the members of the church and the officers of the church was to be strictly observed, for only then could sufficient reverence for priests be established, and only then could control be vested in the hierarchy.

Given this new dawn and his family background, perhaps it is no surprise that James Dunphy opted for a career in the priesthood. His brother John had already taken that path, and was ordained in that landmark year of 1850.[22] Joseph and William would do likewise. James studied humanities and philosophy in St Kieran's College, Kilkenny, before enrolling in the Irish College in Rome on Christmas Eve 1853, to study philosophy and theology.[23] What the twenty-five-year-old thought of the Eternal City is not recorded, but it was not a particularly happy time for him. Because of poor health he did not complete his courses there, leaving the college a year and a half later on 18 July 1855 to return to Ireland to continue his studies in Carlow College where he was ordained in 1857 at the age of twenty-nine.[24]

Archdeacon James Redmond

It was in August of that year that he arrived in Arklow as curate. His parish priest was Fr James Redmond, who had been ordained exactly thirty years earlier. The two men would appear to have had an instant rapport. In a letter to the archbishop, Redmond reported that the new curate had begun well.

"He was nine hours in the confessional last Friday and of these he was 6½ hrs without leaving the box. He appears to be a healthy sensible young man with the spirit of his calling and I anticipate much from his ministry".[25]

Of his other curates at that time, Fr Redmond was also satisfied with the work and demeanour of Frs Deighton and Donovan,[26] but Fr Buckley was a cause of great concern and Redmond wanted him removed.[27] The cause of that concern was Buckley's 'nimia familiaritas cum feminis'. Buckley, it seems, considered priestly celebacy a personal option rather than a professional obligation.[28] In calling for his removal Redmond again cited the virtues of Dunphy:

> I am greatly pleased with Mr. Dunphy. He is pious, sensible and most laborious. I fear it would be too much to expect another like him, but I pray your Grace to send me as efficient a substitute as you can for Mr Buckley.[29]

21

So, despite a relatively late vocation – he was in his mid-twenties when he went to Rome - and disruption of his studies through unspecified ill-health, Fr James Dunphy had found his niche, greatly impressing his parish priest from the outset, a man who would prove to be a major influence on him.

James Redmond was not a man easily impressed. His hundreds of letters to the archbishop and his published correspondence in local and national newspapers show his trenchant views on all matters relating to education, religion and politics. Above all, he believed in the hierarchical structures of the church to which he dedicated his life. He promulgated the necessity of unquestioned episcopal authority, and did not mince his words when condemning priests who did not toe the party line.[30] To him, a unified church was a strong church and no division within its ranks was to be tolerated. He believed in the close alliance of religion and politics and referred to periodicals such as the *Nation* and the *Tablet* as 'pernicious' with 'irreligious tendancies.'[31] He particularly disliked the former which he had no doubt was 'quite prepared to use all means in its reach to cut the Altar out of the way of Republicanism, anarchy & infidelity.'[32] Constitutional nationalism under the control of the Catholic bishops was, he believed, the true goal. 'If the priests of Ireland were united on the principles of O'Connell they would be the moral & effective rulers of the land; but perfection can't be looked for here.'[33]

Rev. Willam Ormsby,
Church of Ireland Parish Rector

When Dunphy arrived in Arklow, the town was rife with poverty. Fr Redmond repeatedly informed his archbishop of the dire conditions of the fishing community. According to him between 2,000 and 3,000 people were on the Poor Law Relief Committee's list of people in need.[34]

It was also a town riven with religious bigotry. Redmond and the Church of Ireland rector, Rev William Gilbert Ormsby, harboured an intense mutual dislike, each accusing the other of poaching parishioners. Redmond referred to Protestants turning to Catholicism as 'converts', but Catholics who became Protestant were to him 'perverts' and 'wretched apostates.'[35] He accused Ormsby of exploiting the widespread poverty, reporting that he was 'buying souls eagerly',[36] and called him a 'vile unprincipled ill-conditioned scoundrel.'[37] On one occasion, while preaching from the pulpit, he 'made [the congregation] laugh at vespers by comparing him [Ormsby] to a monkey practising his antics & showing his teeth but unable to bite within the bars of his cage.'[38] This personal antagonism between the two religious leaders had begun before Dunphy's arrival and continued for many years afterwards, and are mentioned here only because they helped contribute to pivotal events in the story that unfolds in the following chapters. Redmond also made derogatory statements about the Protestant population in general; 'Protestants ... have no real charity,'[39] and yet just three weeks later he felt compelled to write 'the Protestant clergy and shopkeepers [are] co-operating admirably, in fact they exceed the Catholics in zeal to relieve the distress, which is the more creditable to the former as nine-tenths of the relieved are Catholics.'[40]

Acerbic and volatile though Redmond would appear – prone to sweeping statements which he would later contradict if not retract – he was the indisputable leader of the Catholic population.[41] He was their social as well as their spiritual head. In his almost two decades as pastor, he had created a symbiotic relationship with the fishermen in which he represented them in their dealings with secular authority, and even defended their questionable conduct when they were criticised by the archbishop and condemned in the national press.[42] In return, they attended church services in ever increasing numbers and contributed not only to defray the week-to-week expenses but also to the building costs of the new parish church, work on which was begun in 1858. It was consecrated in 1861. He was

23

also on good terms with the local landlords. The Proby family
were Church of Ireland by religion and liberal by political persuasion. During his tenure as parish priest, Redmond had dealings with three of its members who successively held the titles
3rd, 4th and 5th earls of Carysfort, and his relationship with
these men was both amicable and fruitful. This was one of his
strengths, the ability to deal with all the disparate parties that
made up the spectrum of the community - fishermen and arti-
sans, entrepreneurial merchants and landed gentry. The only
party with whom he could not bring himself to negotiate or
cajole was his opposite number, the Church of Ireland rector.

This was the town into which Fr Dunphy arrived in 1857,
and this was the man who would be his mentor for the next
twenty years. Throughout the 1860s, Fr Dunphy went about his
work among all classes of the population, experiencing the day-
to-day simple and sometimes complex realities of the parish,
and giving Fr Redmond no cause to revise his early high
opinion of him.

When Redmond died on 14 May 1877, by which time he
had been promoted to the rank of archdeacon, Dunphy had his
fingers firmly on the pulse of the parish and it came as little sur-

prise when he succeeded Redmond as parish priest the following February. Aged forty-nine, he was at his prime. He was not the inveterate letter writer that Redmond had been. He sent fewer letters to his archbishop and did not enter so eagerly into public correspondence through the national or local press. Nevertheless, he did not hesitate to put pen to paper when the need arose,[43] and he continued the policies and practices of his predecessor to a degree that made the transition almost seamless. For example, he invited the active participation of all the parishioners in the completion of the internal decoration and furnishings of the church, including the installation of the high altar, which was dedicated to the memory of Archdeacon Redmond.[44] The fishermen paid for the acetylene gas lighting; the laity in general funded the installation of the heating system; Peter Boland, a prominent local businessman, donated the stain glass window in the south wall over the high altar; and the organ was installed in 1878 through public subscription.[45] In 1881, Dunphy was largely responsible for the opening of a new convent school, bringing to fruition one of Fr Redmond's dearest hopes.

Since the 1850s, Redmond had been trying to get a convent of the Sisters of Mercy established in Arklow.[46] A group of six arrived in 1866 to help during a serious cholera epidemic, but returned to their house in Rathdrum when the contagion subsided, after which Redmond was more determined than ever to get them back on a permanent basis.[47] He finally succeeded in this in 1876. Dunphy shared Redmond's admiration of the Sisters of Mercy, particularly in their role as educators, and he was instrumental in having a purpose-built convent erected for them adjacent to the church.

Perhaps the most important characteristic he shared with – perhaps even learned from - Redmond was one which a local newspaper later described as his 'labours were not confined to the spiritual needs [of his parishioners] ... they extended to the betterment and uplifting of his people industrially, socially and materially.'[48] He particularly continued the close relationship between the office of parish priest and the large community of fishermen and their families. His years with them as curate, and no doubt the training he received from Redmond, made him all too aware that their frequent bouts of distress were caused as often by adverse weather conditions as by poor catches. While the quantity and quality of fish stocks was beyond their control, the adverse effects of bad weather could be partly alleviated by proper development of the harbour. Dunphy was determined that the necessary improvements to the harbour would be made. In this, he had an important ally, William Proby, 5th earl of Carysfort.

William Proby had not expected to accede to the title. His father, Granville Leveson Proby, had been 3rd earl and on his death in 1868 at the age of eighty-four was succeeded by his eldest son, also Granville, as 4th earl.[49] But Granville junior died in Florence in 1872 while still a young man and William unexpectedly found himself the 5th earl of Carysfort, much to the delight of the Catholic clergy of Arklow.[50] During the cholera epidemic of 1866, William Proby had shown himself to have something of a social conscience, one of the new breed of landed gentry who felt they had responsibilities as well as privileges. After the epidemic had passed, he had the old cemeteries at Castlepark (Catholic) and St Mary's in Main Street (Protestant) closed, having successfully urged his father to

ST. MARYS CONVENT, ARKLOW.

donate a large tract of land for a new cemetery a mile from the town centre. He was appalled at the living conditions in the area known as the Fishery that had given rise to the cholera and believed that one of the responsibilities of a landlord was to provide his tenants with decent living conditions. High principles without the power to implement them are easily held, but in 1872, when he found himself with the power to put those principles into practice, William Proby lived up to his ideals.

Within three years he had plans drawn up for a new village in the Fishery area, and in 1875 the first row of eighteen two-storeyed slated houses were built and became known as Proby's Row, now St Michael's Terrace. Two more phases followed, one of four houses and another row of twenty-four making forty-six in all.[51] Progressive as this move was, it was not enough for William Proby. He also believed that his tenants should have the means to earn a decent living, and he turned his attention to improving the harbour.

Over the course of the nineteenth century the Arklow fishing industry had grown dramatically, as had the trading fleet,[52] but little had been done to improve the harbour. The control and development of the port had been granted to the Hibernian Mining Company, based six miles upstream at Avoca, by an act of parliament in 1792.[53] They retained that control for over eighty years, during which period only piecemeal attempts to construct walls and other infrastructure were made. Throughout the 1820s, 1830s and beyond, many commentators decried the lack of development. None was more frequent or vociferous than the Catholic clergy. In a letter to the *Wicklow News-Letter*, Fr Redmond accused the company of deliberately letting the harbour fall into neglect, but again nothing was done.[54] Seven years later, in June 1876, the government finally announced plans to improve port facilities at Arklow, offering a £13,000 grant and a further £13,000 loan to the mining company, now operating under the name Wicklow Mining Company. Redmond welcomed the news and wrote to the *News-Letter* describing the mining company as 'a dog in a manger, neither eating the hay nor allowing the horse to eat it'.[55] He was further encouraged by the directors' willingness to accept the proposal, but a meeting of the shareholders put paid to any thoughts of celebration. They put so many conditions to acceptance of the offer that the bill was withdrawn at its final stage through parliament.[56] Redmond was incensed. Again he let loose his wrath:

> These shareholders have thus inflicted serious injury on themselves and far more serious injury on thousands in this town taking the shoes from their feet, the clothes from their backs, the food from their mouths, and the roofs from their houses, and exposing them to hunger, nakedness, sickness, pestilence, misery, want and woe. May God forgive the senseless and unChristian authors of such wretchedness.[57]

Blistering though this attack was, it is unlikely that it brought about the change of heart exhibited by the shareholders a short time later. On 22 December, the company directors wrote to the Treasury reminding them of the works they had carried out on the port over the years at a cost of £25,000. That work, they said, had been done in three stages and included the construction of harbour walls and piers. In light of this, they now sought the £13,000 grant and further £13,000 loan which the Treasury had made earlier in the year, on the condition that the company would receive all tolls, that is harbour dues. Before the matter was resolved, Archdeacon Redmond died and Fr Dunphy took the reins of the parish *pro tem*, his position not being formalised for some months to come. In December 1877 nature interceded in such a fashion as to make all proposals ineffectual. A storm raged along this coast, shattering the north pier into pieces. The south pier fared little better, presenting 'an almost similar spectacle, for it is undermined and will collapse in the next storm.'[58] Within a month this prediction came true: 'the last of the old year completed the destruction of Arklow Harbour. The South Pier was washed into the sea; the North Pier has also been destroyed.'[59]

As the new decade dawned Dunphy took control, enlisting the help of the local M.P., William Corbet. Corbet had been elected in 1880 and was a nationalist and a staunch supporter of Charles Stewart Parnell. On 26 November 1881, the *Wicklow News-Letter* reported that the Wicklow Mining Company had agreed to sell their rights to the port for £5,000, not only that but the government was offering a loan of £20,000 and a grant of £15,000 to make Arklow into an efficient port. The following year saw the passing of the Arklow Harbour Act (1882)[60] through parliament, under which the port was to be made operational by the Board of Works, after which it was to be handed over to the management of local commissioners. Tenders were invited for the construction of a 700 ft concrete south pier; a 425 ft concrete north pier; the removal of the debris of the old piers; and the dredging of a channel.

This was the new beginning that Archdeacon Redmond had sought for decades. This was the new hope that William Proby had striven for. Redmond had lived long enough only to see what little infrastructure there had been washed into the sea, and Proby had seen his efforts come to nothing. Now Redmond's successor, James Dunphy, had brought it about through the support of Proby's political enemies. Thus, the economic problem that had been Arklow harbour had become a politicised issue in which nationalist M.Ps. had succeeded where unionist representation had failed. And there, in the middle of it all, was Fr James Dunphy, conflating the economic welfare of his parishioners with nationalist politicians and with himself, the personification of the Catholic church in Arklow.

By the time the new south pier was completed in 1885, the Very Rev James Dunphy, PP, could do no wrong in the eyes of the fishermen and local Catholic businessmen. His twenty-eight years among them seemed to have been steering towards this compass point in his career. He had learned from Archdeacon Redmond the importance of being a temporal as well as spiritual leader. Now that he had succeeded in bringing about a new harbour that would greatly enhance the prospects of the poor as well as the town as a whole, hc knew the debt owed to him. He knew how highly he was regarded. He knew the power that was at his disposal because of that regard. And he knew how he was going to use it next.

It irked him that few, if any, public offices in Arklow were held by Catholics. Over half a century had passed since the passing of Catholic Emancipation, and yet those in control were still largely, if not wholly, Protestant. The early months of 1885 gave him the opportunity to do something about it.

CHAPTER 2:
Home Rule, the Land League, and the National League

Home Rule

James Dunphy's empathy with the fishing community in Arklow was remarkable for a man reared in an agricultural environment. That did not mean, however, turning his back on land-based communities or forgetting the problems they experienced, problems he had seen firsthand as a child and young adult. He was aware of the inequities of landlordism and came to equate the cause for land reform with those for political change and national identity. His opinions in such matters were shared not only by his siblings, as will be seen in due course, but also by his parish priest in Arklow, Archdeacon James Redmond. The three main vehicles for these campaigns were tenants' associations (culminating in the Land League of 1879-1881), the National League and the movement for home rule. It might be said that all three had their origins in the unfortunate Fenian Rebellion.

In the wake of that ill-planned rising against British rule in 1867, prime minister William Gladstone realised that the Irish landlord system would have to be changed to avert further insurrection. The Landlord and Tenant Act (1870)[1] introduced some rights for tenants, such as compensation for improvements made by the tenant and for disturbance on a tenant giving up the land. It was a start, but it did not go far enough, and tenants' associations sprang up throughout Ireland to push for greater reform. In February 1873, an invitation was circulated to the 'Landlords, Clergy and Tenant Farmers of the County of Wicklow, and all others interested' to join a lobby group.[2] It was unlikely that many landlords would accept the invitation, but in extending it to them the organisers could not be accused of excluding them from reform proposals. What is more interesting is the invitation to the clergy. The approval of the clergy of such an organisation would be vital to its success.

The circular was headed *County Wicklow Farmers' Club and Tenants' Defence Association* and it opened with the words:

> It being too evident that the Land Act of 1870 has utterly failed in accomplishing the object for which it was designed, affording, in its present form, neither protection from the caprice and rapacity of the bad Landlord, nor providing any real substantial compensation for the industrious and improving tenant, it cannot therefore be accepted as a settlement of the Land Question, and the necessity for an immediate amendment in its provisions must appear to any fair and impartial mind unquestionable.

It went on to point out that such clubs and associations were being formed throughout Ireland and that two meetings to explore the desirability of forming a branch in the county had recently been held in Wicklow town. At the first meeting it was resolved that a local organisation should be established. A second meeting was then held to take all necessary steps to form such a club, and a committee was appointed to collect information that would be laid before a general meeting of the county. Among the nineteen committee members were four Catholic priests, Revd R Galvin, parish priest of Rathdrum, Revd P Doyle, Revd M Molony,[3] long-time curate and soon to be parish priest of Barndarrig (and who shall figure in the story that is to follow), and Archdeacon James Redmond, parish priest of Arklow. Ten more names were added to the managing committee, two of whom were priests, Very Revd Dr Lee of Bray and Revd Thomas Anderson of Newtownmountkennedy.[4] Of the now twenty-nine committee members, six (twenty per cent) were clergymen. In fact, at this second meeting it was proposed that Frs Molony and Redmond, among others, should address the county general meeting to be held on 24 February. From the outset, then, not only the moral support but the active participation of the Catholic clergy was an important factor in the campaign for land reform.

In the same year as Gladstone's Landlord and Tenant Act, a Dublin lawyer named Isaac Butt also believed that reform was necessary to avoid further bloodshed in Ireland, but he advocated that the necessary reforms should go beyond the restructuring of landlordism. To him, political reforms had to be introduced and he began a campaign for 'Irish federalism', later to be termed 'home rule'. Butt had been a Tory, but had defended Fenians free of charge in the wake of the 1867 rebellion, even though he was a firm believer in constitutional politics being the only means of redressing perceived injustice.[5] In 1870, he formed a loose federation of Irish M.Ps. to act as the 'Irish Party' in parliament, with the aim of establishing home rule for Ireland. It quickly attracted a broad spectrum of support. Remnants of the Young Ireland and Fenian movements, constitutional Nationalists, Protestant Liberals and even a small number of Tories found some common ground in this new departure. In the words of Michael MacDonagh, 'the company may be said to have been in the main Liberal and Conservative with a tang of Fenianism and Orangeism'.[6] At a meeting held in the Bilton Hotel, Sackville Street (now O'Connell Street) on 19 May 1870, two opinions emerged, the Fenian wish for total independence from Britain, and that of the commercial - more loyalist – faction who wanted little more than greater freedom for business interests from Westminster restrictions. Butt summed up the feeling as follows: 'That it is the opinion of this meeting that the true remedy for the evils of Ireland is the establishment of an Irish parliament with full control over our domestic affairs'. He laid out the aspirations in *Irish Federalism, its meaning, its objects and its hopes*. In short, his view of federalism would give Ireland a domestic parliament without sundering the connection between Ireland and Britain. In July, the Home Government Association was formed to push for these aims. 'Federalism' was too new and awkward a word, so 'home rule' became the catch phrase. One of its advantages was its lack of specifity, allowing Fenians and moderates to define it as they understood it.

The movement made steady progress and a conference was held in the Rotunda in Dublin. Some M.Ps. were now recognised as 'Home Rulers', and there were between 800 and

900 delegates, as well as 2500 signatures supporting it. One long-time advocate of federalism was Fr Thaddeus O'Malley who debunked the belief of Orangemen who were already saying that 'home rule would be Rome rule' with the remark 'there is some rhyme in this notion, but not a particle of reason.'[7] The conference went on for four days. Reports of the speeches were published by Swift MacNeil, and its 213 pages are one of the most valuable records of the home rule movement. Twenty-eight of the 103 Irish M.Ps. proclaimed their support for the movement by their attendance, these were mostly Liberals who had been returned in the 1868 election. One of them was Sir John Gray, the Protestant proprietor of the *Freeman's Journal* which advocated home rule and which evolved into the unofficial organ of the Irish Parliamentary Party. The aristocracy had been asked to attend, but they ignored the appeal. The working class were not considered, they were expected merely to turn out and cheer and, should the franchise be extended to them, to vote as directed. The home rule movement was a middle class, professional (including farmers and clergy) and commercial movement. The result of the conference was the formation of the Home Rule League.[8]

Support was also gaining among the Irish in Britain. It was especially strong in the north of England and Scotland, where the Irish were very numerous, but it was in the House of Commons that its strength would be tested.

A general election was held in January 1874 and sixty of the 103 Irish M.Ps. were returned as Home Rulers. This *ad hoc* Home Rule Party consisted of forty-nine Catholics and eleven Protestants, several had been Liberal M.Ps. in the previous parliament, but a few had been Conservative. They came from the commercial classes, ex-parliamentarians, four were members of aristocratic families, and three were Englishmen.[9] This disparate mix agreed to act as a united party when it came to matters affecting Ireland, but in all other matters they were free to act according to their opinions or party, whether Liberal or Conservative. Gladstone lost the 1874 election. The Conservatives were in power with 360 seats to the Liberals'

240, and the sixty Home Rulers lost impact when they separated to sit with their own parties. Those who were Liberal described themselves as such, some with the proviso 'Liberal in favour of the system called home rule for Ireland'. Only one, P J Smyth, described himself as 'a moderate Irish Nationalist'. William Richard O'Byrne was one of the sixty and his election as the first home rule representative for the Wicklow constituency brought an end to the long established Liberal landlord control of the seat.[10] A contributing factor may have been this was the first general election run by secret ballot as laid down in the Ballot Act (1872), so agricultural electors were freed from having to vote for their landlords' candidates.

The first vote in the House of Commons concerning home rule was an attempt to have a committee formed to investigate the degree of support it might have. This took place on 30 June and 1 July, 1874. Sixty-one M.Ps. voted in favour, but there were 458 against. It did little to dishearten the movement as it was an expected outcome, but the members knew that new methods would have to be implemented if progress was to be made. One of these strategies was to cause bitter reaction in the house, even among some of the older home rule M.P.s. On 22 April 1875, Joseph Biggar, the Belfast-born member for Cavan, rose to his feet and began to talk, and talk, and talk, and talk, thereby bringing the business of the house to a halt. Obstructionism had entered the stage. Another event took place in the house that same night, but one that did not seem of particular importance until several years later. It was the night that a young County Wicklow landowner by the name of Charles Stewart Parnell took his seat in the Commons for the first time.

He had been elected M.P. for Meath and there was little to suggest the impact he would have in the years to come. Despite his standing for the constituency of Meath, Parnell had the active support of important members of the County Wicklow clergy, including Fr Galvin, parish priest of Parnell's native Rathdrum, and Archdeacon James Redmond of Arklow,[11] both of whom had been prominent activists in the

County Wicklow Farmers' Club and Tenants' Defence Association.

The ability of Parnell to attract the support of Catholic clergy intent on land reform is often explained by his mother having a strong dislike of England – her father had been Commodore Stewart of the United States navy during the war of 1812[12] – but his paternal forebears had, from time to time, also shown tendencies which might be regarded as being at variance with their social and religious positions. His great grandfather, Sir John Parnell, who had been Chancellor of the Irish Exchequer, was strongly opposed to the Act of Union, although it must be admitted that he was equally strongly opposed to concessions to Catholics in 1793.[13] Charles' father William shared Sir John's opposition to the Act of Union, but was more liberal in his attitude to Catholics. According to Roy Foster, it was 'he who first hit on the subscription idea which funded Daniel O'Connell's Catholic Association ... was close to Catholic activists, and dedicated his one novel to "the Priests of Ireland"'.[14]

Despite these pro-Catholic and anti-British family influences, Charles displayed many of the traits of an establishment figure; he was captain of the Wicklow XI cricketers and a sub-altern in the Wicklow Militia. He was appointed High Sheriff of County Wicklow in 1873, resented being 'mistaken for a Fenian', and once told his mother that he would leave the family home (their Dublin house in Temple Street) if she 'continued to take such an interest in the disloyal and rebellious.'[15] Michael MacDonagh suggests that it was the 1873 home rule conference that won him over and he joined the Home Rule League the following year. Like Isaac Butt, Parnell was a pragmatist who realised the importance of promoting Irish industry and that generating wealth was of paramount importance if home rule was to have any true meaning. In Dod's *Parliamentary Companion* he is recorded as neither Liberal nor Conservative, merely 'Is in favour of the system called home rule for Ireland', and his maiden speech on 26 April 1875 contained the memorable phrase 'Ireland is not a geographical fragment, but a nation.' That, however, was the extent of his input and he remained silent throughout the rest of 1875 and into 1876. Throughout this apparently reticent period, Parnell continued to be on very good terms with the Catholic clergy of Wicklow and their relationship grew increasingly closer.

The Home Rule Party set about preparing Bills on reform of electoral franchise, education, land tenure, poor law, county government, encouragement of sea fishing and reclamation of waste land. None was passed into law. Parnell grew increasingly impatient with the lack of progress and concluded that no measure of autonomy for Ireland would be gained through gentlemanly parliamentarianism. He joined Biggar in his ploy to tie up the business of the house through prolonged and often pointless speeches. Obstructionism had been brought to a new level. Older members of the party, including its founder, Isaac Butt, repudiated the ploy as ungentlemanly and self-defeating. He wrote to Parnell, reprimanding him, but Parnell replied stating that he and Biggar had shown what just two M.Ps. could do. What might not be achieved if all sixty Home Rule M.Ps. followed their example? He cared nothing for the 'feeling of the House' when that feeling was opposed to the interests of Ireland.[16] A few weeks later, Butt sided with English M.Ps. in condemning the obstructionists and in so doing heralded the end of his leadership of the Irish Party. The obstructionists became the heroes of Ireland and Parnell was seen as their leader.

On 1 September 1877, at the Home Rule Confederation of Great Britain annual general meeting in Liverpool, Isaac Butt announced his intention to retire. His softly-softly approach to have a committee appointed to enquire into the demand of the Irish people for self-government had failed three times, in 1874, 1876 and 1877.

The majority of the delegates wanted him to remain at the head of the movement, but they also wanted him to step up the pressure on the government to introduce reforms beneficial to Ireland. Butt knew his day was past and refused to be swayed. He died just eighteen months later, on 3 May 1879, and the only members of the Home Rule party at his funeral were Dr O'Leary and Phil Callan.

Butt was succeeded as leader by William Shaw, who shared Butt's respect for parliamentary convention and process and detested the maverick attitudes of the younger contingent. Parnell's rise, however, was unstoppable and in January 1881 Shaw and eleven other conservative Home Rulers (often disparagingly referred to as 'Whigs') left the party. This suited Parnell, who now took over the leadership with his internal opponents no longer holding him back.

Butt's greatest achievement had been getting most strands of the Irish political spectrum together. He had even brought some of the physical force contingent into the movement, promising that if Ireland did not have its own parliament in five years he would resign as leader of the Home Rule party. Ireland did not have its own parliament in five years and Butt failed to fulfil his promise, so by the second half of the 1870s, the Irish Republican Brotherhood, the physical force forerunners of the I.R.A., were opposed to his strictly constitutional approach. Now leader, Parnell saw that healing this rift was a priority if the movement was to be successful. His initial approaches proved fruitless, but circumstances in early 1879 were to prove fortuitous. Two leading members of the I.R.B., John Devoy and Michael Davitt, asked Parnell to radicalise his plans in a bid to attract the hardliners. Parnell stopped short of entering into a formal alliance with the I.R.B., realising that this would alienate the moderates in parliament and so weaken his position in the Commons. But there was an alternative – an alliance with the newly formed Land League.

Land League
The expansion of the American railway network in the late 1870s saw the opening up of the mid-west grain belt. This, coupled with faster and more regular steam ship routes across the Atlantic, saw Europe flooded with cheap American grain. Irish farm prices fell drastically and small tenant farmers were unable to pay their rents. To compound matters, exceptionally wet

weather throughout 1877 led to potato blight, and memories of the Great Famine of the 1840s were raised. The situation deteriorated further throughout 1878 and by 1879 only one-quarter of the usual potato crop was available for consumption. With non-payment of rent came evictions, especially in the western counties.

It was against this background that a new figure in Irish politics emerged. Michael Davitt was a nationalist and socialist. As a boy he had lost an arm in the cotton mills of Lancashire, in 1865 he joined the Fenians, became organising secretary of the I.R.B. in 1868 and in 1870 was sentenced to fifteen years penal servitude. He served seven of these in Dartmoor, but was then released mainly due to agitation by Butt and Parnell.[17] Back in his native Mayo at the time of the new crisis, he organised labourers and tenants to resist eviction. Perhaps even more impressive was his ability to get results, one of which was a reduction of twenty-five per cent in rents. Encouraged by this, he set about organising the agitation on a national level with two immediate aims, a national reduction in rents and an end to evictions. There was also a long-term aim – the transfer of land ownership from the landlords to the tenants who worked it. He knew that such a national movement would need a high profile figurehead, and in Ireland in 1879 there was no higher profile than that of Charles Stewart Parnell.

Davitt invited Parnell to a meeting of tenant farmers in Westport, County Mayo. Parnell not only agreed to attend, but also to speak. It was immediately clear that he was on the side of the tenant farmers when he said: 'A fair rent is a rent the tenant can reasonably afford to pay according to the times, but in hard times a tenant cannot be expected to pay as much as he did in good times …'[18] A few months later, in October 1879, Davitt founded the Irish National Land League and Parnell consented to be its president. He was now the leader of the Home Rule Party in parliament *and* the agitation for land reform throughout Ireland. He gave the Land League a legitimacy it would not otherwise have had, and it gave him greater political power, having a network that reached into every village and crossroads in the country. The movements not only shared a leader, but a cause; to be a Land Leaguer was to be a Home Ruler and vice versa. It was from this time on that Parnell was known as 'The Uncrowned King of Ireland'.

The league had an immediate impact on landlordism and politics in general. Violent acts across the country became frequent and Parnell's unconvincing condemnation of such acts was to give rise to the general impression of his having a foot in both the constitutional and the physical force camps of the campaign for reform. This ambivalence was probably best expressed by Parnell's right-hand man, Joseph Biggar, when he spoke out against gun attacks on Irish landlords. He regretted such attacks on the grounds that the attackers often missed their targets and hit someone else.[19] Republicans, nationalists and socialists joined the league in great numbers, but perhaps the most important section of the community to give their support to it was the Catholic clergy, just as it had been with the tenants' defence associations earlier in the decade.

A general election was held in early 1880 and William Gladstone's Liberals were back in power with 352 seats to the Conservatives' 237. The home rule contingent increased from its sixty seats to sixty-three, but Gladstone did not need their support as he had in previous governments. His majority gave him freer rein in his dealings with them, a freedom he felt compelled to exercise as the Land League's power increased and their methods grew more violent.

In September 1880, at a meeting in Ennis, County Clare, Parnell introduced a new strategy for dealing with 'land-grabbers', the name given to tenants who took over the holdings of those evicted for non-payment of rent. He called on the local communities to ostracise such people, to ignore them socially, commercially and in every sector of everyday life. The strategy was to become known as 'boycotting', named after Captain Charles Boycott who was its first victim because of his opposition to the Land League. He went further in a speech he gave in Cincinnati, Ohio when he articulated in its clearest form yet what his aim for the country was:

When we have undermined English misgovernment we [will] have paved the way for Ireland to take her place among the nations of the earth. And let us not forget that is the ultimate goal at which all we Irishmen aim ... None of us, whether we are in America or Ireland or wherever we may be, will be satisfied until we have destroyed the last link which keeps Ireland bound to England.[20]

Back in Dublin, he led torch-lit processions through the capital, rallying strength for the twin campaigns of agrarian reform and political independence. Perhaps it was this increasingly hardline approach that spurred his fellow Wicklowmen to action. Up to then, they had seemed content to watch the Land League develop elsewhere, but in December 1880 branches of the league were established in Tinahely, Rathdrum, Arklow, Ashford, Roundwood, and Barndarrig; in Wicklow town in January 1881, and in Baltinglass, Carnew, Newtownmounkennedy and Bray in October 1881. When the Ladies Land League was established as a support structure, branches were opened in Rathdrum, Barndarrig, Baltinglass, Arklow, Tinahely and Roundwood.[21]

Parnell did not garner such support for the Land League, for home rule, and for himself simply by being a local boy – that helped, of course, but it would not have been enough in itself. It was his ability to form and maintain close ties with social and religious leaders that was his forte. Even at the busiest times of his parliamentary life and organisational commitments, he still managed to keep his finger on the pulse of local affairs and events. In 1879 and 1880, immensely hectic years for him on the national stage, he was constantly pushing for the development of the harbours at Wicklow and Arklow. It was with the latter that his relationship with Fr Dunphy grew into one of mutual respect and friendship.

He did not, however, enjoy the same popularity in London. Gladstone felt that the situation in Ireland was getting out of hand and in 1881 introduced the first of a series of legislative measures that would become known as the Coercion Acts, giving special powers to the police and military and suspending some civil liberties. Parnell and other Home Rule M.Ps. spoke for forty-one continuous hours in a bid to bring the House of Commons to a standstill until the Speaker suspended the session, and also suspended Parnell and thirty-five of his followers, including the M.P. for Wicklow, William Corbet. Corbet, accompanied by fellow Home Rule M.P. John Redmond, lost no time in travelling to his constituency and on Friday, 25 March 1881, both addressed a county meeting of the league held in Wicklow town, attended by 'about four thousand people and was marked by great enthusiasm.' The chair was taken by the president of the Wicklow branch of the league, William Byrne, who immediately stated his regret that

> someone better qualified had not been selected to preside. In other places in the county where meetings like these were held it was usual for one of their clergymen – the ever true and faithful friends of the people – to occupy this position. [Cheers][22]

In case anyone was in any doubt, he went on to point out that, although none of the local clergy were present, they were with them heart and soul. This brought more cheers, but failed to explain the absence of the priests. Byrne went on to remark that

> the men of Wicklow might be a little late into the field, but they had proved a trusty reserve. They were ever ready to do their duty and they would do it now in the face of Coercion.

The main tenor of the meeting was one of defiance and opposition to the

> wanton and tyrannical conduct of the Gladstone Government in forging for Ireland the most despotic and cruel Coercion Act that ever disgraced the statutes of the English Parliament.

Redmond addressed the crowd in patriotic terms, reminding them that seven hundred years of oppression by the English had not quelled the spirit of the Irish people. Now, she [England] has sent across the channel to us – instead of redressing the crying evils and wrongs in the landlord system – a coercion bill ... a Coercion Bill to be maintained by brute force, by bayonet, and by buckshot.

Corbet concentrated on their efforts to thwart the passing of the bill, and then went on to condemn one of the principal elements of the act, the suspension of *habeus corpus*, the right to a trial. This 'places it in the power of the Lord Lieutenant to arrest any person, man, woman or child, and to imprison them for 18 long months'.

This was the stick Gladstone used to beat the Land League, but he also dangled a carrot in the form of a new land reform bill, which was passed as the Land Law (Ireland) Act (1881)[23] which contained two very important concessions to tenants; the fixing of fair rents by a judicial court and fixity of tenure. It was a far better bill than many Home Rule M.Ps. could have hoped for, but Parnell urged them to vote against it. In the words of Michael MacDonagh, 'Gladstone and Forster, the Chief Secretary, came to the conclusion that Parnell's purpose was to thwart, for his own political ends, the healing influences of the measure.'[24]

Imprisonment without trial of hundreds of activists and suspected activists had taken place throughout Ireland since the introduction of the Coercion Act. It was now used to get Parnell out of the way, and he was arrested in October 1881 and lodged in Kilmainham Gaol. Incarceration suited Parnell. His image as leader was now enhanced by that of martyr while at the same time he could not be held responsible for the actions of others. Because of its organising of – and often enforcing of – non-payment of rent, the Land League was banned by law. This suited Parnell even more. It had served its purpose well. It had organised a nationwide agitation, had united clergy and socialists, radicals and constitutionalists, but Parnell felt that not only was it too focused on the land question, but that its branches were too autonomous. He believed the ultimate aim – as he had espoused in Cincinnati – was national independence from Britain. He set about filling the gap left by the banning of the league with a new organisation which would build on its achievements, an organisation over which he would have complete control. This was to be the National League.

County Wicklow Property Defence Association
Wicklow landlords also felt the time had come to react to the growing power of the Land League. In January 1882, while Parnell was in gaol and organising the establishment of the National League, County Wicklow landowners were not standing idly by. A notice appeared in the *Wicklow News-Letter* stating that the 'County Wicklow Property Defence Association' was to be established, the aims of which were to protect the rights of 'all kinds of property against organised combinations.' It would protect the rights of individuals to enter into employment without fear of intimidation; it would help landlords to act against the withholding of rent; support shopkeepers and others who were suffering the effects of boycotting; and generally aid anyone 'desireous of withstanding the advance of Communism.'[25] Its membership was open to 'all loyal persons, without reference to religion or politics.' Finances, or the lack of them, would not be a barrier as the amount of subscription was entirely voluntary. The instigator of this reaction to the legally defunct but still active Land League was William Brabazon, 11th earl of Meath, who lived at Kilruddery near Bray. He urged the establishment of local branches and promised that names of members would not be published without the members' consent.

The National League
Elsewhere outside the walls of Kilmainham a degree of calm was restoring itself. Many former Land Leaguers were satisfied to accept the level of rents fixed by the courts. This, coupled with the return of potato crop yields, saw a lessening of agrarian outrage. By the beginning of 1882, the time had come for Parnell and Gladstone to review the situation. The result of this review became known as the Kilmainham Pact. Parnell agreed to cool

the situation even further and Gladstone agreed not only to tackle remaining landlord-tenant injustices, but also to look sympathetically on Ireland's national aspirations. Parnell was released from Kilmainham Gaol in April 1882 and soon his replacement for the Land League, the National League, came into being.

This new organisation, along with the sympathetic ear of Gladstone, looked promising for home rule. Chief Secretary Forster opposed Parnell's release and resigned when Gladstone refused to be swayed. He was replaced by Frederick Cavendish. Within weeks of his arrival, in May 1882, Cavendish and his under-secretary, Thomas Burke, were murdered in Phoenix Park. Gladstone could not now be seen to show too close a relationship with Parnell and his National League. The question of home rule, so alive with prospects in April, was taboo in May. Three years were to pass before the question could again be raised.

CHAPTER 3:
Fr Dunphy's fiefdom

In the nineteenth century, the Roman Catholic parish of Arklow stretched from the Avoca river in the north to the Castletown area in the south, and from the Irish Sea in the east to Woodenbridge and the slopes of Croghan Kinsella in the west.[1] In all it compromised 18,689 acres, or twenty-nine square miles, taking in all of the fifty townlands in the civil parish of Arklow, thirty-six of the thirty-eight townlands of the civil parish of Inch, and twenty-nine of the thirty-three townlands of the civil parish of Kilgorman. Fr Dunphy's parish, therefore, straddled the county boundary into north Wexford. According to the 1881 census, the total population in this catchment was 6,970, of which 5,882 (84.4 per cent) were Catholic.[2] These parishioners were served by three churches. There was the parish church in Arklow town and two chapels, one at Johnstown, four miles to the west, and another at Castletown, six miles directly south of the town.[3]

The Johnstown chapel had been built in 1803 and the one at Castletown in 1806, replacements for earlier structures destroyed by local loyalists in the aftermath of the 1798 rebellion.[4] Fr Dunphy knew them both well, but was particularly familiar with Castletown as he had served his early years in Arklow as curate there.[5] Its poor condition had troubled him for some time, and in 1884 he advertised for builders to view plans for a new church and invited them to submit tenders.[6]

The foundation stone was laid just three months later, on 8 June 1884 and what a day it was. A large procession left Arklow at midday, with 'banners bearing national and religious mottoes and devices.' Carriages and carts of all shapes and sizes were decked out in evergreens and flags. Along the route, decorated archways had been erected and the numbers of walkers swelled, joined by groups at each crossroads. The ceremony was performed by the archbishop, Cardinal Edward McCabe, who arrived in a two-horse covered carriage, but there was no doubt as to who was the hero of the day. Fr Dunphy's praises were sung, and he in turn sang the praises of the Arklow fishermen who had donated £100 towards the expected total cost of £2,000. Parish priests came from Ballygarrett and Kilanerin in County Wexford, from Wicklow town and Rathdrum. No doubt the presence of a cardinal was a major attraction, but reports of the occasion confirm that James Dunphy was the central figure.

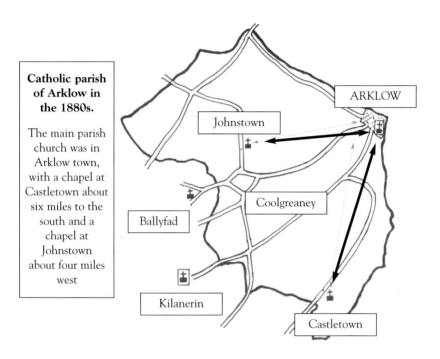

Catholic parish of Arklow in the 1880s.

The main parish church was in Arklow town, with a chapel at Castletown about six miles to the south and a chapel at Johnstown about four miles west

ARKLOW

Johnstown

Coolgreaney

Ballyfad

Kilanerin

Castletown

Like his predecessor, Dunphy believed in the importance of the parishioners congregating in the churches, rather than practising their religion at home. Attendance at mass and other ceremonies was not optional, but integral to their religion. The annual 'mission' – a week-long series of sermons, confessions, prayer and devotional reflection – were attended by crowds of up to two thousand, and many undertook to abstain from alcoholic drink, some for life but most for specified periods.[7]

Not only was he responsible for the three churches and their congregations, but he was also in control of the several Catholic schools throughout his parish, a task about which he was passionate. Throughout his career, he saw school building and education as paramount to his mission. He saw to it that young girls as well as boys had adequate national school facilities. The main boys' school was, and still is, on Coolgreaney Road. This was a mile or more distant from the populous area of the Fishery in the eastern area of the town, so a small school was held for those children in rented rooms near the harbour.[8] Fr Dunphy felt that this *ad hoc* arrangement was unsatisfactory and in 1900 had a purpose-built school erected on Harbour Road for boys aged four to eight, after which they were considered old enough to walk the mile or so to Coolgreaney Road. As the girls' national school was in the middle of the town at St Mary's Road, it was not deemed too far for the girls of the Fishery to walk to it. The depth of his belief in the importance of education is reflected in the amount of space he devoted to it in his letters to the archbishop.

To help him run this sizeable parish with all its plans, problems and complications, he had four curates. Their names changed as they were transferred to other parishes for one reason or another, but as 1885 dawned they were Fr James Flavin, Fr M McGrath, Fr B Dalton,[9] and Fr Laurence Farrelly. Fr Flavin had been ordained in 1882, and Arklow was his first parish.[10] Fr Farrelly was slightly older than Flavin and had a great deal in common with Fr Dunphy, but apparently lacked Dunphy's capacity for self-control. He did not mince his words,[11] and was known as a 'thorough paced Nationalist.'[12] He was curate in Athy, County Kildare before moving to Arklow and his role there

> in the hot days of the Land League will not soon be forgotten by friend or foe, by evicted tenant or merciless landlord. His ultra-activity was rewarded by his being sent to the comparatively quiet and staid parish of Naul.[13]

His demeanour in the 'quiet and staid parish of Naul', County Dublin either satisfied the archbishop that he had cooled his ardour and was now ready for normal duties elsewhere, or the archbishop thought that the parish priest at Naul had been unsuccessful in calming the volatile Farrelly. One way or the other, Farrelly was sent to work under the rather formidable Fr James Dunphy at Arklow. As will be seen, his conduct in 1888 and 1889 would suggest there was little reformation in his hot-blooded character. Whether still hard-line or humbled, Fr Laurence Farrelly was transferred to Arklow and was given responsibility for the Castletown section of the parish, just as the building of the new church was under way. He was, of course, present at the laying of the foundation stone and at the consecration of the church on 18 November 1885. Fr Farrelly will figure prominently in this story.

Fr Dunphy's relationships with the priests of neighbouring parishes were good. His brother William was parish priest in the parishes of Rathdrum and Avoca between the years 1870-1888, and would later be parish priest of Barndarrig. William had also shown himself to be a strong advocate of tenants' rights, and had displayed courage on several occasions during evictions at Redcross, where he had stood against 'landlord tyranny, rapacity and eviction.'[14] The parish of Barndarrig ten miles north of Arklow was run by Fr Michael Molony. Like Farrelly and William Dunphy, Molony shared many of James Dunphy's views but was more circumspect in pursuing them. It will be remembered that Molony had been prominent in the County Wicklow Farmers' Club And Tenants' Defence Association in the early 1870s along with Fr Dunphy's predecessor and mentor, Archdeacon Redmond. With such pro-tenants' rights and nationalist neighbours and colleagues, James Dunphy's own views were strengthened. Not that he needed affirmation to be true to his own ideals, but it did help.

The Very Rev Fr James Dunphy was a priest of the old school. He believed in the authority of position and his twenty years as curate to Archdeacon Redmond confirmed his view that the parish priest had an inalienable right not only to be respected but to be obeyed by his curates and the laity. Remarks in his letters to his archbishop in Dublin reflect this; 'the body of the people are of [the] poor class and have to look up to their priests for everything', and 'the fishermen ... usually follow me.'[15] He was even accused of claiming the right to control the

Fr. James Dunphy, c.1890

temporal and spiritual lives of non-Catholics: '... we, who claim the temporal as well as spiritual power over you as well as these poor creatures, will settle this matter with you.'[16] His curates, especially Fr Farrelly, shared this belief in the necessity of clerical leadership of the laity – '... with some little management the fishermen of Arklow will be found where they have always been – on the side of their Archbishop and priests.'[17]

Apart from his clerical equals and subordinates, Fr Dunphy had a coterie of middle-class Catholics who acted as his lieutenants in the day-to-day world of business and administration. Among the more important of these were Daniel Condren and James Hannigan,[18] both of whom were, among other things, members of the Arklow Dispensary and Sanitary Committee, of which much more at the appropriate junctures.

As stated in chapter 1, 'his [Dunphy's] labours were not confined to the spiritual needs [of his parishioners] ... they extended to the betterment and uplifting of his people industrially, socially and materially.'[19] He had seen how Archdeacon Redmond had involved himself in the promotion of employment and no doubt remembered when John Morrison, an Englishman who established a chemical works on the north side of the river in about 1870, had had difficulty in getting the support of the agents of lords Carysfort and Wicklow without bribing them, had written;

> This placed us in a dilemma, but there was the consolation that though those more directly in power opposed us, the poorer classes headed by the priests gave us much assistance, favouring the project in every way.
> The latter would allude to the undertaking at the alter [sic] on Sunday mornings (perhaps certainly from pecuniary motives) in the most glowing language, they visited the Works frequently, and they seemed ever ready to do us a good turn or give us any assistance in their power, and in the most priest-ridden country in the world, the moral influence of the Roman Catholic Clergy possesses immense weight. Indeed, had the Priests and the Agents combined, perhaps they would have stopped our operations entirely.[20]

Dunphy's tireless work in developing the harbour, and in establishing a small business concern manufacturing straw covers for bottles which employed about fifty girls, are testimony to his continuing Redmond's temporal as well as spiritual leadership.[21] The bottle covers, or 'envelopes' as they were referred to, were used to protect bottles in transit and, until Dunphy set up the Arklow factory, they had to be imported from Belgium and France. The editor of the *Wicklow News-Letter*, William M'Phail, was particularly impressed by this development and was fulsome in his praise of Fr Dunphy's enterprise, even though politically they were on opposite sides of the fence. It had occurred to Dunphy that a considerable number of the fishermen's daughters would benefit from such work. A local Catholic businessman, identified only as Mr. Fogarty,[22] allowed Fr Dunphy to use an unoccupied store-house as the factory premises. A woman was brought down from Dublin for a week to teach the Arklow girls the relatively basic skills required for the work, and markets for the finished product were secured. The wages were small, on average between four and five shillings a week, which equated to about half of a labourer's wage, but Dunphy's main aim was not to establish a commercial enterprise, but to give employment to the unemployed – 'to enable the younger and weaker branches of the poor fishermen's families to contribute something to the family resources.'[23]

The *News-Letter*, however, was not always so supportive of Dunphy's control over his parishioners. In March 1885, it carried what initially looked like another glowing report of his benevolent influence: 'A few weeks ago we had occasion to remark in congratulatory manner upon the satisfactory moral tone of the townspeople of Arklow as instanced in the scanty charge sheet at the local police court for some time past.'[24] It continued in similar fashion, extolling in particular the sobriety of the general populace. M'Phail even praised the recently concluded Catholic mission for its strong advocacy of the cause of temperance. No less than two thousand people had taken a temporary pledge of abstinence from alcohol and seemed to be fulfilling their promises. These opening plaudits were soon overturned as the report went on to decry the apparent lack of priestly leadership in other matters. It denounced the –

> series of cowardly attacks which have been made upon a respectable and well-known inhabitant of the town, simply because he chose to exercise his right of thinking and acting independently, in place of sacrificing his judgement and conscience at the altar of religious prejudice and political fanaticism.

The victim of these attacks was Mr T Kavanagh, who had been insulted and threatened in the street, burned in effigy, had tar barrels 'lighted in derision' before his house, his boats were damaged, and 'every device that ignorant malice and bigotry could invent has been employed to outrage and injure him.' The newspaper was not accusing Fr Dunphy or his curates of taking an active role in these disturbances, but they did stand accused of failing to intervene, and

> [t]he lower classes of Arklow are more amenable to the [influences of the Catholic church] than perhaps any community in Ireland, and a word from the Catholic clergy would have prevented the occurrence of any such scenes of ruffianism.

M'Phail also blamed the police for not acting to protect Kavanagh, but it is telling that he obviously believed that the secular authority could not have wielded the same degree of power over the perpetrators as the parish priest. He went on to use the incident to accuse the promoters of political 'Liberty' – meaning, no doubt, the advocates of home rule – of hypocrisy, turning to violent and intimidatory acts when someone refused to toe the party line.

> It shows how the wirepullers of this combination require each of their adherents to barter away his independence as a man, his dignity as a reasonable creature, and to degrade himself to a mere automaton.

According to M'Phail, Kavanagh was a Catholic member of the Arklow Dispensary Committee, but I could not find his name in the membership list in the minute books of the Rathdrum Board of Guardians in February or in the new committee voted in on 1 April 1885. He had, again according to M'Phail, recently voted against the other Catholic members of the committee, and by extension against the wishes of Fr Dunphy. M'Phail now used the attacks on him to attack the growing association of nationalist politics and Catholicism:

> In Arklow a certain party appear to have made some such proclamation as this: 'It is impossible to be a good Catholic without being an advanced Nationalist – it is equally impossible to be an advanced Nationalist without introducing religious prejudice and party bitterness into the simplest details of social intercourse. And those of our faith who refuse to subscribe in all obedience to this combined creed, we will not only ostracise and treat with contempt, but punish by injury and insult at every opportunity'. What a monstrous outrage that such a system of tyranny should be shamelessly practised in the name of Faith and Fatherland.

M'Phail's use of such vague terms as 'certain party', 'appear to have made', and 'some such proclamation' render the accusation woolly, but the tone of the piece leaves no doubt that he believed that such was the case, and he further believed that it raised grave doubts about the ability of such people to rise to the 'dignity as a free nation'. It is unlikely that Fr Dunphy or his curates cared for M'Phail's opinion, but M'Phail had a point; one word from Dunphy would indeed have brought the intimidation of Kavanagh to a halt, but he had chosen not to issue that word. Perhaps he felt that Kavanagh deserved to be taught a lesson.

Dunphy's position in the religious, social and commercial life of the town and parish was a powerful one. It might be no exaggeration to describe him as the most powerful man in the area. The vast majority of Catholics gave him unquestioning support, but even many Protestant businessmen recognised his ability to get things done and had no difficulty in acknowledging his primary role in matters of general benefit. An example of this cross-community acknowledgement took place in May 1885 when he chaired a meeting in the Marlborough Hall to hear the reading of an engineer's report of damage done to the new harbour works in a recent storm. It should be noted that those named as being present were a fairly even mix of Catholic and Protestant, and although the motion that Fr Dunphy should take the chair was made by a Catholic, P. Kavanagh, it was seconded by Mr Black, manager of the local branch of the Bank of Ireland,[25] who was a son of the Church of Ireland rector at Inch, five miles south of Arklow.[26] One of the purposes of the meeting was to form a committee that would keep the local M.P., William Corbet, informed as to the condition of the works so that he might make representation to the Treasury as required. No one was better qualified to chair the meeting than Dunphy. Over the years he had worked relentlessly with Carysfort, Corbet, Parnell and others to have the developments approved and funded. Once again, he had managed to conflate his role of spiritual leader with that of community activist. Not only that, his curates Farrelly, Flavin and O'Donnell were also in attendance, as was William Dunphy, his brother. The meeting was concerned with who was responsible for the poor design and construction of the harbour developments and does not really concern us here. What is important is the almost automatic choosing of Dunphy to chair it, particularly as it was a mixed attendance of Catholic and Protestant, of nationalist and unionist. His acceptance by the audience as chairman is perhaps indicative of his proven concern and commitment to the town's economic well-being. It is equally interesting, however, that none of the town's Church of Ireland, Methodist or Presbyterian clergymen were present, and their absence added to the impression that this secular gathering, as with so many others, was being controlled by the local Catholic Church.

There was one sphere, however, over which he had not yet been able to gain control, the very important Arklow Dispensary and Sanitary Committee.[27] It irritated him that in an overwhelmingly Catholic country such as Ireland, Catholics were grossly under-represented in public office and on public bodies. The Arklow Dispensary Committee was a case in point. Of its thirteen members the majority had always been Protestant, and it was no coincidence that the medical officers elected by the committee had also always been Protestant. But in 1884 there was a change of personnel and although it is not possible to give a definite religious profile, it was more finely balanced than before. As parish priest, and as a warden of the committee, Dunphy recognised that this was the opportunity he needed to increase his influence over it.

To understand the importance of the dispensary committee at that time it is necessary to outline the system of public health then in place.[28] There had been a system of public health in Ireland since the mid-eighteenth century which was overseen by the grand jury of each county. A county infirmary had been opened in Wicklow in 1766, and in 1805 the grand jury was authorized to give grants to dispensaries in rural districts. By the middle of the century these were widely distributed throughout the county, administered by committees of management, supported partly by subscription and partly by grand jury grants of equal amount. The economic viability of a dispensary district, therefore, depended mainly on the level of voluntary subscriptions raised. This meant that while some dispensary districts could manage to carry out their duties, others could not. Fever hospitals were also established, the one in Arklow being opened in 1818.

After the introduction of the Poor Law (Ireland) Act[29] in 1838, many public health responsibilities were transferred from county grand juries to boards of guardians which were management committees compromised of ratepayers. Arklow was in the Rathdrum Poor Law Union and public health matters in the town were therefore the responsibility of the Rathdrum Poor Law Board of Guardians. In 1851, the old grand jury dispensary system was also placed under the board of guardians, resulting in a rudimentary medical service being more widely available than ever before. More legislation expanded and improved the system. For example, in 1863 dispensary doctors were made registrars of births and deaths, so for the first time accurate statistics of mortality could be compiled. In 1864 compulsory vaccination of children against smallpox was introduced, and in 1872 a new central authority for local government and health services was established. This Local Government Board put the emphasis on prevention rather than cure in matters of health and the Public Health Acts of 1874 and 1878 were introduced as measures to promote sanitation. Under their provisions poor law guardians became rural sanitation authorities and in certain cases urban sanitation authorities.

> A new code was established to deal with water and sewerage schemes, removal of nuisances, scavenging control, infectious diseases, burial grounds and other sanitary matters and the slow fight to prevent disease, rather than contain it, began in earnest.[30]

The position of medical officer, which also included the responsibilities and title of sanitation officer, was vital within this structure. He – and at that time, and for many decades to come, it was invariably 'he' – was in the front line, not only in treating sickness and disease but in being vigilant in eradicating conditions which could give rise to them. With such responsibility and the necessity of treating patients in outlying areas, the holder should ideally have been young, fit and committed to the new focus on prevention. These requirements were particularly needed in the Arklow dispensary district, which with 6,390 inhabitants was the second largest in the union, and areawise covering 16,796 acres or 26.3 square miles, was the largest.[31]

As 1885 dawned, however, the medical officer for the Arklow dispensary, Dr. Stopford William Halpin, was neither young nor fit. He may have been committed, but being in his eighty-second year his flesh was probably weaker than his willing spirit. On 24 February, James Hannigan, honorary secretary of the committee and a Catholic who would prove to be a staunch supporter of the parish priest, wrote to the Rathdrum Board of Guardians, informing them that he had received notification from Dr Richard Halpin that his father was seriously ill. A meeting of the committee had been called and had appointed Dr French to act in *locum tenens*.[32] Three days after that letter was written, Dr Halpin senior died, leaving the position of medical officer open. Another meeting of the dispensary committee was held on 5 March where it was proposed and agreed that the election of a replacement medical officer be held on 4 April, and that the honorary secretary was to advertise the post.[33] In the meantime, Dr French was to remain in the position from 21 February until 4 April at a salary of £3.0.0 per week.

This was the opportunity Dunphy had been waiting for. For the first time, there was a real chance of having a Catholic doctor appointed to this important position and he had no intention of letting it slip by. It was time to rally his troops. He could not afford to have any break in the ranks and it is interesting that it was about this date that the attacks on Kavanagh took place. If M'Phail was right and Kavanagh was a member of the committee and had been attacked because of his failing to toe the party line, then Dunphy would have had to let the intimidation proceed if he was to tighten his grip on the dispensary committee, particularly as the appointment of a new medical officer was about to take place.

No sooner had Dr Halpin's death been announced than strings were stretched taut, ready to be pulled. Not only was there a real chance of a Catholic doctor being appointed medical officer for the district, but it is highly probable that Dunphy even had a candidate in mind. It will be remembered that the parish priest of Barndarrig to the north of Arklow, Fr Michael Molony, was on very good terms with Fr Dunphy. Molony had a nephew who was a doctor in London, a young man who would be a very suitable candidate for the position.

CHAPTER 4:
Dr. Michael J Molony

Michael Joseph Molony was born on New Year's Day 1861[1] in the village of New Inn which lies half-way between the towns of Cahir and Cashel in south Tipperary. In the northwest corner of the cemetery which surrounds the village's Catholic church is a group of monuments to the Molony/Moloney family, sometimes spelt with an 'e' and sometimes without, who were well established in the general area. Michael's grandparents, Daniel Moloney and Catherine O'Neill had married in the church, or in its predecessor, on 16 February 1808,[2] and they had at least six children. There was Michael (1812),[3] Andrew (1820), Judith (1822), Mary (1823), Honora (1826) and Daniel (1829), Moloney being spelt with an 'e' in all cases.[4] The fact that only one child, Michael, is recorded in the gap of twelve years between the marriage and the baptism of Andrew in 1820, coupled with the more regular and frequent spacing of Michael's subsequent siblings, raises the probability that there were other children whose baptismal records are either elsewhere or have been lost. Michael became a priest, eventually becoming pastor in the County Wicklow parish of Barndarrig. He has already featured in this story and will feature again from to time to time. For now, it is the youngest son Daniel who requires our attention.

Daniel studied medicine, becoming a licentiate of the Royal College of Surgeons of Ireland in 1854 at the age of twenty-five.[5] The following year he took a position as surgeon with the government emigration service before transferring to the transport service during the Crimean war. In 1857, he was on a British naval gunboat on the Danube; the entry in *The Medical Directory* says 'HM Gunboat', but 'gunboat' was a type of vessel and no royal navy vessel ever bore it as a name; neither is there a record of Daniel Moloney's service, but this would not have been unusual as such periodic services by civilian doctors were not normally recorded.[6]

His taste for travel didn't last long, however, and he returned home where he married Ellen Slattery. There is no record of the marriage in the Tipperary records, but she is listed as the mother of his nine children.[7] As it was the norm at that time for marriages to take place in the bride's parish, it is possible that they were married outside the diocese. There is also the ever-present possibility that they were married locally and that the record was either never made or has been lost. The young doctor and Ellen were to have Michael Joseph (1861),[8] Mary (1862), George Mark (1863), Daniel Joseph (1864), Daniel (1866), Thomas Joseph (1869), Joseph Clements (1870), Clara Margaret (1873), and Josephine Mary (1875). All their surnames were also spelt with an 'e', although later references to those who feature in this story are usually 'Molony'. Another interesting aspect of their names is the fact that 'Joseph' was given to four of the six boys and the feminine Josephine to the last girl. The presence of two Daniels suggests that the first born Daniel died in infancy and the next boy born to the family inherited the name, which was a common practice in the nineteenth century.

The different addresses in the records show that at the time of both Michael's baptism in 1861 and Mary's in 1862 the family residence was at New Inn, but this changed to Cashel in 1863, James Street, Cashel in 1864, and John Street, Cashel in 1869 and subsequent years.[9] Mary's godfather was recorded as Daniel's oldest brother, Revd M Moloney, who was already a curate at Barndarrig. It is Daniel's first born, Michael Joseph, who is of most importance to this story, and from this point on the form 'Molony' – the form he used himself – will be used for his surname.

Nothing is known about his pre-school life, but it can be assumed that being the son of the local doctor would have given him some economic security and social standing. The houses of John Street were handsome two- and three-storeyed slated buildings which announced that their inhabitants were of the 'respectable' variety. Halfway along its length stood, and still stands, the Church of Ireland cathedral dedicated to St

John the Baptist. At the other end, just across Main Street, was the bishop's palace, now a hotel. His familiarity with these Protestant surroundings and church-goers would stand him in good stead, fostering an outlook that differed from the them-and-us mindset of many he would meet in later life. As Roman Catholics, the Molonys would have taken a short-cut from John Street through the narrow Agar's Lane to Upper Friar Street to attend another St John the Baptist church, this one Catholic. Looking down either John Street or Upper Friar Street, towards the northwest, it is impossible to miss the impressive architectural remains on the Rock of Cashel, ancient seat of the kings of Munster; its round tower; its medieval cathedral where many of the town's citizenry were massacred in 1647 by Cromwell's henchman Lord Inchiquin, better known as Murrough-of-the-Burnings; and the gem that is Cormac's chapel. Here were the symbols of Irish identity, cultural, political and religious covering a period of a thousand years and more. Did these august surroundings impinge on the young boy's consciousness? Who can tell? Too often the problem with growing up in the constant presence of reminders of past greatness is not that familiarity breeds contempt so much as it breeds indifference. The Rock and its ruins were simply *there*, just as the shops on Main Street were there.

His middle-class family and environment gave him opportunities denied to many; one of these was access to a good education. Four miles south of Cashel is Rockwell College, a private secondary school run by a Catholic religious order, the Holy Ghost Fathers. Just when Michael first entered Rockwell, or if he had undergone private study or had attended another school previously, is not known. Rockwell's early records are incomplete and do not record him as a student, but his academic record in Queen's College, Cork (now NUI Cork) gives his 'place of education' as Rockwell.[10] Some sources state that he also attended Blackrock College in Dublin, but their extensive archive does not bear this out.[11] Rockwell was a logical choice. It had a good reputation, was very near his home and his father, Daniel, was medical advisor to the college.[12] Today, the school's mission statement speaks of fostering a 'Christian Community of freedom and love which respects the rights and uniqueness of each pupil, as well as promoting respect for civil authorities and a concern and care for one another.' The school motto promotes '*Inter Mutanda Constantia* – (constancy in the midst of inevitable change) –through fidelity to Christ and His Church, openness to the future and attentiveness to discerning the Spirit of God at work in successive generations.' Among the virtues it aims to inculcate are 'justice and peace … genuine charity … mutual forbearance, pardoning, sharing, ever hospitable and free from prejudice.' Although these heady aspirations are taken from today's mission statement, it is likely that they were also the watchwords of the college ethos in the 1860s and 1870s, and may well have been influential in shaping the adult life of the young Michael Molony. Perhaps the following extract is the most telling:

> We count the following as constitutive parts of our mission of evangelisation: the integral liberation of people, action for justice and peace, and participation in development. It follows that we must make ourselves the advocates, the supporters and defenders of the weak and the little ones against all who oppress them.[13]

When these words are compared with the words his friends and supporters had inscribed on the monument they erected over his grave, it would appear that Molony took them to heart and tried to live his life by them.

In 1878, at the age of seventeen, he was enrolled as a first year student in the Faculty of Medicine in Queen's College, Cork. His parents' residence was given as Cashel, but Michael was recorded as living at 1 Charlotte Quay (now Father Mathew Quay), Cork. No name was given to indicate with whom he was living, and his father's name is mistakenly recorded as David instead of Daniel. Michael also appears on the rolls as a second year student in 1879-1880 and as a third year student in 1880-1881. During those years he also appears to have had some practical training in the North Cork Infirmary.[14] His name then disappears from the record.[15] The reason for this disappearance is he transferred to the Royal College of Surgeons, Edinburgh, where he took his final examinations on 1 November 1882. His academic record there shows that 'being examined in Anatomy, Surgery and Pharmacy found duly qualified to practise these arts and received Diplomas having paid the usual fees to the Treasurer.'[16] The college president at that time, and the man who would sign and verify Molony's election, was Sir William Turner, probably the foremost teacher of anatomy in Britain in the latter part of the nineteenth century, and who was also president of the general medical council. His marks were anatomy 50, physiology 55, chemistry 50 which, out of 100, seem to have been fairly standard results for the period. Molony obtained what was known as the 'Double Qualification', which provided licentiateship of both the Royal College of Surgeons and the Royal College of Physicians of Edinburgh. Licentiates were often apprentices for three or more years, and had to have attended courses as well as attendance at surgical operations (which perhaps explains his presence at the North Cork Infirmary) at an approved university by recognised professors or at a school with teachers who were fellows of one of the medical colleges. They then attended the college for further examination by the fellows.[17] In the same year he also became a licentiate in midwifery and is recorded as attending Surgical Hall and Royal Infirmary, Edinburgh.[18] He was registered as a doctor on 19 December 1882, and appeared in *The Medical Register* for the first time in 1883, four names below his father's entry. Both father and son gave their address as Cashel.

Cashel might well have been Michael's official address at that time, but he did not spend much of 1883 there, for he is recorded as holding the post of assistant surgeon in the London boroughs of Camberwell and Islington, and shortly afterwards was one of a specially commissioned medical team sent to Tunstall, Slingsby in Yorkshire and Tredegar in Wales, where he was senior assistant surgeon at Tredegar Mine and Ironworks.[19] It was while he was in Tredegar that he began contributing articles to professional journals. His paper on 'Fracture of the Base of skull, followed by Encephalitis, Ataxia and Aphasia', a case study based on an incident there in 1883, was published in *The Lancet* in 1884.[20]

Dr Michael Joseph Molony was at the start of a promising career and his first permanent position was about to be offered to him. It was an offer that would bring him back to Ireland.

The seventy-three-year-old Very Revd Michael Molony, parish priest of Barndarrig in County Wicklow, was uncle to this promising young doctor working across the Irish Sea. It does not overtax the imagination to believe that he was aware of Fr Dunphy's long-held ambition to have a Catholic doctor treat the poorer people of Arklow; nor is it unreasonable to assume that he mentioned this most eligible young physician and surgeon, his nephew, to Dunphy. Not only could he vouch for his professional suitability, but could also expound on the young man's personal qualities, his respectable family in Cashel, his upbringing as a good Catholic and his desire to secure a position back in Ireland, back among his own people. There is no direct evidence that this actually happened, but what would have been more natural? Fr Dunphy needed a good candidate, Fr Molony could suggest one.

Whether Dr Molony learned of the opening by letter from a close family member such as his uncle, or by reading an advertisement in the professional press is immaterial. All that matters is learn of it he did, and he wanted it. His father had been medical officer for the dispensary district of Tullemaine in the Cashel poor law union for many years,[21] so he knew what it entailed. He was aware that, as medical officer of Arklow, he could satisfy any moral drive he might have towards administering to the poor, while also fulfilling any financial ambitions he may have harboured as the position left ample opportunity to develop a private practice, as well as allowing time to enter into contractual agreements with local businesses.[22] He applied for the job and was duly called to interview.

Before the interview took place, however, a new Arklow dispensary committee was elected on 1 April for the coming

Dr. Michael J. Molony

year, although it was in fact merely a re-election of the outgo-ing committee. As far as can be ascertained, there were seven Catholic and six Protestant members of the committee as well as ten wardens, one of whom was Fr Dunphy.[23]

Normally, meetings were held at noon on the third Thursday of each month, but an extraordinary meeting was held on 4 April to select the new medical officer. There were six candidates, but only two were duly placed for nomination; Dr Richard Halpin, son of the recently deceased medical officer, and Dr Michael Molony. The Catholic majority on the committee should have put Fr Dunphy's mind at ease as regards the outcome, but he was unsure as to how one of the Catholics, Owen Fogarty, would vote, but he need not have been concerned. With seven votes for Molony and six for Halpin, Dunphy's candidate was appointed at £120 per year.

No doubt the young doctor, still only twenty-four years of age, was delighted with his success, but he could not have been more pleased than Fr Dunphy, who was ecstatic. He had at last brought his influence to bear on the appointment of a public officer and the following day, 5 April which happened to be Easter Sunday, he wrote to Dr Walsh, acting Catholic archbishop of Dublin:

> The result of yesterday's election was – we have a Catholic doctor over our poor people. It was hard to work Mr Fogarty – He would not give the others of the Committee his views or unite his actions with theirs, yet they acted all along as one man in obedience to my wishes. Public opinion ran very high in all this country - so that had a distinct effect on Mr Fogarty. I am most proud of the <u>result</u> and we have given a stab to <u>Freemasonry</u> in these quarters it won't forget a while. Lord Carysfort came all the way from London to back <u>his</u> man. We beat him by [illegible]. If we could only unite our <u>Forces</u> in every Parish we would soon pull down ascendancy. I am happy to tell you that we are all as one Family in this Parish that way – <u>The Priests & the</u> <u>People for ever</u> since the days of King William. A Catholic Doctor but could get a fart[h]ing in Arklow – We are contesting all the positions at Public Boards by electing the men of our own choice – Lord Carysfort has been creating ex-officios to part[?] us of the type of Owen Fogarty & Daniel O'Connell – grandson of the Liberator – and other <u>Idiots</u>.
> Thanks for your sound advice in these transactions. Hoping we may soon hear of the Selections of the Holy See of the future Archbishop of Dublin.[24] Wishing you a Happy Easter –

> I am yours very truly, James Dunphy.[25]

From the tone of the letter there can be little doubt that, whatever the mood of the acting archbishop, James Dunphy was having a very happy Easter indeed. He had, after all, secured 'a Catholic doctor over our poor people', and seems to have missed the irony of his establishing his own freemasonry in order to give a 'stab to Freemasonry in these quarters.' The fact that Molony supported home rule and was a member of the central branch of the National League would not have gone unnoticed, endearing him even more to Fr Dunphy. The central branch had many American and British, as well as Irish based, home rulers on their register.[26] In 1889 Molony was also to state that he had been working for the national cause for ten years both in England and Ireland.[27] A final point regarding this letter is the fact that Dunphy refers to Lord Carysfort coming from London to back 'his' man, Dr Halpin. There can be little doubt that Dunphy therefore regarded Molony as being *his* man, but Michael Molony was to prove that he was no one's man.

Just when or how Dr Molony was informed of his selection is not recorded, but that is also of little importance. A more annoying lack of information concerns his marital status. There is nothing to say if he were married or single, or if he had children at the time of his appointment. Despite exhaustive research in English, Welsh and Scottish records of births, marriages and deaths, no suitable matches have been found. Later brief references, as will be seen, did mention 'a wife', but no details, such as her name, when and where they met, if they had children, have as yet been discovered. Married or single, he lost no time in taking up the position of medical officer for the dispensary district of Arklow.

CHAPTER 5:
Molony settles in

The town into which the twenty-four-year-old Dr Michael J Molony arrived in April 1885 was neither prosperous nor populous. It was a fishing port whose importance had grown a great deal in recent decades, but it suffered the economic vagaries that fishing invariably entails,[1] and a significant portion of its 4,777 men, women and children were frequently destitute.[2] Many people had left the town in the 1870s, resulting in a seven per cent drop in population since the 1871 census figure of 5,178, and it would continue to fall by another twelve and a half per cent to 4,172 in 1891.[3] There was, however, a growing trading fleet and boatbuilding industry.[4] The harbour improvements spearheaded by Fr Dunphy, supported in parliament by nationalist M.Ps. William Corbet and Parnell in the early 1880s, had not been as effective as had been hoped, with some of the infrastructural developments washed away by storms and the rest generally taking longer than expected. Work on the piers was still in progress when Molony took up his position as medical officer.[5] Non-maritime related industry consisted in the main of the Arklow Manure Works, also known as the Arklow Chemical Works founded by John Morrison in about 1870,[6] and a few small enterprises which were mostly inconsequential.

From time to time, short-lived attempts to provide employment for the poor were made. One of these was the straw bottle cover factory established by Fr Dunphy mentioned in chapter 3. But in early 1885, there was an air of hope on the employment front, and Charles Stewart Parnell was again at the centre of it. In December 1884, he leased Arklow Rock from the earl of Carysfort. The Rock, as it is more simply and popularly known, was an 800 feet high dolerite plug of an ancient volcano[7] a mile south of the town, and plans were in place to begin quarrying it on a large scale within the year, thus bringing significant employment to the area.[8]

The layout of the town was straightforward and might best be explored through Molony's eyes. The railway had reached Arklow in 1863[9] and it is probable that this was how he arrived. Emerging from the station, he would have had his first view of the several hundred yards of straight road that led to the town centre. The first building he passed was on the right side, a building with which he would become very familiar, the combined fever hospital and dispensary erected in 1818. Next came a few dwelling houses and a small Protestant school erected by the local landlord, William Proby, earl of Carysfort, again all on the right-hand side and all of recent vintage. Beside these was a steep-roofed larger structure, too big and barn-like to be a private residence. This was the Marlborough Hall, built in 1878 as a town hall and community centre. The town commissioners used the venue for their meetings, but were later to transfer to rooms in the courthouse a short distance away. Local lore suggests that the nationalist commissioners felt the courthouse would be seen as a more independent venue for town commission meetings. After all, the hall had been erected at the expense of the local unionist landlord and named in honour of a recent visit to the town by a British Tory peer of the realm, John Winston Spencer Churchill, 7th duke of Marlborough, lord lieutenant of Ireland from 1876 to 1880, and grandfather to the future British prime minister Winston Churchill. The Marlborough Hall was to prove much more successful as a venue for non-political entertainment and fundraising functions. Next came St Mary's, the new convent of the Sisters of Mercy, opened in 1881 mainly due to the persuasive entreaties and fundraising powers of Fr Dunphy and his predecessor Archdeacon Redmond. The last building on the right side of this railway station road, which here joined the town centre, was the Catholic parish church dedicated to Saints Mary and Peter. On the left-hand side, facing St Mary's convent and the west side of the church, was a respectable terrace of two-storeyed, slate-roofed houses. This had been constructed just four years earlier, the same year the convent was built, replacing a row of tiny mud-walled thatched cabins.[10] It too was

The light-coloured house was Molony's home during his years in Arklow

named in honour of the recent lord lieutenant, Marlborough Terrace,[11] although some of the residents refused to use this politically-charged name and opted for the older one of Chapel Lane.[12] The end house nearest the railway station, number 8,[13] was to be Molony's new home.

It was more than adequate accommodation, boasting a drawing-room, dining-room, study, hall, four bedrooms, a kitchen, and pantry. At the rear was a small shed to house a side car and horse.[14] He was leasing it from William Kavanagh, and its previous occupant had been the late Dr Stopford Halpin, the recently deceased medical officer whose role Molony had now assumed.[15] It might be said that Molony had not only stepped into Halpin's professional shoes, but also into his domestic slippers.

His first few days were no doubt given over to familiarising himself with Arklow and its environs. To reach the town centre, all he had to do was turn left as he closed his front door and walk 150 yards along Marlborough Terrace (or Chapel

Lane) and into the irregularly shaped open space that served, and still serves, as the town square. Two prominent buildings dominated this space, the Catholic parish church dedicated to Saints Mary and Peter, which still stands and serves the same purpose today, and the much older Royal Irish Constabulary barracks from which the square takes its name, Parade Ground. The barracks was built in about 1720 on the ruins of a Norman castle. The adjacent open space served as the parade ground where the small army garrison, usually amounting to no more than twenty officers and men, trained and drilled. With the formation of the Royal Irish Constabulary (R.I.C.) in the 1830s, the garrison was replaced by the new force.

The barracks took up the entire north side of Parade Ground, stretching from almost the railway bridge in Upper Main Street to the courthouse, which still stands at the northeast corner of Parade Ground. The courthouse had been built in the 1860s and, as stated above, apart from its judicial functions it would also serve as the home of the town commissioners, and until 2009 was the home of the commissioners' administrative offspring Arklow Urban District Council, now Arklow Town Council. On the south side, beside the church was the home of the parish priest, Fr James Dunphy, which stood on what is now the front lawn of the present parish priest's house. The local branch of the Bank of Ireland marked the end of Parade Ground on this side. Parade Ground was the town's centre for religion (at least for Roman Catholics), law and order (R.I.C. barracks and courthouse), and finance (the only bank in town at that time). It was here too that public meetings and demonstrations were held.

The main commercial area lay to the east. Main Street started at the bank and sloped downwards flanked on both sides by fine two- and three-storeyed buildings. Businesses of various types stood shoulder-to-shoulder here. Drapers, bakers, public houses, a hotel, post office, general grocers and butchers all added to the air of a busy town. There was a market house, and four fair days a year.[16] Roughly one-third of the way down the street, on the right-hand side, was the Protestant parish church

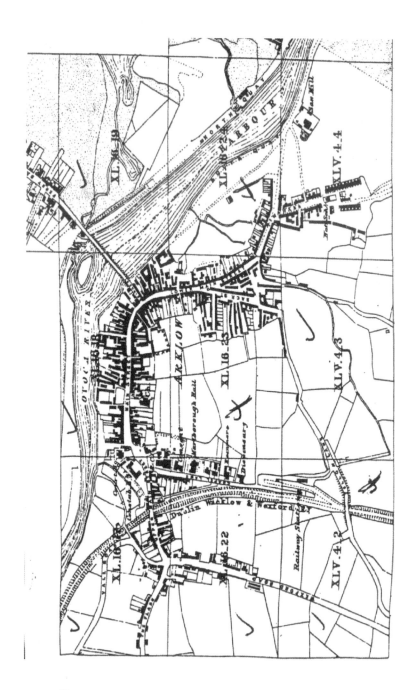

Arklow as it appeared when Dr Molony first saw it. (Source: OS map 1887)

of St Mary's, directly opposite a disused graveyard of the same name.[17] The graveyard had been closed in 1866 in the wake of a virulent outbreak of cholera.[18] Lanes of overcrowded dwellings, housing some of the poorest people in the town, linked Main Street to the river Ovoca.[19]

At the bottom of the sloping street, the way veered to the right, following the curve of the river. On this bend, Bridge Street led to a bridge of nineteen arches giving access to Ferrybank, a prosperous area where businessmen and shipowners resided. East and south of Bridge Street, Main Street gave way to Lower Main Street. It too boasted fine modern buildings, but they were mainly residential rather than commercial and the farther Molony walked along it, the more noticeable did diminishing standards become. The lanes off both sides of Lower Main Street were as poverty stricken and congested as those off Main Street, they were also more numerous. By King's Hill the houses grew steadily smaller and more dilapidated. Stone-built slated buildings became less frequent and low thatched roofs on mud-walled cabins became the norm in the triangular area of Back Street, Old Chapel Ground, the Brook and all their adjacent lanes.[20] This architectural homogeneity continued into Tinahask, Harbour Road, Gregg's Hill and the general area referred to as the Fishery. It would have been immediately obvious to Molony where he would spend most of his time treating the poor.

West of Parade Ground was little better. Upper Main Street reflected Lower Main Street in that the farther Molony walked from Parade Ground the less salubrious the buildings became. By the time he reached the area known as the Flash, where Upper Main Street met the Wexford, Vale and Coolgreaney Roads, congested lanes of houses mostly unfit for human habitation mirrored the enclaves of the Fishery. It was clear that he was going to be a very busy man – even without the rural section of his bailiwick of over twenty-six square miles, much of it on hilly terrain accessible only on horseback. The only areas of apparent affluence were Marlborough Terrace where he would live, Parade Ground, Main Street and the

Gregg's Hill 1890, showing the type of house in which the majority of Arklow people lived at that time. [Source: Lawrence Collection, NLI]

aforementioned Ferrybank on the north side of the river. Ferrybank consisted of a single double-sided street where well-to-do Catholics lived cheek-by-jowl with well-to-do Protestants, just as poor Catholics lived cheek-by-jowl with poor Protestants in the congested lanes of the Flash, the Brook and the Fishery.

In these circumstances, perhaps it was fortunate that he lived near his base of operations. The dispensary rooms were housed in the fever hospital, a couple of hundred yards from his house in the direction of the railway station. Molony wanted to begin work as soon as possible, and the dispensary committee were eager to have him do so, but there was an unforeseen problem. On 22 April 1885, James Hannigan, honorary secretary of the dispensary committee, wrote to the Rathdrum Board of Guardians to inform them that the fever hospital committee had requested that the dispensary vacate its rooms there.[21] No reason was given, certainly none that might suggest that Dr Molony had already stepped on toes, although, as will be seen, ruffling feathers was not beyond his personality. Perhaps they were simply peeved at Molony's selection as medical officer. Although there is no direct evidence to support this, it is not too difficult to imagine the still conservative-led hospital committee making things difficult for the now nationalist-led dispensary committee. The guardians' response was that a settlement should be arrived at as quickly as possible. A second problem was raised three weeks later while the first was still under negotiation, and this difficulty was deemed to have been caused by a breach of procedure on Hannigan's part as secretary of the dispensary committee. He wrote to inform the guardians that an inventory of surgical instruments had not been taken when Dr French had taken up the interim position between the demise of Dr Halpin and Molony's appointment. Now, he wrote, only a few instruments remained in the dispensary and the dispensary committee were obliged to order a new supply. The guardians were not pleased with this contravention of protocol and ordered that copies of the dispensary regulations be distributed to the various dispensary districts in the union.[22] Perhaps such teething problems were to be expected, but they were unfortunate incidents with which to start Molony's tenure.

His primary responsibility, and one he lost no time in addressing, was the care of the ill, but while engaged in this, he too soon upset the board of guardians in Rathdrum. A patient had dislocated a shoulder and Molony was called. On preliminary examination, he assessed that relocation could not be carried out without chloroform. The application of chloroform as an anaesthetic was a tricky undertaking in which the doctor applying it could himself be overcome by the fumes. For this reason it was normal practice to have two medical men present, the administrator and a qualified assistant. Molony sent for his rival-at-interview Richard Halpin. Halpin was rapid in his response and competent in his assistance.[23] If any personal rancour existed, none was shown. A week or so later Molony called on another local medic, Dr James Ryan, to assist in the removal of a tumour from a Mrs Long.[24]

When Halpin submitted a bill for five guineas (£5-5-0), the guardians were furious both at his apparent greed and at the new medical officer's equally apparent ignorance of the importance of fiscal management. They ordered that Halpin be paid no more than £1-1-0 and that in future, when time allowed, medical officers must call in other public health doctors for assistance rather than those in private practice.[25] Although Molony was not specifically named in this decision, it was ordered that he be informed by the dispensary committee that the guardians were not happy. Molony understandably felt that he was being reprimanded, and Michael Joseph Molony was a not a man to allow a criticism to go unchallenged. He wrote to the guardians stating that, as the 'patient was in torture' he had called in the nearest help rather than let the patient suffer while another medical officer was dispatched from somewhere else to assist. While this exchange was in progress, Dr Ryan submitted a bill for £2-2-0 for his assistance in Mrs Long's tumour case. The guardians refused to pay either Halpin or Ryan more than £1-1-0. Both doctors refused to accept this and continued for months to submit bills only to meet with the same response. Molony added fuel to the fire when he submitted a bill of his own for attending a petty sessions hearing regarding a health nuisance. He was seeking £2-2-0 as he did not consider this to be part of his normal duties. The guardians claimed that it had been made clear to him that such attendances were part of his duties and that such expenses were included in his salary. Molony refused to accept that decision and re-entered his claim for re-imbursement. Again the guardians refused to entertain it and were supported by the Arklow dispensary committee who stated that all Molony's expenses must come from his salary, except those allowed by the Registration and Vaccination Acts. Again he resubmitted the bill, but as in the case of the other doctors' claims it seemed to disappear into the ether. One good piece of news in July was the decision of the fever hospital committee to allow the dispensary to continue to use rooms in the hospital.

As medical and sanitary officer, Molony had several areas of responsibility apart from his direct treatment of injuries and ailments. Various improvements in the government's approach to public health in the 1860s and 1870s had seen the introduction of compulsory vaccination of children against contagious diseases. Many people were suspicious of vaccination and refused to comply with – or, in most cases of non-compliance, simply ignored – the law. Molony was a strong believer in the scientific approach to medicine. To him, prevention was far superior to cure and anything that would help avert an epidemic of cholera, chicken pox, typhus or other contagion to which the primitive, overcrowded living conditions gave rise to was to be embraced. During his tenure as medical officer he repeatedly urged the board of guardians to pursue defaulters in this matter.

Another string to his hippocratic bow was the detection and eradication of potential health hazards. Indoor sanitation was a novelty in 1880s Arklow. It was non-existent in the homes in the lanes and crowded enclaves, where waste was simply left outside the door.[26] However, there was effluent among the affluent as well. Molony took all these breaches of health regulations as seriously as he took the necessity of the vaccination of children. If he reported the poor for non-compliance, he also reported the well-to-do. Among the latter was a neighbour in Marlborough Terrace, Mrs Benkey, whose house lacked a proper drainage system and thereby was 'causing a nuisance' – in today's parlance, it stank.[27] Dr Halpin, who also lived in Marlborough Terrace,[28] did not escape Molony's attention either, despite his assistance in resetting the dislocated shoulder. Molony reported him for having an open drain on his property. The more cynical might suspect that Molony was retaliating for the exorbitant bill submitted by Halpin, but Molony's reporting of Halpin's less than state-of-art drains was made in

May, a month before Halpin submitted his bill. Both Halpin and Benkey were ordered to have the necessary work carried out.

From these cases, it must be inferred that Molony was single-minded in his duty. When he saw breaches of regulations which he was charged to uphold, he did what he felt bound to do, irrespective of who was involved. While such individual actions were undoubtedly necessary, Molony soon realised that improvements were needed on a systematic scale. In October 1885, just six months into his tenure as medical officer, he began a campaign for an improved sewage system and a general clean-up of the town.[29]

There was a serious cholera scare in various parts of the country in September, and the Local Government Board ordered that medical officers were to inspect crews of ships arriving from ports where cholera had been confirmed and to

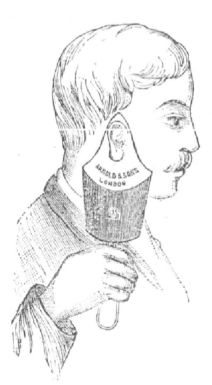

make sure that there was adequate accommodation for cholera victims. Molony wrote to the board of guardians stating that the earl of Carysfort, chairman of the dispensary committee, was refusing to allow cholera patients into the fever hospital, but that he had instructed his agent to arrange some suitable building should cholera break out.[30] Thankfully, no outbreak occurred in Arklow at that time.

By the end of his first year in the job, few could have been in doubt about Molony's ability, integrity, and commitment. They might have been even more impressed with his other activities had they known of them. 'Time management' may not have been an expression or even a concept then in vogue, but his ability to serve such a large dispensary area and still manage to keep abreast of developments in his profession was remarkable. But he did even more than that. He not only read the latest views and discoveries in the medical journals, he also found time to write articles for them. For example, his piece about his own invention of 'an aural reservoir', a device used in syringing ears which left an unassisted surgeon's hands free to carry out the process, was written during his busy first year in Arklow and was published in *The Medical Press Circular* in May 1886.[31] And he still found time to play, joining the committee of the Arklow Athletic and Aquatic Sports, helping to organise their annual sports day on 15 August.[32]

In the light of subsequent events, this apparently inno-cent, even praiseworthy, participation in a healthy community activity may have contributed to a cooling of relations between himself and Fr Dunphy. Like most events in Arklow in the 1880s, even a sports day could be politicised. Molony was an intelligent man and cannot have been oblivious to the power plays that were going on around him. He could not have been unaware of the behind-the-scenes dynamics that had resulted in his being appointed medical officer, but even if he were Michael Molony was not a man to plan his actions to suit another's purpose or faun for another's approval. When he decided on a course of action he did so because he felt it was the proper course of action. He had already shown this trait in his professional role and would show it in his political and private roles time and time again, irrespective of who was pleased and who was not.

Like many powerful men, James Dunphy could show his peevish side. His relationship with his clerical neighbour, Fr Michael Molony in Barndarrig, hit a bumpy patch in June 1885, two months after the arrival of Molony's nephew, when one of the Arklow curates, Fr Flavin, was transferred to Barndarrig. Dunphy wrote to Bishop Walsh to air his annoyance at the move. Walsh was still interim administrator of the diocese until a new archbishop was appointed to replace the recently deceased Cardinal McCabe.

> The present staff of curates were working very harmoniously and were giving great satisfaction ... I wish the likes [of] Fr Molony would learn to train young men and not be coveting his neighbour's goods.[33]

This letter, perhaps insignificant in itself, raises several questions. Was Dunphy's annoyance at Fr Molony a short-lived flare-up, a peeved reaction to Molony's 'poaching' of Fr Flavin? Or was it a manifestation of some underlying problem between them? Was it merely another step in an already fractious relationship? It should be remembered that Fr Michael Molony was Dr Michael Molony's uncle, and if the erstwhile apparently friendly relationship between the two priests was beginning to slip into acrimony, would it have tainted Dunphy's relationship with the young doctor? It is a difficult question to answer because it may have been something of a chicken-and-egg situation in that the reverse could also hold true; there is the distinct possibility that from the start the relationship between the young medical officer and Fr Dunphy had not been all that either might have wished. Perhaps Dr Molony's independent spirit – which was already widely recognised and would manifest itself time and again in the months and years ahead – was something Fr Dunphy had not bargained for. If this is assumed to be the case, perhaps a growing antipathy between these two important pillars of the community was the cause rather than the effect of the declining friendliness between the two priests. In short, was Dunphy annoyed at Fr Molony for foisting the recalcitrant Dr Molony on him?

It is clear that in March and April, Fr Dunphy had approved of the young man, endorsing his candidature for the post of medical officer. The members of the dispensary committee who had voted for Molony had 'acted all along as one man in obedience to my [Dunphy's] wishes.'[34] His endorsement was probably based on three factors: one, Molony was appropriately qualified for the job; two, Molony was a Catholic; and three, Molony was a member of the National League. Nothing in the doctor's professional capacity could have brought about a change of heart in Dunphy. He was competent and diligent. But what of his Catholicism and political allegiance? Molony would later unequivocally state

> that in ecclesiastical and spiritual matters I need hardly say that I bow most respectfully to the opinions of the clergy, but not being a professional flunkey who wants to scrape up a few patients by hanging on and toadying to the local clergy, I decline to be dictated to in purely temporal, and above all on local municipal questions by the clergy or anybody else.[35]

Even allowing that this was written four years after his arrival, there is ample evidence to show that this was his stance from the outset. Given this attitude, Dunphy may have felt cheated in having what he would regard an apostate (at least politically speaking) rather than a devout follower urged upon him by a neighbouring parish priest. And if so, would he not have been as annoyed with the recommending uncle as he was with the nephew? This is conjecture, but the possibilities are interesting.

A couple of months after Molony's arrival, Dunphy was given another reason to suspect that he had made a mistake in supporting his candidature for the position of medical officer. In July 1885 Dunphy wrote to Alexander Taylor (sometimes spelt Tailyeur or Tailyour), Carysfort's estate manager, seeking the use of the 'Town Hall' – this was the Marlborough Hall and should not be confused with the courthouse – for a fundraising bazaar in aid of the construction of the new chapel at Castletown.[36]

> The time I will require it about the 15th of August and for three days. I have circular [sic] tickets issued for about that time. Will you kindly let me know if I can have the use of the Hall at that time, and for the space of three days.

It is obvious from the fact that the tickets had already been printed that Dunphy assumed he could use the hall as it suited him, but Taylor's reply was not the one he expected. He said that Carysfort would be happy to rent the hall to Dunphy on the usual terms of £1 per day, and a deposit of £5 to make good any damage that may be done, but the hall would be available only on the 13, 14 and 15 August, or the 18, 19 and 20th. Dunphy was not pleased and he informed Taylor that the tickets were issued for the 15, 16 and 17th and it was now impossible to alter them. Taylor responded by saying that he could not be held responsible for the issuing of dated tickets before the dates had been agreed. The reason that the hall would not be available for the 16th was that the 16th was Sunday, 'on which the hall is not allowed to be used for any purpose, and the 17th being Monday, it is not available on that day, as it is required for Lady Carysfort's weekly Clothing Club'. Dunphy does not appear to have replied to this. It was a blow to Fr Dunphy's ego as well as to his plans.

To compound matters, the first date for which Dunphy was seeking use of the hall, Saturday 15 August, also happened to be the day of the annual sports in which Dr Molony was participating as a committee member. The clash could hardly have been coincidental. Fr Dunphy and his curates were eager supporters, indeed promoters, of activities which would bring improvements in the general welfare of the community. Surely the annual sports day should have fallen into this general description? Yet, of the twenty-plus committee officers and members, not one clergymen – of any persuasion – was included. Could this absence be explained by the fact that the chairman of the sports committee was the earl of Wicklow and the vice-chairman was his agent Robert Hudson? The earl of Carysfort and his agent, Alexander Taylor, were also on the committee, and the surnames of the other members suggest that a large majority were Protestant in religion and unionist in politics. This suggests two possibilities; either Molony's sole interest in the sports day was its intrinsic value as a stimulus to healthy living as well as being a good day out, or he was making a statement of some kind. One way or the other, while the parish priest was looking to hold a fundraising event for Castletown chapel, Molony was cavorting with the Protestant unionists of the sports day committee.

CHAPTER 6:
National politics and local division

The year 1885 was a momentous one for national politics in Ireland. The horror of the murders of the lord lieutenant and his under-secretary in the Phoenix Park in 1882 had sufficiently receded from public consciousness for Parnell and his party to push the question of home rule once more. During the three-year hiatus, a number of changes in the electoral system had been made and these strengthened hopes of success for the home rule movement. The most important amendment was the Reform Act of 1884,[1] which provided for the extension of the household franchise throughout Ireland, allowing all male householders, even those who owned or rented just a single room, a vote. This major development had the effect of increasing the electorate from 224,018 to 737,967.[2] Many of the new Irish voters were Catholic and were numbered among the poorer classes sympathetic to home rule. The act also reorganised the constituencies, with the result that Ireland was given twenty-five extra seats. County Wicklow had been a single constituency returning two M.P.s, but was now divided into two new constituencies, East Wicklow and West Wicklow, each returning a single member to Westminster, so even though it was restructured it did not get any of the new seats.

Parnell had used the 1882 to 1885 period well, refining and consolidating his party at national level. The days of a loose federation of Irish members working together on some aspects of legislation and breaking ranks on others were gone, and Parnell made it clear that any candidate running on the home rule ticket must promise to sit, act and vote with the party as a whole, and to resign if the majority of the party felt that he had broken that promise. This concentration at national level, however, gave rise to complaints that he was no longer interested in the grass roots of the nationalist movement, and at local level it was the individual branches rather than the central branch of the National League or the parliamentary party that controlled the movement. The league had been growing slowly since its formation in 1882, with 371 branches in 1883, but it mushroomed in 1885. By July it had 818 branches and over 1,200 by the end of the year.[3] Both Gladstone's liberals and Lord Salisbury's conservatives were very aware of the mounting impetus of nationalism in Ireland, and both realised they would have to woo Parnell and his followers.

Charles Stewart Parnell

Things came to a head in June 1885 when Gladstone's government were defeated in a parliamentary vote on a budget amendment. Gladstone resigned, an action which normally would have precipitated an immediate general election, but the constituency changes of the Reform Act were not yet fully in place and several months were to pass before an election could be held. Salisbury and his Conservative Party formed an interim administration. Parnell believed that the Irish party would hold the balance of power after the election, in which case they would be in a position to bargain as never before. Gladstone's liberals made noises in support of home rule if the Irish M.Ps. sided with them, but were careful not to articulate details. The conservatives, on the other hand, gave the impression that they were in favour of not renewing the coercion acts which had been introduced for three years in 1882 if the Irish M.Ps. sided with *them*. Calculating numbers as the election drew near, Parnell let it be known that he favoured an alliance with the conservatives. This may seem an amazing choice, considering that the liberals were, by and large, more kindly disposed to Irish affairs than the tories, but it was a shrewd political calculation. It was a move by which he hoped enough Irish votes in England would swing towards the tories, not enough to give them a safe majority, but enough to ensure that the liberals would not have a safe majority either, thereby creating a stalemate between the two major parties with the Irish party in the position of power broker. It was a calculated strategy that was to return to haunt him later.

The entire country was alive with expectation, anticipation and speculation, and the people of Arklow were not oblivious to these national and regional goings-on. The town was as captivated and as obsessed by them as any other town or village in Ireland. The Land League had established a branch in Arklow in December 1880 and its off-spring, the National League, was no less popular among Arklow's Catholic nationalists. Relatively speaking, Parnell was a local boy. His family home at Avondale was a mere ten miles away on the outskirts of Rathdrum. He was well known in Arklow even before his espousal of the development of the harbour, the unsatisfactory progress of which he was repeatedly raising in parliament and at functions in London.[4] His opening of the quarries at Arklow Rock at the end of 1884 and his plans to expand them were a cause of hope for those seeking employment.[5] But most of all, he was a personal friend of the parish priest, Fr James Dunphy, with whom he had worked so well on the harbour project. Parnell had that magic touch, the ability to cross social and reli-gious divides. This Protestant landowner was accepted by Catholic landless labourers and fishermen throughout Ireland. How could the town of Arklow not be a Parnell stronghold? Of course there were unionists to be found in their midst, quite a few of them, enough to be a real presence, but Arklow, like the rest of the Rathdrum poor law union and the Wicklow parlia-mentary constituency in which it was placed, was a home rule town.[6] Such was the nationalist control of the Rathdrum union that in the 14 March 1885 edition of the *Wicklow News-Letter*, the editorial was headed 'Board of Guardians or Land League Committee?' In the 2 January 1886 issue, the editor castigated the nationalist Arklow town commissioners for narrow self-interest. Politics were in the air, in the houses, in the pubs, and in the streets. Even the names of the boats in the fishing and trading fleets in the late 1800s - *Green Flag, Robert Emmet, Daniel O'Connell, Irish Leader, Charles S Parnell, British Queen, Prince Albert, Royal Sovereign, Royal William, Prince of Wales* - bore evidence of rival allegiances.[7]

In October, the *Wicklow News-Letter* editorial stated that the 'flood of political oratory continues, and on both sides is not likely to abate, until the new Parliament assembles.'[8] It went on to announce that the conservatives were united in their ideals and stood in stark contrast to the 'varied schools of politicians which make up the heterogeneous opposition.' This harmony augured well for a conservative victory against the 'Radicalism and Socialism of the time'. In an adjoining column, a report appeared under the heading 'The Ram "Priestcraft"'. It was an account of the admonishment of a member of the Avoca branch of the National League, a Mr Wolohan, for his attendance at sheep sales organised by the earl of Carysfort. Wolohan's defence was there had never been any objection to his attendance at these sales before, which had been held in the same location for the previous five years. The main objection to the attendance of any National League member on this particular occasion was the fact that Lord Carysfort's prize ram 'Priestcraft' would be on display, the name of which was deemed by the league to be offensive to Catholics. Wolohan's first line of defence was neither Carysfort nor his agents had named the animal, but had purchased it two years earlier for seventy-two guineas. Nor was it to be sold at the event, although his offspring were for sale but, he asked, 'where was the great harm in that?' He agreed that a decision by the league branch not to attend the sales had been taken at the previous meeting, but as he had not been present at that meeting how could that decision be binding on him? He had not been informed of it, and he certainly would not have gone to the sales if he 'thought it would have been any discredit to them, or [was] against the interests or the wishes of the branch'. This gained him some support, eliciting 'hear, hear' approval. So he decided to introduce his second line of defence saying that the only reason for his being there was to see who was attending the sales

> 'and it would have been well if a man had attended for the same purpose from Barndarrig, Rathdrum, Arklow, Aughrim, Bray, and, in fact, all the surrounding branches. They should have given a proper list of all parties who should not have been there, and not have picked out a few'.

He concluded by saying that he would have supplied such a list except that as he was attacked, he would only defend himself and leave the matter as it stood. The branch secretary replied that all the names that had reached him had been published and that the branch had attained its objective of holding up 'to the scorn of their fellow-men the petty meanness and narrow-minded bigotry of their would-be despots.' In light of Wolohan's explanation, no further action was taken against him.

It is clear that 'petty meanness and narrow-minded big-otry' was not restricted to one side or the other and that the entrenched states of mind were deepening and mental barri-cades were springing up everywhere, even when it came to something as mundane as attendance at sheep sales.

Beside the above report was a longer piece headed 'Meeting of Loyalists of East Wicklow'. The sub-heading had an ominous ring to it, 'preparation for the conflict', almost a gear-ing up for war rather than getting ready for an election. It con-cerned the response to a circular published by the earl of Meath, who lived in Kilruddery House on the outskirts of Bray, calling on Wicklow unionists to form 'a loyal and patriotic union' to counteract the progress of home rule.[9] That response, according to the reporter, was 'of the most encouraging charac-ter, and demonstrated beyond all doubt that the spirit of consti-tutionalism in this country is stronger than ever it was.' At the meeting, Meath described William Corbet, the home rule M.P. for Wicklow – without actually naming him – as a 'leader of anarchists and communists'. Corbet, the most unlikely commu-nist in the county, raised the matter in the Commons in January on two points; one, he argued that, as lieutenant of the county, Meath had no right to become actively involved in party poli-tics and, two, had even less right in call-ing the sitting M.P. names.[10] The same newspaper carried an advertisement calling on labourers to use their newly-acquired voting rights to vote for home rule.[11] The battle lines were unequivocally drawn.

The home rule candidate for East Wicklow was one of

MR. W. J. CORBET, M.P.

the two sitting M.Ps. for the now defunct Wicklow constituency, the above-named William Corbet, whose residence was at Spring Farm, Delgany in the north-east of the county; their candidate for West Wicklow was the other sitting M.P., James McCoan. Both had been first elected to parliament in 1880 as home rulers. Now, in the summer of 1885, Corbet's opponent was the unionist landlord Colonel Charles George Tottenham. The result was almost a foregone conclusion; Corbet emerged victor polling 3,385 votes to Tottenham's 1,000.[12]

Nationwide, the home rulers did well, winning eighty-five of the 103 Irish seats, they also won a seat in Britain bringing their total representation at Westminster to eighty-six seats. This gave Parnell the balance of power he'd planned for, as the liberals had won 335 seats and the conservatives 249. The liberal leader, the seventy-six-year-old William Gladstone, immediately entered into negotiations to win the home rulers' support. The price was straight-forward, and Gladstone publicly announced his support for home rule, although he again avoided giving precise details of what that would actually mean and entail. Not all liberals were in favour of this measure. Joseph Chamberlain and others split from the majority of the Liberal Party over it, believing it to be the beginning of the break-up of the empire, and styled themselves 'liberal unionists'. Lord Hartington, brother of the lord lieutenant murdered in Phoenix Park in 1882, felt that the Irish were temperamentally unfit to govern themselves, a harsh but perhaps understandable opinion in the circumstances. The tory Randolph Churchill, whose father was the duke of Marlborough after whom Arklow's Marlborough Hall and Marlborough Terrace had been named, was particularly vehement in his condemnation of home rule, travelling to Belfast to 'play the Orange card', stirring up loyalist passions at a very large gathering of unionists in the Ulster Hall in February 1886. He urged them to organise and prepare so that home rule would not come upon them 'as a thief in the night'. Soon afterwards, in an open letter he wrote a phrase that was to become a loyalist mantra; 'Ulster will fight and Ulster will be right.'

At various times in the nineteenth century, Orange lodges had ironically been banned under legislation aimed at curtailing Catholic gatherings. For example, on 19 July 1823 the Unlawful Oaths Bill was passed, banning all oath-bound societies in Ireland including the Orange Order which was nominally dissolved only to be soon reconstituted. In 1825 a bill banning unlawful associations largely directed at Daniel O'Connell who had revived his Catholic Association, compelled the Orangemen once more to dissolve their association. When Catholic Emancipation was granted in 1829, the Orange Order feared that Catholics could not only become members of parliament but that if there were enough of them elected they could hold the balance of power and thereby bring Roman Catholic influence into the laws of the land. This was something they would not countenance and Orange lodges reinvented themselves, becoming more militant than before. The Orange Order's fortunes waxed and waned, its strength lying in the strength of opposing factions, and the establishment of the Land League gave it a new impetus. The prospect of home rule gave it a more potent *raison d'être* than it had had in decades.

James B Caldwell of Main Street, Wicklow called on all Protestants of both sexes and aged over sixteen in the county to sign a petition to both houses of parliament against the granting of home rule.[13] In March, a very large loyalist turn-out was seen at a meeting of the Wicklow branch of the Irish Loyal and Patriotic Union.[14] If this push was meant to intimidate home rulers it failed, and in April Arklow town commissioners wrote to Parnell, Gladstone and John Morley (chief secretary for Ireland) pledging their support for home rule, and acknowledgements were received from this trio at the next commissioners' meeting in the Marlborough Hall.[15]

Despite the departure of some leading liberals from the party's ranks, and the opposition of the tories, and the growing militaristic utterances of the Orange Order, Gladstone forged ahead. On 8 April 1886, he introduced the Home Rule for Ireland Bill. It was debated again on 7 June, but was defeated the following day by 341 votes to 311. Even if it had been passed by the commons, it would have been defeated in the House of Lords, but the important point was that the home rule for Ireland question had finally been debated and voted on in parliament. Its defeat was not an end but a beginning. Nevertheless, the setback caused Gladstone to dissolve parliament and another general election was held.

The 1886 election came just eight months after the 1885 election in which eighty-six (eighty-five in Ireland) home rule M.Ps. had been elected. It was to result in a major turnaround of fortunes. Lord Salisbury's conservatives had entered into an electoral pact with Hartington's liberal unionists although no formal coalition came of it. The conservatives won 316 seats and the liberal unionists seventy-seven, giving a combined total of 393. The liberals had lost 127 seats, bringing their total down to 192 and this, even when combined with the Irish party's return of eighty-five seats (they had lost the single seat in Britain) the conservatives had a clear majority and home rule was dead for the foreseeable future.[16]

*

Back in Arklow, Fr Dunphy had kept a reasonably low profile in all these political to-ings and fro-ings. In November 1885, William Corbet's nomination was endorsed by the parish priests of Newtownmountkennedy, Ashford, Wicklow and Bray, but Dunphy's name does not appear in connection with it.[17]

Perhaps he was busy with parish business and the construction of the new church at Castletown in particular might have been on his mind. As mentioned earlier, the foundation stone had been laid by Cardinal Edward McCabe on 8 June 1884, and it was expected that he would also consecrate the church when it was completed, but fate decreed otherwise. McCabe died on 11 February 1885, and was replaced pro tem by Dr William Walsh. Dr Walsh was officially appointed McCabe's successor to the see of Dublin on 3 July 1885, and as incumbent archbishop it was he who celebrated the consecration of

Castletown chapel on 15 November of that year – just as the 1885 general election was about to take place.[18]

Walsh's appointment had been hailed as a triumph by Irish nationalists as his sympathy for their cause was well known. He was a strong advocate of home rule and agrarian reform, whereas his predecessor had had little knowledge of rural life and little empathy with the Land League or its successor the National League. McCabe had continually denounced agrarian outrages and disapproved strongly of withholding rents.[19] Walsh was equally vocal, but his voice was supportive rather than condemnatory.

Even on the day he consecrated Castletown church, Walsh did not refrain from clearly showing those present where he stood politically. After the religious ceremonies had been completed, a public meeting took place outside the new chapel, at which several addresses were made to him. One of these was on behalf of Gorey town commissioners – Gorey lies just five miles south-west of Castletown – in which reference to past sufferings of Catholics were made and, more pointedly, reference was also made to the fact that all magistrates at the Gorey petty sessions were 'of the minor religion' as were the Gorey poor law guardians. They spoke of the inhumanity of landlords, and thanked Walsh for his recent statement that religion and patriotism go hand-in-hand. The archbishop replied, saying that he was

> glad to allow his priests take part in the great movements of the day ... They must all struggle to remove indefensible inequalities that had so long oppressed Catholics in the field of education ... [there is a case in Arklow] in which a landlord was hindering the building of a school. The remedy for the evils of landlordism was the extirpation of landlords, and we now have the leaders to achieve that.[20]

The landlord in question was the earl of Carysfort and his 'hindrance' concerned the location of a proposed school. Dunphy wanted the ground beside the convent, but Carysfort wanted that particular site for a project of his own. The wraggling went on for months, but Dunphy eventually got his way.[21] So, even when Dunphy was not appearing at political meetings, his role as parish priest, particularly under this new archbishop of strong home rule and National League leanings, was closely aligned with political rhetoric.

Molony also seems to have been concentrating on his professional rather than his political work – and making waves as he did so. There is no evidence to show he had taken even a passive interest in the election or its outcome. Neither, however, is there evidence that he didn't and, as will be seen, he did become very involved at a later stage. The question here is if, as he later claimed in 1890,[22] 'for ten years [I] have done all [I] can for the advancement of this country in England and Ireland', why did he not take a more active role at this crucial time in national, and indeed nationalist, politics? It is probable that he had joined the league while still living and working in England between 1882 and 1885. A list of those attending a central branch meeting in Dublin clearly shows that it catered for members based in England, America and elsewhere.[23] In the late 1880s and particularly in 1890, he signed letters to the press not only with his name but also as 'member, central branch, Irish National League', whenever he felt it appropriate.[24] Yet from the time of his arrival in Arklow he had kept his distance from the local branch. Had the Arklow group, 'formerly, no doubt, a bona fide branch of the Irish National League [become] long since repudiated and cut adrift by that body', as the *Wicklow News-Letter* would later claim?[25]

In March 1886, when the country was awash with political opinion and high tension, Molony was writing to the board of guardians in Rathdrum complaining about the poor state of the lanes of Arklow and the Brook area between Lower Main Street and the river, and he urged that immediate remedial work be carried out.[26] The guardians claimed that such repairs were not part of their duties; where homes had insufficient sanitary arrangements, the medical officer should have had notice served on the owners and occupiers. On 19 April, the dispensary committee, probably at Molony's insistence, requested the guardians to gravel and repair Arklow lanes as soon as possible. The guardians gave the dispensary committee permission to do the work on the condition that the cost did not exceed £40.[27] A few days later, Molony reported eight people who had failed to have their children vaccinated and requested that 'energetic steps be taken to enforce compliance with the law.'

At the same time, however, there was a complaint that Molony had not attended the vaccination clinic at Ballykillageer, about six miles west of Arklow, on three consecutive days. He denied neglect of duty, citing several emergencies which he had to deal with and which could, he warned, happen at any time. And so the litany of Molony's reports of breaches of health and safety regulations went on, even to his reporting a house in danger of falling down at Ballykillageer, and two piggeries leaning against dwellings in Arklow's congested lanes.[28] In October, the local government board and the Arklow town commissioners seemed to vindicate Molony's constant complaints about the poor condition of the lanes and the general dirt of the town. The latter warned that 'the present filthy condition of the town, Main Street included ... will lead to disease'.[29] The following week Molony again complained about the general unsanitary condition of the town, reminding the guardians of his many previous letters. The dispensary committee also increased pressure for something to be done. The town commissioners' warning of impending disease proved justified when scarlatina broke out.

Perhaps it was this that prompted the local government board to accuse the guardians of making no effort in November, the same month in which Molony made another twenty-five reports of health hazards in the congested areas of the town. The guardians responded that they issued twenty notices to those in breach of health regulations, that disinfectant had been distributed, and that the outbreak of scarlatina 'has greatly subsided', but a few weeks later (27 November) the local government board more-or-less twisted the guardians' collective arm to request the governor of the Arklow fever hospital, which was reported as being unoccupied, to use it for scarlatina cases for the duration of the epidemic.[30] Molony was so exasperated with the lack of response to his letters and reports to the guardians that he appears to have opted for writing directly to the local government board. This going over their heads did not endear him to the guardians and, as procedure had to be observed, the local government board had to report his correspondence with them to the guardians, resulting in a new degree of mutual antagonism in their dealings.

On 20 November the guardians ordered Molony to report on the number of scarlatina deaths and also to furnish figures of the weekly mortality rates in Arklow before the outbreak; exactly a week later Molony told them to get the information themselves in the registers of births, marriages and deaths. The guardians insisted that he do it. It was, after all, one of his duties under the act of 1863 which made dispensary doctors the official registrars of births and deaths.[31] They must also have told him how to carry out disinfection and fumigation procedures, for on 4 December it was recorded in the guardian minutes that Dr Molony thanked them for their 'extremely valuable suggestions as to disinfection and fumigation', and informed them that those measures had been regularly adopted by him 'for these several months past. Also the hospital is always open to fever patients, but the people don't want to go in'. As regards the mortality figures, Molony wanted to know how much he would be paid for furnishing them. The guardians replied, nothing – just do it.

This bickering between the guardians and their Arklow medical officer was sheer pettiness, and eventually the guardians were informed that between 1 July and 1 December 1886, twenty cases of death by scarlatina had occurred in Arklow, along with three from diphtheria, five from whooping cough, and thirty-five from other causes. At least the lanes were at last being cleaned. The sanitary officer, John Evans, reported that twenty-seven lanes, courts, alleys and back streets had been cleaned up. But this did not satisfy Molony who wrote; 'the erection of 3 or 4 ashpits and the cobbling of a few dilapidated surface channels will fall a little short of the improvements required', and he urged them again to act on his earlier recommendations. He again complained of 'the very inferior quality of water in Arklow for drinking and culinary purposes', and suggested that samples of the water of several pumps and wells be submitted to Sir Charles Cameron for analysis.

It was all very tedious, particularly when set against the backdrop of the political milieu, but it is significant that it was such matters which seemed to be of primary concern to Molony at a time of national, regional and local tension and uncertainty. Perhaps one of the reasons for his throwing himself so wholeheartedly into his work was to avoid getting entangled in the politics of division. Avoiding such entanglement was impossible in Arklow at that time, as he was soon to discover.

In October 1886, a storm wreaked havoc with the local fishing fleet,[32] causing the midland-born Molony to realise the sudden devastation that can visit a fishing community. The river swelled to its widest and highest in living memory, tearing old hulks from their moorings near the bridge and sweeping them downriver at a tremendous rate. They hit into newer, functional boats and vessels in the congested river, breaking them from their moorings and pushing them seaward. It was four o'clock in the morning, but the river walls were lined with people, watching their livelihoods being carried downstream, between the piers and out into the storm-tossed open sea. The lifeboat was launched from the new purpose-built house near the south pier. The floor of this house was a steep slipway which extended directly into the river for speed of launch, but the violence of the river at this point was such that a direct launch was impossible. The crew and helpers manhandled the boat, the *Out Pensioner*, down to the end of the pier to launch her from the beach. Five times the men timed their push forward to take advantage of a receding wave, and five times they were beaten back onto firm ground. The sixth attempt proved successful. As well as the lifeboat crew, the *Out Pensioner* carried upwards of thirty volunteers to take rescued boats to safety. When the long night was over and the storm had abated, the totting up of costs began. Twenty-three of the fishing boats had been either damaged or completely wrecked, putting more than 170 men out of work. One of the boats had been repaired just four months previously at a cost of £40. The owner had had to borrow to pay that bill, now he was left with nothing. The total damage was estimated to be £3,600. The *Wicklow News-Letter* reported:

> Arklow, having struggled against a series of adverse circumstances will take many a long day to get over it and will depend upon the kindness and goodwill of the outside world. Many industrious families will look in vain for bread during the rigours of the approaching winter.[33]

Molony was deeply moved by the event and, despite his heavy workload, he became involved in the fundraising campaign that followed. A subscription list was opened and over the following weeks, the *Wicklow News-Letter* kept its readers abreast of the growing fund. Local musicians and vocalists organised concerts, £50 was sent by the Shipwrecked Fishermen and Mariners Royal Benevolent Society, a sum which Queen Victoria matched. Concerts were held in Wicklow and Gorey as well as in Arklow. Most of the music was provided by the Original White-Eyed Christy Minstrels, who must have been wonderful if their music was half as good as their name. Within three months £1,516-10-8 had been raised. There was still £2,000 of a shortfall, but seldom had the community come together so wholeheartedly.

Another concert was held in the Marlborough Hall on 27 December. Molony was recorded as chairman of the committee, whether of this single event or of the entire fundraising campaign is not stated. Mr J K Twomey, 'a man well thought of in the musical world', was master of ceremonies, introducing twenty-two different acts. The songs chosen were bound to strike a chord and everyone joined in the singing of 'The Mariner', 'Anchored', 'Pull Away', 'Man the Lifeboat', and the 'Midshipmite' [sic]. As already stated, the duke of Marlborough, when lord lieutenant of Ireland, had officially opened the hall in July 1878[34] and, lest anyone forget this noble connection, the

Marlborough family coat-of-arms hung above the stage. It had never been properly secured and was in constant danger of falling from its position and causing injury. The caretaker removed it for the duration of the concert, as he had done in the past. William M'Phail, editor of the unionist *Wicklow News-Letter*, heard of its removal and complained to the organisers. Dr Molony wrote to M'Phail, his annoyance at the editor's petty-mindedness clearly in evidence.

> The success of the concert has demonstrated that people of all parties here can unite and pull together for a good project, independent alike of religious and political 'lines of cleavage'. This is a step in the right direction and indicates that even in Arklow modern progress is beginning to make itself felt. It is, therefore, to be regretted that you should have sought to make political capital out of a very trifling incident, more especially as the matter was fully explained by me to your representative on the evening of the concert.[35]

This short letter gives an insight into how Molony felt about certain matters. It shows that he had little time for the 'religious and political "lines of cleavage"', which were holding Arklow firmly in the past, and saw mutual respect and community loyalty as characteristics to be fostered. It affirms the independence he displayed by joining the committee of the annual sports day soon after his arrival, and again by his becoming vice-chairman and treasurer of the committee of the Arklow Amateur Aquatic & Athletic Sports in August 1886. He believed greater good would come from co-operation than from division.

Not everyone, of course, shared that view. Many believed that social and political change could only be brought about through confrontation. Likewise, there were those who believed that the status quo could only be maintained through confrontation with the would-be reformers. These opposing confrontationalists were about to enter into a protracted and bitter few years. The usually quiet area of Ballyfad and Coolgreaney, just six miles west of Arklow, was to be the unlikely gladiatorial arena – one which was to attract national and international focus in the twin campaigns for home rule and the abolition of landlordism.

Agricultural prices had been falling for some time. By January 1886 the situation had reached crisis point and tenants throughout the country were seeking reductions in rents. Not all landlords were unsympathetic to these requests. On his Coolattin estate in the south-west of County Wicklow, Lord Fitzwilliam immediately consented to a fifty per cent reduction.[36] On the other hand, William Brabazon, the earl of Meath - the instigator and leader of the County Wicklow branch of the Loyal and Patriotic Union and whose estates included lands in the village and hinterland of Aughrim - flatly refused to entertain such a proposal, threatening action against defaulters. There was a weak promise of his considering reductions *after* the rents had been paid.[37]

By the end of the year, unrest among the tenants of the Brooke estate at Ballyfad, near the village of Coolgreaney, was about to erupt into a maelstrom that would make the area one of the major focal points of the tenants' rights and home rule movements.

Few people in the locality would remain untouched by it.

CHAPTER 7:
The Coolgreaney evictions

Six miles south-west of Arklow lies the county border locality of Coolgreaney[1] and Ballyfad. Both villages, little more than a mile apart, are in County Wexford, fiercely so when the Wexford hurling team is doing well. Some of the neighbouring townlands however are in County Wicklow. Likewise, some of the townlands form part of the parish of Kilanerin in the diocese of Ferns, and some are part of the parish of Arklow in the diocese of Dublin. Catholics in the Kilanerin parish can attend mass and other services at Our Lady of the Nativity at Ballyfad, while those in the Arklow parish townlands can attend St David's at Johnstown. They can, of course, go to whichever church they prefer, or according to which mass times suit them best. Little has changed since the 1880s. Then, St David's at Johnstown was administered by the curate Fr Pierce O'Donnell (often spelt O'Donnel) and the parish priest was Fr Dunphy in Arklow. O'Donnell's counterpart at Ballyfad was Fr Lambert, curate to Fr William O'Neill, parish priest of Kilanerin. All these men will feature in the following pages.

The principal landlord in the area was George Brooke, a Dublin wine merchant who had purchased his property from the Forde family in 1853.[2] The Fordes were of Welsh extraction and had been in the area for almost three centuries, and the estate was centred around Ballyfad House, about two miles west of Coolgreaney. Little remains of the house now, the last vestiges having recently been bulldozed for agricultural purposes. In the eighteenth century the Forde family had another estate near Downpatrick in County Down, where they built a mansion which they named Seaforde near the village of Clough.[3] Although they retained their Coolgreaney estate, Seaforde became their principal residence although some members of the family continued to live in Ballyfad House. By the mid-nineteenth century the head of the family was Revd Brownlow

Forde, who had his 5,000 acre Ballyfad estate and his 19,000 acre estate in County Down. The former comprised the townlands of Askinch Upper and Lower, Ballyfad, Barrack Croghan, Coolgreaney, Coolgreaney demense, Croghan Mountain, Croghan Middle and Upper, Forchester Upper and Lower, Glenogue South and North, Gurteen Upper and Lower, Knockgreany, Knockbawn, Monereagh, Moneyribbon, Newtown Upper and Lower, Oulart, Rathpierce Upper and Lower, and Rathpierce Hill.[4] Some of these were in the Catholic parish of Arklow and some in the Catholic parish of Kilanerin.

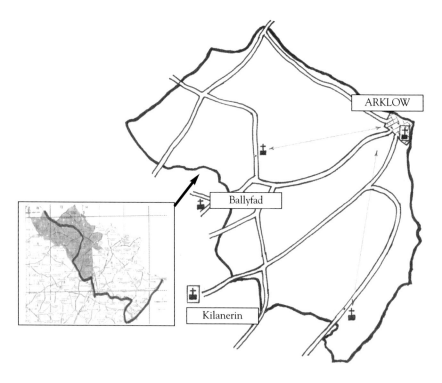

The Roman Catholic parish of Arklow and (inset) the Brooke estate straddling the parish boundary with Kilanerin

The estate was run by an agent, a Mr Owens, but in 1850 it was decided that the family should take direct control of affairs and Owens was replaced by a junior Forde. It was not long before eviction notices were served on almost twenty families, and a general air of unrest among the tenants ensued. Hopes of improvement in landlord-tenant relations came when the Fordes sold the estate to George Brooke, but these hopes were short-lived. Folklore has it that the Fordes falsified rental returns, making the estate revenues appear more lucrative than was really the case. When Brooke tried collecting the exaggerated rents the tenants refused to pay. Some compromises must have been arrived at as no immediate all-out disputes took place and for the next three-and-a-half decades an uneasy peace was observed. The land agitation of the 1870s and 1880s were to bring the simmering unease back to the boil.

The failure of the Home Rule for Ireland Bill in parliament in July 1886 meant a refocusing of the nationalist movement on tenant rights once more. Parnell's concentration on home rule meant that others had become prominent in the land question. One of these was William O'Brien, a Cork-born journalist who became editor of the National League journal *United Ireland*.[5] He was well-known for his militancy and had served time in jail under the coercion acts, but shortly after his release in 1883 he was elected M.P. for Mallow in County Cork. In 1886, he and John Dillon devised a system to force landlords to reduce rents which tenants could no longer pay. The secretary of the National League, Tim Harrington, refined the idea into a very potent weapon for tenants. It was called 'The Plan of Campaign' and it was published in *United Ireland* on 20 November 1886. Under this policy, tenants were to seek an abatement in rent; if this was refused the tenants were to pay their rent, less the requested reduction, to a committee of trustees appointed by the campaign organisers. The funds collected in this way would then be used to promote the plan and to aid evicted tenants.

The tenants of the western section of the Brooke estate saw this development as the answer to their years of discontent. They contacted their parish priest, Fr William O'Neill of Kilanerin, who in turn contacted William O'Brien for advice.[6] O'Brien explained the pitfalls of the plan, that it was high risk and could greatly injure tenants who took part, and because of this it should be looked upon as a last resort. At a meeting of the Coolgreaney branch of the National League it was decided to invite some members of the Irish parliamentary party to be in attendance on the next rent day in order to carry out the Plan of Campaign should all attempts at compromise fail. Two M.Ps., Sir Thomas Esmonde (South Dublin constituency) and Thomas Mayne (Mid-Tipperary) agreed to attend. Esmonde was a County Wexford landlord with an estate at Ballinastraw, just a few miles south of the Brooke estate. He had recently converted to Catholicism and was an ardent home ruler. Such was his position in the organisation that he would later travel to Australia with other leading members to promote the cause.[7]

The day of the showdown was 15 December 1886. Mayne arrived in Arklow by train and was met at the station by an enormous crowd. The Arklow home rule band played and he was greeted by Fr Dunphy and his curates Farrelly, Dillon and O'Donnell. Wagons and carts were ready and waiting for the procession to Coolgreaney and on their arrival there they were met by the tenants of the Brooke estate. Also waiting to meet them were Fr O'Neill of Kilanerin and his Ballyfad curate Fr Lambert. The Gorey brass band had also travelled to augment the musical element of the day's proceedings.

In the village's National League meeting room, eighty of the tenants agreed to offer the estate rents due less a reduction of thirty per cent. They knew that this would be refused, but the offer must first be made before any other action could be taken, and a deputation was sent to the rent office to meet the estate agent, Captain Edward Hamilton who, like Thomas Mayne, had travelled from Dublin that morning. The rent office was in the house of a bailiff on the estate, where Hamilton, George Freeman, the estate's head bailiff, and a process server met the tenants' representatives.

Just who was part of that deputation is difficult to say. According to Fr O'Neill, it was he and Fr Patrick Dillon, one of the Arklow curates, who called to see Hamilton, and that Hamilton refused to discuss the matter, ordering them 'not very

Arklow Home Rule Band on its way to support the Ballyfad tenants.

civilly, to leave his office.' But according to Hamilton there were 'four priests, a reporter of the *Freeman's Journal*, some local reporters, and four of the tenants,' but Fr Dillon was not one of them or, if he were, Hamilton said that he did not remember him there.[8] It is possible that he confused the names Dillon and O'Donnell. Hamilton later wrote that these men

> rushed into the room; and the priests in the rudest possible manner (the Rev P Farrelly, one of them, calling me "Francy Hynes' hangman," and other terms of abuse) informed me that unless I re-instated a former Roman Catholic tenant in a farm which he had previously held, and which was then let to a Protestant, and gave an abatement of 30 per cent., no rent would be paid me that day.[9]

Farrelly's alleged reference to 'Francy Hynes' hangman' recalled the execution of Francy Hynes for murder in County Clare in 1882. He had been evicted for non-payment of rent and his holding was taken over by James Lynch. Hynes called for a boy-cott of Lynch, which was generally observed. John Doolaghty had been a herdsman for Hynes and, ignoring the boycott, con-tinued to work for the new tenant despite warnings from local land leaguers. Sometime later, Doolaghty was murdered. Hynes was arrested, found guilty and hanged. All the way through his trial he protested his innocence and it was widely believed that a grave miscarriage of justice had been carried out.[10] Farrelly's outburst showed that he regarded Hamilton as part of a general conspiracy against Irish Catholic tenants.

Hamilton's letter continued saying that he asked if he had no alternative but to concede, to which Fr Dunphy, whom Hamilton claimed was present, replied 'None other; do not think, sir, we have come here to-day to do honour to you.'

> The Rev. P. O'Neill [sic] spoke as he always does, in a more gentlemanly and conciliatory manner, and I therefore, as the confusion in the room was great, offered to discuss the matter with him, the Rev. O'Donel, C.C., and the tenants, if the other priests, who were strangers to me, and the reporters would leave the room. This the Rev. Mr. Dunphy declared they would not do, and I accordingly refused further to discuss the matter.
> After they left the house, one of the tenants, Mick Darcy, stepped forward and said, 'Settle with us, Captain.' I replied, 'Certainly, if you come back with me into the house.' The Rev. Mr. Dunphy took him by the collar of his coat and threw him against the wall of the house, then turning to me with his hand raised said, 'You shall not do so; we, who claim the temporal as well as spiritual power over you as well as these poor creatures, will settle this matter with you.'

The graphic quality of the letter suggests clear memory, but it does contain some inaccuracies: Fr Farrelly's first name was Laurence so the initial 'P' is incorrect; Hamilton twice refers to Fr William O'Neill as 'the Rev. P. O'Neill'; and the placing of the apostrophe in 'Hyne's' suggests that Hamilton thought the man's name was Francy Hyne when it was in fact Francy Hynes. These may be minor points, but they do cast doubt on Hamilton's attention to, or memory of, detail. Head

106

bailiff George Freeman's recollection of that meeting, perhaps not surprisingly, tallies very well with Hamilton's account.[11] Several months after the event, he told an American diarist, Henry Hurlbert, that Hamilton was prepared to talk with O'Neill and O'Donell and the local people. Like Hamilton, Freeman regarded the matter as being no business of the Arklow priests. He described Dunphy as 'a high-tempered man', but did not recount Dunphy's alleged assault on Darcy. Freeman blamed such 'outside people [for making] all the trouble', and Dr Dillon (as Fr Dillon is almost invariably referred to in most sources) 'was as busy as he could be till the evictions were made in July. And then he was in retreat. And I believe, sir, it is quite true that he wanted the Bishop to let him come out of the retreat just to have a hand in the business.'

The entire deputation then walked out and as they were going towards their wagonettes, the process server opened a package and tried to serve the tenants with writs. On seeing this, Fr Farrelly shouted 'Don't take that paper!' None did, and all headed back to the meeting room in the village.[12]

Whatever about the conflicting details of the meeting and its immediate aftermath, the various accounts seem to agree on what happened next. Back in the National League offices in Coolgreaney, Esmonde asked if they were now prepared to adopt the Plan of Campaign. There were loud cries of 'Yes!' He reminded them that the plan entailed certain risks and sacrifices and asked were they prepared to abide by them, again the reply was 'Yes'. Mayne then produced a black bag and collection of the rents (less the thirty per cent) began. After two hours £600 had been paid, which was £70 short of the total reduced rents due. Each tenant's liability was checked against the official rent book by Mayne and Fr Dillon, while Esmonde, Dunphy and O'Neill took the money, which would be used in the months ahead to house evicted tenants. There was no going back, and the tenants resolved:

That we, the tenants of the Brooke Estate, proclaim our unswerving allegiance to the principals [sic] of the Irish

National League, and our confidence in the Irish Parliamentary Party and its illustrious leader, Mr C S Parnell.

That we declare our undying resolve to refuse to pay unjust exorbitant rents while at the same time declaring our readiness to pay that rent which the immense fall in the value of produce enables us to pay.

That we believe the offer made by us to-day to Mr Brooke and rejected contemptuously by his agent, Mr Edward Hamilton, to be a liberal offer, and that by offering more we should deprive ourselves of the means of support to preserve which is our first duty to ourselves and our families.

That we hope the tenants of the neighbouring rack-rented estates will take courage from our action to-day, and resolve not to pay their rents without a solid and substantial reduction.[13]

The success of the Plan of Campaign across the country was such that on Saturday, 18 December, within a month of its introduction, the privy council in Dublin Castle declared it an 'unlawful and criminal conspiracy.' They warned that anyone promoting or taking part in such action would be liable to prosecution. Not only that, the privy council reserved the authority to seize all monies raised and all documents relating to the collection.

This proclamation was no more than a red rag to a bull. The day after it was decreed, a mass meeting was held in Gorey. It was primarily a protest demonstration, but it had the air of a carnival with music provided by the Gorey brass band, the Gorey fife and drum band, the Riverchapel band and the Ballybeg band. Once again, the Catholic clergy were out in force. Canon Furlong, parish priest of Gorey, gave his permission for his curates to be present, and Fr O'Neill of Kilanerin also attended. Fr Dunphy's name does not appear, but his curate at Castletown, Fr Farrelly – who had called Brooke 'Francy Hynes's hangman' – was not only present but was one of the speakers. O'Neill reminded the crowd that 'the priests were the moral guides of the people, and he believed they would never be perfectly united unless the priests were at their head ... He believed that the priests ought to be with the people and lead them on'.[14] Significantly, the lord mayor of Dublin, Timothy Daniel Sullivan, made the trip specially. His support showed that land agitation was more than a rural problem, as representative of the largest conurbation in the country his presence gave testimony to the importance of the event as a milestone in the cause of wider nationalist politics.

Impressive though this meeting was, it did not intimidate Hamilton. Not only was he agent for the Brooke estate, but he was also one of the leading lights in the Property Defence Association, the landlords' response to the Land League and National League. He called on Dublin Castle to help him fight the Plan of Campaign at Coolgreaney. For reasons best known to themselves, they refused but advised him to evict some of the better-off tenants before negotiating with the others through the parish priest. Hamilton was incensed, saying that the parish priest was 'at the bottom of the whole business', but it is not clear which parish priest he was referring to, Dunphy in Arklow or O'Neill in Kilanerin. He then threatened to get a thousand Orangemen who would support him in evicting every tenant who subscribed to the Plan of Campaign.

Hamilton's bombast was not substantiated, but he did begin piecemeal evictions, and once again the Catholic clergy took an active role in thwarting him. When an eviction party of bailiffs and helpers were spotted heading towards a tenant's holding, the priest would ring the bell and a crowd of neighbours would assemble to help protect the evictees or at least cat-call and intimidate the evictors. When evictions were carried out, in many cases the evicted family returned to their former home and reoccupied it illegally. Even when this did not happen, solidarity among their neighbours made it extremely difficult for replacement tenants – 'land-grabbers' – to take possession. This meant that the estate received no rent at all on the holdings in question and the land was allowed to fall fallow. Such boycotting was arguably the league's most powerful weapon. Some of the braver, or perhaps simply more desperate, replacement tenants tried to defy the ostracism imposed by the locals, but they eventually had to leave the area.[15]

One counter-measure available to landlords was their legal right to seize tenants' property such as livestock in lieu of withheld rents. As the new year got under way, the tenants of the Brooke estate decided to pre-empt such seizures by taking their livestock to Gorey to be auctioned on Monday, 3 January 1887. When Hamilton heard of this, he had the following notice put into tenants' houses and posted in public places:

PUBLIC NOTICE

Whereas a sale has been announced to take place at Gorey
Fair on
Monday, 3rd January, 1887, of
ONE THOUSAND HEAD OF CATTLE
Belonging to the tenants upon the estate of
GEORGE F. BROOKE, ESQ.

over which I, the undersigned, am authorised agent. And whereas, I have been advised by counsel that such sale, auction, or otherwise, forms part of the illegal conspiracy known as "The Plan of Campaign" and that any person, whether auctioneer, tenant, or purchaser, who takes part in such auction or sale, will be guilty of a criminal act, and the sales and purchases will be illegal and invalid. Now I hereby give notice to all whom it may concern, that any person taking part in such auction or sale will be held responsible for his acts; and that any money paid in pursuance of any such auction or sale, and any cattle purporting to have been purchased at such auction or sale will be dealt with according to the law.

Edward C. Hamilton
1st January, 1887.
40 Lower Dominick Street, Dublin.

On the night before the fair, 2 January, Arklow fishermen showed their solidarity with the tenants by keeping a watch on Hamilton's home. They were equipped with foghorns from their boats and they sounded these to warn tenants that Hamilton had left the house and may have been on his way to seize property. He did leave the house on one occasion during the night, but his purpose was merely to put up the posters described above. The sales went ahead the following day regardless, and tradition states that the fair was one of the largest ever held in the town. Hamilton walked through the crowd protected by a cordon of police and hired bodyguards. By two o'clock in the afternoon nearly all the stock had changed hands, and when all transactions were completed a public meeting was held with John Dillon, one of the architects of the Plan of Campaign and sitting M.P. for East Mayo, being the main speaker. A skirmish had been won, but it was only the opening engagement of what was to prove a protracted battle in a wider war.

In February, the Irish Court of Appeal declared the Plan of Campaign illegal and Hamilton lost no time in taking direct and swift action. On the 28th of the month, accompanied by twelve 'emergency men' and a back-up of over 100 R.I.C. officers, Hamilton made his way to the home of a blacksmith on the estate, John O'Neill. It is claimed that O'Neill owed no rent, but he had refused to carry out work for a boycotted tenant. His cottage was heavily barricaded and a couple of harrows were embedded in the ground at the doorway. Despite these defences, the 'emergency men' tried to force their way in with pick-axes, while O'Neill hurled abuse at them from a small loft window. Several hundred of O'Neill's friends and neighbours stood around voicing support of their fellow tenant and their anger at Hamilton and his hirelings. As they pressed closer, the police tried to hold them back, using their batons and severely injured one of the crowd, Peter McCarthy. Only the timely arrival of Fr O'Neill saved further injury by calming the situation. O'Neill, the blacksmith, finally agreed to leave his home with his wife and their five children, 'and their furniture, bedding and food as well as a few hens were thrown out after them.'[16] Hamilton, his bailiff George Freeman, the 'emergency men', as the eviction crews were known, and the police then moved on to the next family to be evicted and then the next.

When they came to William Ford's house they found that

111

not only had he erected iron gates across the door, but he had moved a donkey and cart into the house as a further obstruction. He had, apparently, dismantled the cart, brought it inside bit by bit, reconstructed it and then brought in the donkey which he harnessed to it. It was an added nuisance for Hamilton's men and caused great amusement among the lookers-on, but all obstacles were ultimately removed and Ford, along with his wife and two children, left the house. Hamilton offered him the option of staying on as caretaker of the cabin, but Ford refused it. He was able to do this because the local organisers of the Plan of Campaign had used some of the money collected to erect temporary housing in a field adjacent to Ford's home. Ford and his neighbours picked up his furniture and carried it across the road to his new accommodation. That was the last of four evictions carried out that day.

In March John Dillon, M.P., advised the Brooke tenants to plough their fields as if the state of unrest did not exist. Tenant farmers from miles around arrived with their ploughs over the following week as a mark of respect and solidarity.

The situation deteriorated over the following months and came to a head when a new chief secretary for Ireland was appointed. Arthur Balfour was a nephew of the prime minister, Lord Salisbury, and was regarded with some ridicule by many of his parliamentary colleagues, even by some members of his own party. He was considered a 'hot-house flower' and a 'popinjay'. His rather effeminate qualities had earned him the nickname 'Clara' at university.[17] But Balfour had recently curtailed the Scottish Land League, proving that his detractors greatly underestimated him. His enthusiasm for introducing and enforcing harsh legislation prompted nationalist M.Ps. to bestow a new nickname on him, and 'Clara' became 'Bloody Balfour'. In the Perpetual Crimes Act he introduced some of the most drastic coercion measures on the British statute books, one of which was the abolition of trial by jury. Hundreds of people were arrested. The act was condemned by the Irish Catholic hierarchy since it was to become a permanent part of the law and did not have to be renewed annually by parliament. The ultimate

Armed Police protecting Ballyfad House

Catholic hierarchy however, the papacy, was uncritical of the measures. Balfour followed this up by proclaiming the National League and suppressed its branches.

While all this was in progress at national level, there had been relative peace on the Brooke estate, but that was to change at the beginning of July. On Tuesday, 5 July, 150 policemen were drafted in from south Wexford and 100 soldiers of the 12th Suffolk regiment from the Curragh arrived at Ballyfad House, where a temporary camp was erected. A large number of cavalry under Captain Sylvester also arrived. This was to facilitate major evictions and suppress expected resistance. Many tenants had barricaded the inside of their homes with tree trunks and boulders, even earth works had been thrown up around the houses. The following day Hamilton and a large party moved to evict Patrick Kavanagh in the townland of Newtown. Kavanagh, aided by neighbours and supporters, had made his home virtually impregnable, and the large crowd of onlookers jeered the emergency men's efforts to gain entry. It took half-an-hour to dislodge enough of the barricade to allow access and the Kavanagh family were ejected. Before the day was over, five families had been evicted. Eight more were turned out the following day, and so it continued for several days. In some cases there was little resistance, but in others scalding water was poured on the attackers and physical force was used by both sides. Patriotic slogans such as 'You may evict us from our homes, but you cannot evict the spirit of nationality from our hearts', and 'Death before dishonour' were shouted, and at one stage the crowd sang 'God save Ireland', which had been written in honour of the Manchester Martyrs by Timothy Sullivan, the Dublin lord mayor who had travelled to support the tenants' livestock sales in Gorey at the beginning of the year. At each house evicted tenants called for cheers for the Plan of Campaign.[18] The evictions continued into July and were not only national but international news. M.Ps. were present at some of the evictions, so too was Michael Davitt. In one of the several photographs of these major events, Davitt stands out from the crowd in a light grey suit. A 'Mr Holmes' told Henry Hurlbert his account of it:

> Mr. Davitt, who was present, stood under a tree very quietly watching it all. 'He looked very picturesque,' said Mr. Holmes, 'in a light grey suit, with a broad white beaver shading his dark Spanish face; and smoked his cigar very composedly.' After it was over, Dr. Dillon brought up one of the tenants, and presented him to Mr. Davitt as 'the man who had resisted this unjust eviction.' Mr. Davitt took his cigar from his lips, and in the hearing of all who stood about sarcastically said, 'Well, if he couldn't make a better resistance than that he ought to go up for six months!'[19]

One of the provisions in the Plan of Campaign was for selected tenants to pay full rent so that they would be in legal good standing and could therefore allow temporary accommodation for evicted tenants to be erected or adapted on their holdings. Michael Kavanagh of Barrack Croghan was one such tenant. He had ten evicted families in his outhouses which had been

Michael Davitt, in the light grey suit, at the Coolgreaney evictions.

converted into makeshift dwellings. On 28 September, the estate's head bailiff George Freeman arrived at Kavanagh's farm with an armed group of seventeen emergency men. When one of the emergency men tried to get over the gate to the farmyard, an evicted tenant, John Kinsella, hit the gate with a pitchfork, Freeman then pulled a revolver and shot Kinsella dead. Two volleys of ten or twelve shots each followed, but miraculously no one else was hit.[20] When the tenants took cover inside the house, the emergency men seized fourteen head of cattle. An inquest into the killing was held two days later and continued, with adjournments, until 12 October when a verdict of wilful murder was returned. At the subsequent trial however it was found that there was no *prime facie* case against Freeman. No one was ever convicted of the murder of John Kinsella, whose monument stands in Kilninor cemetery. Michael Kavanagh later successfully took an action against the estate for the recovery of his cows, proving that the emergency men had no legal right to be at the farm that day.

Although many, if not most, Catholic clergy throughout Ireland supported the National League, the upper echelons of the church, particularly abroad, were dubious about its methods, especially the use of the Plan of Campaign and boycotting. The Vatican sent Archbishop Persico to Ireland to see the situation for himself and to report back with recommendations. Persico travelled throughout the country from July 1887 until January 1888, consulting not only with prominent members of the Irish hierarchy, but also visiting some of the flash points. He was scheduled to visit Arklow in October, the plan being to arrive in the town early so he could talk with Fr Dunphy and other priests in the area and also to see the situation in Coolgreaney for himself. Archbishop Walsh was to accompany him. News of his anticipated arrival spread throughout the town and the surrounding countryside. This was an emissary of the pope and

Fr. Patrick Dillon, DD, Arklow curate

preparations were soon in place to award his visit due pomp and circumstance. The houses and streets were decorated in green boughs, bunting and triumphal arches.[21] From early in the morning crowds had left their rural homes to converge on the town. Nationalist M.Ps. William O'Brien and John Dillon, instigators of the Plan of Campaign, arrived early on the day and were given an enthusiastic welcome by the large crowds. Word reached the welcoming committee, however, that the papal envoy was delayed in Dublin and would not arrive until much later in the day. It was a setback, but the plan to visit the evicted tenants at Coolgreaney was proceeded with.

The group included Fr James Dunphy, Fr Dillon, Fr Farrelly, Fr O'Donnell who was the Arklow curate based at Johnstown, Fr O'Neill of Kilanerin, Fr William Dunphy, and

East Wicklow M.P. William Corbet. Two particularly interesting figures in the group were Wilfred and Lady Blunt. Blunt was
an English landlord whose sympathy lay with Irish tenants.

A meeting was held at which Fr Dillon presided. He
praised Gladstone's referring to the murder of John Kinsella,
and once again intertwined the Catholic church with the home
rule and land reform movements in very specific terms:

> As of old the blood of martyrs was the seed of the Church, so
> the blood of Kinsella and other slaughtered peasants through-
> out the country would be the seed of nationality springing to
> life throughout Ireland.

Corbet, perhaps wishing to reclaim the political aspect of
the movement, pointed to a notice on the wall of one of the
huts, 'Strike Together', and urged his listeners to continue
doing that, as they had been doing and as their forefathers had
done in the rebellion of 1798.

Wilfred Blunt then spoke, joking about being an English
landlord. He said that the plight of the Coolgreaney tenants
had aroused great sympathy not only in Ireland but also in
England and wider afield. He compared the role of English
landlords with that of their Irish counterparts; the former
invested in their properties and took little from them, the latter put little into their properties and took everything. It was
the tenants of Ireland who built and maintained farms and
holdings. He then touched on the subject of perceived lawless-
ness in Ireland. As a Catholic himself, Blunt said he knew that
the Irish people were not lawless by nature. He cited their
adherence to the rules of their church as proof of this. There
was a reason they broke or ignored the laws of the land. These
laws were inflicted on them from outside their own country.
They ignored the plight of the Irish tenant, so different to that
of the English tenant. Respect for the laws of the land in
Ireland would only become a reality when the law for Ireland
was drafted and enacted in Ireland, and that would come with
home rule. Blunt was cheered and applauded, with shouts of

'There should be more like you', and the visit came to a triumphant end. What a pity that Persico had missed it all.

The envoy did not arrive in Arklow until eight-thirty that night, by which time the group who had gone to Coolgreaney were long back in the town. Despite the disappointment and frustration his delay had caused among the vast crowd, his appearance raised the spirits and he was met by bands and banners and 'an immense assemblage', and a torch-lit procession led him from the railway station to Fr Dunphy's door.

Their hopes of papal approval, however, were soon to vanish.

CHAPTER 8:
Extremists and moderates

Terms such as 'extremists' and 'moderates' are weighted, often telling more about those who apply the labels than about those who are labelled. They also imply the existence of an accepted base-line from which degrees of belief and behaviour can be measured. For most people that base-line is the law of the land, but what if the laws are 'inflicted on [the people] from outside their own country', a situation identified by Wilfred Blunt at Coolgreaney and recounted in the last chapter? What if the laws are iniquitous and oppressive? Such a base-line can measure only what is legal and illegal, not what might seem justifiable. In difficult circumstances, one man's 'extreme' is another man's 'total conviction'; one man's 'moderation' is another man's 'half-heartedness' or even betrayal. They are merely indicators of perception within differing realities. Inappropriate and unsatisfactory as these labels may be, however, they were used in the sources consulted in researching this story. For that reason they are used here, with the warning that they should be accepted cautiously.

In April 1888, the belief of many, if not most, unionists that 'home rule would be Rome rule' proved premature when the pope, Leo XIII, issued a papal rescript condemning both the Plan of Campaign and the practice of boycotting.[1] The paper also ordered all clerical involvement in these activities to cease. This was a major blow to the Catholic clergy of Ireland, and to the more conservative Catholic laity. It will be remembered that the pope had sent Archbishop Persico to Ireland to see the situation first hand and to report back with recommendations. Persico had travelled throughout the country from July 1887 until January 1888, arriving in Arklow one evening in October, too late to visit the evicted tenants at Coolgreaney but early enough to be led by torch-lit procession to Fr Dunphy's house. The result of his fact-finding mission was now made public - the

119

Catholic clergy were ordered to step back from further involvement. Greatly disappointing as this was, worse was to come. Two months later, on 24 June, Pope Leo addressed all the Irish bishops in an encyclical, *Saepe nos*, reiterating and expanding on his condemnation of these weapons used so tellingly by the National League.[2] Many priests were conscience-stricken and reluctant to ignore the commands of their pontiff. The same crisis of conscience was faced by many of the Catholic laity who had to ask themselves: should the campaign continue once it had been condemned by the Vatican? There were others, however – clerical and lay – who looked upon the encyclical as an unwarranted intrusion into Irish affairs.

Much of the anger stemmed from the belief that the papal ruling was based not on moral considerations, but on political expediency. It was no secret that the Vatican was in the process of establishing full diplomatic relations with Britain for the first time since the Reformation, and it was suspected that part of the package deal was papal assistance in quelling the Plan of Campaign by banning clerical participation. In short, it was felt that the Irish tenantry were being sacrificed as pawns in this particular game of international chess. But it wasn't as clear cut as that. Some of the senior Catholic hierarchy in Ireland, supported by Cardinal Manning in England, had approached the Vatican for a ruling on aspects of the land movement which concerned them and several of these were very happy with the papal response.[3] The covering letter which accompanied the encyclical, written by Cardinal Monaco, head of the branch of the Vatican civil service known as the Propagation of the Faith, was particularly galling and included:

> The justice of the decision will be readily seen by anyone who applies his mind to consider that a rent agreed upon by mutual consent cannot, without violation of a contract, be diminished at the mere will of a tenant, especially when there are tribunals appointed for settling such controversies and reducing unjust rents within the bounds of equity after taking into account the causes which diminish the value of the land ... Finally, [regarding boycotting] it is contrary to justice and to

charity to persecute by a social interdict those who are satisfied to pay rents agreed upon, or those who, in the exercise of their right, take vacant lands.

Persico, who had seen conditions here for himself, later tried to distance himself from the encyclical, commenting that:

> I had no idea that anything had been done about Irish affairs, much less thought that some questions had been referred to the Holy Office, and the first knowledge I had of the decree was on the morning of the 28 April, when I received the bare circular sent me by Propaganda. I must add that had I known of such a thing I would have felt it my duty to make proper representations to the Holy See.[4]

By-passed or not, soon after his return from Ireland Persico was appointed vicar of the Vatican seminary and was made cardinal within five years.

Almost immediately, convoluted arguments as to why Catholic clergy and laity could ignore the papal decree were being formulated. One argued that the ruling was based on adhering to the rule of law, but 'so-called law ... expounded by Irish judges and enforced by British bayonets is no law at all' and thus the decree was rendered inappropriate to the reality of the situation of Irish tenants.[5] It soon became evident that the Arklow clergy were probably in the disgruntled-with-the-pope (or at least the disgruntled-with-the-decree) faction, for they carried on as if *Saepe nos* had never been drafted let alone circulated, and Fr Farrelly – he who had memorably, if melodramatically, accused Edward Hamilton of being 'Francy Hynes's hangman' – was to the fore in continuing the fight regardless.

Although by mid-summer of 1888 the Brooke estate at Ballyfad was quieter than it had been for some time, evicted tenants were still living in temporary accommodation, wooden huts erected by the National League and in converted outhouses of tenants in good-standing with the landlord. And evictions would still continue there for another couple of years. It should be remembered, however, that evictions were not restricted to that estate. For example in the townland of Coolmore, about five miles north of Arklow, Thomas Waldron, a tenant of John O'Connor, had to leave his holding because of rent arrears.[6] O'Connor was a butter-buyer based in Dublin whose business had prospered and he decided to invest in real estate in County Wicklow. On purchasing the land he discovered that Waldron was two years behind with his rent. Waldron's wife claimed that she had offered to pay something off this but the offer was rejected. The Waldrons left the property without resistance or causing trouble and the matter seemed to be at an end. Members of the local branch of the National League, however, felt that yet another injustice had been perpetrated and needed to be avenged.

A meeting was called for Sunday, 19 August 1888, in the grounds of the parish priest's house right opposite the R.I.C. barracks in Arklow. Among the crowd of about 500 was a police note-taker, Constable Mulvany, and he was literally 'among the crowd' because the organisers would not allow him access to the platform, and he had to have the protection of a cordon of constables to carry out his duty.[7] To make matters worse, the weather was extremely inclement. These factors were introduced at a subsequent trial in an effort to cast doubt on the accuracy of Mulvany's record of what was actually said. Among the speakers to condemn O'Connor's eviction of Waldron were the Arklow curate Fr Laurence Farrelly and the Avoca (usually spelt Ovoca at that time) curate Fr Michael Clarke, both of whom were later summonsed to appear in court for inciting the use of boycotting against O'Connor and others.

At the beginning of September, the *Wicklow News-Letter* relayed information from another publication: 'The Barony of Arklow in the County of Wicklow has been proclaimed under the Crimes Act, and we understand that it is probable that some important prosecutions will take place in connection with recent proceedings in the district.'[8] It was an accurate prediction, and to avoid repetition it is best to proceed directly to the trial.

The summonses were issued on 12 September and both

men were to appear on Thursday 20th. In the intervening eight days, the air was palpable with tension or, as the *News-Letter* would have it, 'excitement'. By the time the court-day arrived, there was a sense of preparation for battle about the town. The windows of nationalist-owned shops were shuttered. 'Crowds of men, women and boys paraded the street cheering, groaning and blowing horns, and the din and confusion which prevailed can be better imagined than described'. An extra force of 100 R.I.C. were drafted in and, as anticipated, a pre-trial meeting was held in the chapel yard at which an estimated 600 attended. Fr Dunphy took the chair. Predictably, the crowd had come not to bury Farrelly and Clarke, but to praise them. Addresses were presented by the Arklow, Barndarrig, Castletown, Wicklow and Ashford, Annacurra, and Ovoca branches of the National League, and also by Arklow town commissioners and Wicklow town commissioners. Farrelly and Clarke were the first to be charged under the new Criminal Law and Procedure (Ireland) Act (1887)[9] in this part of the country and as such were potential martyrs to the cause.

Farrelly responded. 'Words could not convey the feeling which overwhelms me'. It was, he said, the proudest day of his life because he stood there as one battling tyranny. He believed he did not deserve such honour as he did only what thousands of priests in Ireland would do. As it was, it merely happened that he and Fr Clarke were to be the first two priests 'in the county to be selected for Balfour's prison'. He stood by what he had said and was prepared to take the consequences. This brought forth rousing cheers and applause, which were repeated after Fr Clarke said more or less the same thing. At this point in the proceedings, the road and footpath became blocked by a very noisy crowd and Captain Slacke, in charge of the R.I.C., directed the area cleared, but this was easier said than done. The women in the crowd fought with the police while the men cursed and threatened. Order was soon restored, however, through the joint actions of Fr Dunphy and, surprisingly, the local rector Revd Richard Carmichael Hallowes, who will feature in this story shortly and very prominently. Hallowes' action was surprising not so much for his taking it, but that he was present at the meeting at all. He was no supporter of home rule and, as will be seen, had as little time for the Catholic clergy as they had for him. It was reassuring to see the two men working in unison even if only for a brief period. It was an outburst that could have been avoided and even the *Wicklow News-Letter* felt that Slacke had over-reacted.

The meeting dispersed and the two heroes in the eyes of the crowd, defendants in the eyes of the law, made their way to the courthouse 100 yards away. It is the same courthouse that is used today and it is easy to imagine the lack of space on such an occasion, which is why the doors were closed to the general public after the seating capacity had been reached. The importance of the event can be gauged from the presence of three M.Ps., twenty priests (eight parish priests and twelve curates), town commissioners, presumably their wives and daughters who might have been the 'ladies' referred to in the report and reporters, including one from the *Manchester Guardian*.

Fr Farrelly and Fr Clarke faced four charges: 1) inciting the populace to boycott John O'Connor; 2) inciting the populace to boycott others; 3) taking part in the boycotting of John O'Connor; 4) taking part in the boycotting of others. Up to the introduction of the Criminal Law and Procedure (Ireland) Act, boycotting was a civil offence which allowed the victim to sue the perpetrators for financial loss and other damages, but the new legislation made it a criminal offence and, if found guilty, Farrelly and Clarke could face prison sentences. It was also conducted by a special court, one without a jury of their peers. The evidence was to be weighed by two sitting magistrates, in this case John S M'Leod (or McLeod or MacLeod depending on how the various reporters preferred to style it) and Albert T Meldon. Prosecuting counsel was Mr Ryan, Q.C., defending counsels were both prominent home rule M.Ps. and National League members who were also barristers, T M Healy and Tim Harrington. It will be remembered that Harrington was the man who had refined the Plan of Campaign.

When the clerk announced that the court was open,

Fr Laurence Farrelly

Healy interjected: 'The court may be open, but the public are excluded'. M'Leod agreed to open the doors, but he would allow only as many people to enter as would not constitute dangerous overcrowding.

The case was quickly outlined: – O'Connor's eviction of Waldron, Waldron's acceptance of the eviction, the 'interference' of the National League, and the meeting in Arklow on 19 August. The crux of the matter was what Frs Farrelly and Clarke had actually said at that public meeting. Was the language used either intended to or liable to incite a boycott? Ryan quoted Farrelly as recorded in Mulvany's notes taken on the day:

> There is no law in this world, nor in the next I think, that will oblige you to deal with any man against your will; there is no law to compel me to sell my butter to Johnny O'Connor. Now if you put two and two together it will make four.

Although there was no explicit urging of people to boycott O'Connor in those words, Ryan asked the magistrates to do as Fr Farrelly had suggested, 'put two and two together.'

Quite a bit of the first day, Thursday, was taken up by legal argument, haggling over various aspects of the case and little progress was made. The case was adjourned until twelve-thirty the following day. Again, large crowds gathered outside the courthouse, while inside Mulvany took the stand again and read from his notes, particularly those relating to Fr Farrelly's speech:

> ... my friends, it will not do if you do not hunt the land grab-ber; ay, and hunt the landlord–exterminator. But, my friends, as long as you don't make the place hot for these parties, so long will they reign and rule in your midst. And why would you give money to your enemies? It is treason, I think, for any English firm to sell ammunition to a power at war with Great Britain. Therefore it is treason to the Irish cause for you to give money to anyone who is not united in your cause, let him be Protestant or Catholic; and if he is not united with me none of my money will he ever possess!

Farrelly's idea of boycotting did not end with social and economic ostracism. He said that when O'Connor was approached by his local priest to negotiate Waldron's case, O'Connor had replied that he would not be 'priest-ridden': 'The time might come,' said Farrelly, 'when he would give all the farms of which he was possessed to have a priest by his side and God knows a priest may not be with him then.'

Clarke's words, again as recorded by Mulvany, were along the same lines but were even more damning of landlordism, especially when the landlord, as in this case, was Irish. Most landlords, he said, were foreigners reared to hate the Irish, but here was a man by the name of O'Connor who sided with them against his own people.

The case was adjourned until the following day when there was little to be done but to announce the verdict. On re-sitting the next morning the magistrates found that both defendants were guilty of the charges and as it was a precedent in this part of the country, they imposed sentences of six weeks' imprisonment without hard labour on both priests. There was some hissing in the court but surprisingly little other reaction. The bench did, however, agree to refer the case and verdict to the Exchequer Division seeking clarification on the word 'induce' in cases such as this. Could 'induce' mean something more law-abiding and acceptable than 'incite'? It was in effect an appeal and it turned the hissing to cheers, but the result of that appeal would not be known for another four months.

*

As early as December 1885, two and a half years before the above incident, the editor of the *Wicklow News-Letter* had remarked on the 'varied schools of politicians which make up the heterogeneous opposition' [that is, home rule supporters].[10] This heterogeneity was becoming more marked as the campaign became more intense. For some National Leaguers in the town, the extremes to which the cause was being taken by others was distasteful and self-defeating. One of these moderates was Dr Michael Molony. Molony's political leanings were nationalist and he was a member of the central branch of the National League. This begs the question why did he not transfer to the local branch on his arrival? The answer might have been that he felt that the Arklow branch was already too aggressive for his liking and had already gone beyond the pale of acceptable behaviour in forwarding the aims of the league. This was certainly his view by 1888, when he described them as 'terrorists'.[11]

From the time of his arrival in the town, he had shown that he did not live his life according to other people's expectations of him. He preferred to decide matters for himself and align himself with whom he saw fit – irrespective of politics or religion. This trait was most evident in his involvement in sports and social occasions. It might be recalled that in the aftermath of the 1886 storm which wrecked many fishing boats in the harbour, he had written of how people of all parties here can unite and pull together for a good project, independent alike of religious and political "lines of cleavage". This is a step in the right direction and indicates that even in Arklow modern progress is beginning to make itself felt.[12]

It might also have been noticed that he had kept a very low profile during the Coolgreaney evictions, although the Brooke estate was in his dispensary district. His name appeared only in his capacity as medical officer for the district when he certified that Michael Kavanagh, the eighty-seven-year-old father of soon-to-be-evicted tenant John Kavanagh could not be removed from the house.[13]

By the autumn of 1888, Molony felt the time had come to try a new political avenue. He was a founder member of, and may even have instigated, the Arklow Independent Ratepayers' Association, a mix of Catholics and Protestants, moderate nationalists and conservative unionists. He was certainly chairman and chief spokesman of this new entity. Its stated aim was to take sectarianism out of politics, find common ground and to build on it for the greater good on a purely local level. In October 1888, just weeks after Farrelly's trial and sentencing, some of the seats on the town commission were up for election, and the independent ratepayers put forward four candidates in the Arklow ward; Richard Hudson, a Catholic and long time town commissioner and also a member of various committees, the *News-Letter* described his politics as 'nationalist'; Patrick Maher, harbour master, Catholic and nationalist; James Tyrrell, shipowner, Protestant and unionist; and John Tyrrell, shipbuilder, Catholic and nationalist. There was also one candidate in the Ferrybank ward, Samuel Marshall, Methodist, whose political stance was uncertain. The *News-Letter* praised this cross-community approach and urged voters, whether Catholic or Protestant, nationalist or unionist, to vote for whomever they felt was the most capable and most deserving, but it did not list the candidates proposed by the local branch of the National League. The newspaper quoted Molony's reasons for this new departure:

We, the independent ratepayers, are the Arklow nationalists, properly so called. The Arklow branch of the league is simply a clique, banded together for purposes of local terrorism, out of touch with the central branch, and representing no-one but themselves. Our object is to sweep away every vestige of local terrorism; until we do that we will never lay down our arms; but in order to do it we must have the active support of every independent ratepayer, be he Catholic or Protestant, national-ist or unionist. In the meantime, no amount of vulgar slander and loud-mouthed ignorant abuse will turn us one hair's breadth from our resolve.[14]

M'Phail, the editor, echoed these sentiments and wished the new party well, ending with the phrase 'any form of terrorism is objectionable. Petty local terrorism is simply execrable'. The 'terrorism' which Molony and M'Phail referred to were inci-dents such as the intimidation of Kavanagh in March 1885 for not keeping to the party line, the naming-and-shaming policy of publishing names of National League members who attend-ed particular sheep sales, boycotting business premises, and ostracising individuals and entire families.

Another member of this middle-ground and, it has to be said, conspicuously middle-class group was Thomas Troy.[15] If Fr Dunphy had felt betrayed by 'his' doctor, he must have been doubly disappointed in Tom Troy. As Troy's role in this story will be an important one, it is best to give something of his background here. He was born on 15 April 1860, making him about eight and a half months older than Molony. His family had been in the town for several generations. His grandparents were Anthony Troy and Rose Beakey, who had two sons, Thomas, born 1818, and Michael Anthony, whose date of birth is unknown but who married Anne Furlong on 31 May 1857.[16] The Troys and the Furlongs had several businesses in the town, at least one shop and two pubs, but they also had shares in small trading vessels and fishing boats, owning some outright. They were financially 'comfortable' and socially acceptable, number-ing among their friends the parish priest, Archdeacon James Redmond. Redmond was so close to the family that he agreed to be godfather to their first-born, Michael Anthony, in October 1858. When their second son, Thomas, was born in 1860, Redmond's curate, Fr James Dunphy was godfather to him. A third child, a daughter named Roseanna Maria followed in 1862.

There is little information about Thomas' early years, but it is clear from his choice of career that he was lured to the sea. This is hardly surprising as both his paternal and maternal families were seafaring people and owned several local fishing boats and trading vessels.[17] He learned his profession well, progressed to mate and later skipper and became owner of the *Frances Jane*, an eighty-six ton schooner which had been built in Tusket, Nova Scotia in 1858.

Captain Troy and Dr Molony had a great deal in common. They were roughly the same age; they were both young middle-class professionals; they shared a political outlook that marked them out as moderates in an increasingly hostile environment; and they both loved to play to the gallery when the opportunity arose. An example of this could be seen on 26 December 1887, the annual St Stephen's night 'Concert for the Poor' which was held in the Marlborough Hall. The programme gives an interesting glimpse of an evening's entertainment at that time, but that is not the sole reason for giving it in detail here. The reason for such detail is to show its content and beg the question why should anyone boycott it – an allegation made by the editor of the *Wicklow News-Letter*. There were to be twelve acts, each performing two pieces of song or poetry.

> Mr Donnelly will sing 'The Romany Lass' and 'A Warrior Bold'; Mr Kerr will recite 'Virginia' and the 'Execution of Montrose'; Mrs Kerr will sing 'Thou art so near' , and 'The Dim Hills Far Away'; Mr Harry Twomey will sing 'She's coming Home to-morrow'; Mr O'Connor will sing 'Oh! Stay with me', and 'Let me like a Soldier fall'; Mrs Gaynor will sing 'Bid me Good-bye', and 'La Serenata' (with violin obligato); Mr J H Long will sing 'The Old Brigade'; Miss Saville will sing 'At the Ferry'; Mr J K Twomey will play (violin solo) 'Fantasia on Irish airs'; Mr T J Troy will recite 'The Combat'; Dr Molony will sing

'His Lordship winked at the Counsel' and 'Killaloe'; Dr Byrne will sing 'The Heart Bowed Down', and 'The Stirrup Cup'.

And all this for a mere two shillings, one shilling, or sixpence as generosity allowed or pockets dictated. Some interesting points arise from the names of the performers. The Mr Kerr referred to was manager at the Parnell Quarries; J K Twomey was a solicitor who acted as election agent for several local unionist candidates in general elections; Troy was a prominent local businessman and sea captain; and there were the two doctors. There is a distinct middle-class feel to the line-up, and it might be ungracious to point out the absence of lower class participation in the show, but it is a factor that leaps off the page. Tickets were available from the following shops, 'Troy's, Hall's, Donnelly's, Wilson's, Annesley's, Hanagan's, James Bolger's; and at the doors of the Hall'.

Not only did Molony sing but he was also a member of the organising committee. The programme, as set out in the newspaper the previous week, seems to have been an aspirational list rather than a hard-and-fast running schedule as there were several changes in songs and poems. Neverethless the Wicklow News-Letter reported the event in glowing terms.

> The audience was not only a large one – exceptionally large in fact – but was thoroughly representative of creeds and classes and of all the diverse shades of politico-local colour which have recently contributed so much to the enlivenment of the good old town of Arklow.
>
> Doctor Molony gave his great topical song, 'Just in the Old Sweet Way', showing some free all-round hitting and securing a vociferous encore. Later in the evening, his rendition of the rollicking song 'Killaloe' brought to a close an entertainment which was, perhaps, the most successful of its kind ever given in Arklow.[18]

But, as appears to have been the constant state of affairs in Arklow at that time, some petty-minded ill-will was not too far away. According to the *News-Letter*, the evening was a tremendous success despite '[t]he miserable attempt to boycott a concert in aid of a local charity which was made for politico-municipal and pseudo-religious reasons.' The editor did not say who was behind the alleged attempted boycott, but the absence of Catholic clergy from such an event, when they were so active in other areas of social concern, might explain the 'pseudo-religious' reference. What were Dunphy's feelings towards his god-son? Would he have seen the reciter of English poems as a turn-coat? Perhaps Dunphy forgave him these slippages in the light of Troy's undoubted support of Parnell and the home rule move-ment. Whatever Troy's relationship with his godfather was at this point, it could not have been improved by his joining Molony in the new political party.

Also, why did Molony change his mind about the songs he was to sing? He was scheduled to perform 'His Lordship winked at the Counsel' and 'Killaloe', but while he stuck with the latter, he replaced the former with a 'topical … free all-round hitting' rendition of 'Just in the Old Sweet Way'. What prompted this substitution and what 'all-round hitting was involved'? In the best tradition of the Christmas pantomime, did he coat not-so-veiled attacks on prominent local figures in a veneer of jocular entertainment?[19]

Perhaps the one priest of the parish who could still move seamlessly between factions was Fr P J Dillon, whom everyone seemed to regard as a man of fairness, high-intellect and pos-sessing a capacity for dealing rationally even with those with whom he disagreed.[20] It will be remembered that Fr Dillon had been in the thick of things during the Coolgreaney evictions, and no one on the nationalist side had ever questioned his com-mitment to the cause, but he still had the ability to deal with extremists and moderates alike. It was a blow, therefore, when it was announced that he had been appointed 'one of the prin-cipal professors of Newark College, New Jersey.'[21] Perhaps it is not surprising that he should look to the United States for a new beginning. As Henry Hurlbert had written, Dillon was deeply interested in what was going on there in science, in pol-itics, in all matters.[22] Without his bridge-building skills, the chasm between the factions was bound to widen. The *News-*

Letter summed it up when it said that his many friends would be pleased to hear of his appointment to such an important position, but he would be greatly missed. Many of those friends differed from him in religion and politics, and the high esteem in which he was held by all classes was 'the result of his thorough honesty when meeting his political opponents and the superior learning which he possessed.'[23]

Three weeks later, the *News-Letter* published an account of the presentation of an illuminated address to Fr Dillon by the Arklow Independent Ratepayers' Association on the eve of his departure for America. The address was the work of Tom Troy's wife, Mary, and was 'a model of artistic elegance.' It spoke of Dillon's universal popularity, his eloquence and patriotism and 'single-hearted devotion to the cause of Ireland'. It praised his independence and in his 'scorning narrow-mindedness and petty bigotry, you have done much to banish forever the curse of sectarian rancour which had for so long been as a very plague in our midst'. It was signed by Molony, John Storey, Richard Howard, Richard Halpin, Hugh Byrne, John Donnelly, and T J Troy. Admittedly, illuminated addresses by their nature are sycophantic, and the word 'patriotism' was trotted out by every faction with equal fervour as suited their own particular viewpoint, but Dillon does seem to have had universal appeal. He was going to be a loss in the months and years ahead, even if only to try putting a stop to the internal squabbling of nationalists. It proved a wise move from a personal point of view, because in March 1890 the *Wicklow People* carried the following piece from the *New York Sun*:

> The Rev Dr Dillon of Newark, New Jersey, who preaching the sermon at the dedication at the altars in the Carmelite Church on Sunday, is said to be one of the most popular orators of his Church in this vicinity. He is noted for his clearness of both his pronunciation and his logic. He was formerly an editorial writer in Dublin, and like a good many more patriotic Irishmen, has served time in one of Her Majesty's prisons. He was in a week only, however, as he won his case on appeal. He has been in America about a year.[24]

An example of the squabbling he was turning his back on was recounted in the *News-Letter* of 1 December 1888, just two weeks before Fr Dillon departed. Richard Hudson was a member of the Independent Ratepayers' Association and had successfully contested the October municipal elections under their banner. He was a landlord, renting out houses around the town. In October he evicted one of his tenants, John Culleton, and the nationalist *Wicklow People* immediately castigated him for the action:

> ... not being satisfied with joining the unionists and opposing the nationalist candidates at the recent municipal elections, [Hudson] has now, to prove his fealty to his patrons, assumed the role of evictor by evicting John Culleton, who paid his rent punctually, because he had the hardihood to condemn Hudson's actions and sympathise with the Nationalist party.[25]

Hudson wanted to state the case from his perspective and it is interesting that he should use the columns of the unionist *News-Letter* to do so. He said that for the previous four years Culleton had been renting a portion of a house in Lower Main Street from him and another house at the rere at the weekly rent of three shillings and sixpence. Part of the floor had been concreted, and Culleton proposed that he would construct a wooden floor in the kitchen. Hudson agreed and, according to him, a price of ten shillings was settled upon. This was not to be paid directly, but to be off-set against any rent outstanding if Culleton should cease to rent the premises. In October 1888, Hudson evicted Culleton, but stated that it was not through a question of political leaning or private spleen but simply 'a question of pigs and pigs only'. Culleton had set up a pigsty just five yards from the house, 'to the great discomfort and, at least, nasal inconvenience to his neighbours', who, in that very congested part of town, were close-by. Acting on requests from the neighbours, Hudson asked Culleton to move the sty to the bottom of the yard, some thirty yards away. Culleton did not accede to this request. In July, a tenant who occupied a front room in the house left and Culleton asked if he might rent that room along with those he already rented, and a rent of just sixpence a week was agreed, although the previous tenant had been paying one shilling and sixpence. This brought Culleton's total rent to four shillings, but gave him possession of the rooms he was already renting, the newly acquired front room, and the house at the rere from where he conducted his boot and shoe business. Culleton then transferred his place of business from the house at the back to the front room, and installed his pigs in the rere building. It was this use of the premises to which Hudson objected. Culleton had been a prompt payer of rent up to this disagreement, but now, according to Hudson, he failed to continue making payments, and so the eviction took place and there was still an outstanding amount of eighteen shillings and four pence – it did not state if this included the ten shillings due to Culleton for laying the wooden floor. It probably didn't, because when Culleton left he took up the floor and took it with him. Not only that, when he had been laying it, he had found it necessary to break up the concrete floor with a pick to allow room for the timber-floor joists, now Hudson had neither the wood floor nor the original concrete floor.

This incident might seem farcical in itself, but it demonstrates the ludicrous situation that was developing between the nationalist elements. Hudson's resorting to the unionist *News-Letter* to make his point confirmed his opponents' belief that he had completely jumped the political divide.

Worse was to come.

CHAPTER 9:
Widening the divide

In January 1889 the Exchequer Division of the law courts considered the cases against Fr Laurence Farrelly, curate of Arklow, and Fr Michael Clarke, curate of Ovoca, as charged and convicted by the Arklow magistrates M'Leod and Meldon the previous September. They were particularly concerned with the magistrates' request for clarification of the word 'induce' in relation to cases of boycotting, and to review the magistrates' verdict and sentencing in the light of an agreed definition. The outcome was not good news for the priests for it was decided that 'induce' could be construed as 'incite' and was therefore a criminal act under the new law. It was also felt that the sentences imposed were justified and were to be carried out.

Warrants for the arrests of Farrelly and Clarke were issued ten days later.[1] At two o'clock on the morning of 28 February, Fr Clarke was arrested at his lodgings in Dargan's house in Avoca. There was no resistance and no disturbance was caused. Fr Farrelly, however, was unwell and the warrant against him could not be served. In fact, a month was to pass before Farrelly was taken into custody, and the protracted event was an unseemly, highly charged series of actions that brought honour to no one, but bestowed on Farrelly enhanced status among the more militant National Leaguers in the Arklow area.

At three o'clock on the morning of Tuesday, 26 March 1889, several members of the R.I.C. in the barracks in Wicklow town were roused from their beds by their officer and told to dress in plain clothes. Eleven constables and four drivers, under the command of district inspector Shaw from Bray, travelled in four horse-drawn police cars towards Arklow. Their route was a roundabout one, taking in Rathnew and Redcross, at each of which more constables joined the party. The route became even more indirect when, instead of travelling straight to Arklow via Barniskey or the Dublin road, they passed through

Avoca, Woodenbridge and Thomastown to enter Arklow from the west, on the Coolgreaney road near the cemetery. Their destination was Lamberton Cottage, a house about two hundred yards nearer the town.

Lamberton Cottage stood opposite what is now Lamberton Grove, but at that time was about a quarter of a mile outside the town and was the home of Fr Laurence Farrelly. Farrelly had been expecting their arrival for some time and had taken several measures to make their task an awkward one. When head constable Martin arrived at the scene, he knocked on the door and demanded admittance. The voice which responded was that of Farrelly's servant, Mary Merna, who asked what he wanted. When Martin replied that he had a warrant for Farrelly's arrest she asked him to read it to her through the door. This he did, but still she refused to admit him. While Martin urged her to co-operate, some of the constables made their way to the rear of the house and tried forcing their way in through a broken window – whether the window had been bro-

Fr Farrelly's house, drawn by Brian McKay c. 1985. It was demolished in the 1990s

137

ken before their arrival is a moot point. What they found was reminiscent of the barricades erected inside the homes of tenants about to be evicted, but on a much smaller scale. A plank or other piece of timber was jammed between the window and the opposite wall. It was more a joke or perhaps a symbolic alliance of Farrelly's situation with those of evicted tenants than a real effort to avoid arrest, and the police quickly gained entry and removed other half-hearted barricade material from behind the front door to allow the rest of the police in.[2] A search was made of the small house, but it was soon obvious that Farrelly was not there.

It was at about this juncture that Fr Dunphy 'chanced by' [*Wicklow News-Letter's* words, my inverted commas]. He returned to the town centre and within minutes the chapel bell could be heard. In a very short space of time, an estimated crowd of 2,000 people had assembled outside Fr Farrelly's house. They surrounded the police, shouting and hooting. Stone-throwing followed and several of the constables were injured in the first few volleys. Still the stones flew and the injuries grew more numerous and more serious. The *News-Letter* made the point that the policemen were armed, but could not produce their weapons without the express order of their officer. The editor wondered if men should be expected to show such restraint 'when they are almost stoned to death.' Some of the crowd tried to curb the stone-throwers and were successful enough to allow the police the opportunity of fleeing towards the safety of the barracks at Parade Ground, by which time all had received injury to a greater or lesser degree.

News of the debacle was telegraphed to other R.I.C. centres and 150 reinforcements were despatched to Arklow by train. These received the same stone-throwing welcome as the earlier arrivals and also made haste for the protection of the barracks, although in the scuffles they managed to arrest two of the women. The large crowd remained outside the barracks all day, their shouting and threatening behaviour complemented by the continuous ringing of the chapel bell directly across the road. At one point, the large force of armed R.I.C. officers sent

Arklow at the time of the events related in this book.
Right of centre is the Catholic church, with the R.I.C. barracks directly opposite.
(NLI, Lawrence Collection, c.1890)

a servant girl from the barracks to the shop for refreshments. A group of men in the crowd outside called her names and threatened her with physical violence. The situation calmed as the day progressed and by three o'clock in the afternoon it was deemed safe for fifty police officers who had travelled from Wexford to return there. They were stoned as they made their way from the barracks to the railway station. They drew their batons and a street battle took place with severe injuries on both sides. That, however, was the end of the day's events and all the drafted-in police returned to their home bases.

The question remained, where was Fr Farrelly while all this violence and mayhem was taking place on his account? There was no sign of his accepting the consequences of his words as he had promised on the day of his trial. Instead, he had left his servant alone to deal with the police at his house and he had stayed in hiding rather than bring an end to the many injuries sustained in the violence on the streets. According to the *News-Letter*, it was rumoured that shortly before midnight he had been told of his imminent arrest and so he left his cottage and moved into Fr Dunphy's house. Wherever he was, the matter could not be allowed to rest there. There was a warrant for his arrest, and it would have to be served.

Two days later, on Thursday 28 March, twelve policemen were expected to arrive in Arklow on the eight o'clock evening train. They alighted and were getting their baggage together when Fr Farrelly arrived on the platform and enquired if any of them had a warrant for his arrest. The sergeant in the group replied that he hadn't, to which Farrelly responded by saying that in that case he would surrender himself to them at the barracks at ten o'clock the following morning. He then turned to leave the station. There was a large crowd gathered yet again, and their appearance must have made the twelve policemen very apprehensive, especially in the light of the previous forty-eight hours, but Farrelly told the crowd to go to their homes. At first, they appeared to do just that, but then stones were being thrown once more and the police counter-attacked with their batons. Other R.I.C. made their way from the barracks to help and when peace had been restored fifteen policemen and an unknown number of civilians had been injured.

The next morning Farrelly did give himself up as promised. Watched by a crowd of upwards of 2,000, Fr Dunphy accompanied him to the barracks, where they rang the bell for admittance, a strange thing to do as the gate was wide open. When the duty officer appeared, Dunphy demanded to see the officer in charge. It was agreed at that meeting that Farrelly should make his own way to Wexford gaol the following day to begin his six week sentence. At least, that was one version of the event. William Corbet had a different take on it and he asked the chief secretary to the lord lieutenant of Ireland in the House of Commons if he were aware that Constable Satchwell had grabbed Fr Farrelly by the throat in front of a large, excitable crowd. Mr William Johnston, M.P. for South Belfast, responded by asking if Fr Farrelly had been the worse for drink that morning, as he had been violently ringing the bell when there was no impediment to his entering the barracks.[3] Satchwell had denied grabbing the priest by the throat but he did admit to stopping him ringing the bell continually and violently. Whatever the truth of the matter, Fr Farrelly did take the ten o'clock train to Wexford, Frs Dunphy, Manning and O'Donnell travelling with him for moral support.

It had been a tawdry, shameful affair in which dozens of people had been injured, some seriously, and it was merely luck that had prevented death. Twenty people had been arrested, twelve men and eight women, but the magistrate dealt with them leniently. Four of the cases were withdrawn, four summonses had not been properly served so could not be pursued, and the remaining twelve defendants were each bound to the peace for six months on £10 in their own recognisance and two sureties of £5 each.

*

There was no way back now for the moderates, those who felt that the cause of nationalism was being dragged through the mire. If they harboured any hope that the imprisonment of priests would make the more extreme element review the direction their militancy was taking them, those hopes were dispelled by the reaction to the release of Fr Clarke from Wexford gaol on 11 April. He was reported as looking well and in good spirits as he stepped outside the prison. As with Farrelly's sentence, Clarke's had not included hard labour, but inside he had even refused to engage in the menial tasks which were part of any prisoner's lot. He also refused to mix with the ordinary inmates as he deemed such mixing to be degrading to his social position.[4] Clarke obviously agreed with the positioning of priests on a higher social level than the laity, as decreed by the Synod of Thurles. Perhaps to men like Clarke a jury-less court was fitting, for what would constitute a jury of his peers – twelve priests? He took the train to Avoca, being greeted by cheering crowds as it passed through the stations along the forty-mile route. It halted at Arklow so the large gathering could give him a rousing welcome home before it brought him the last six miles to Avoca. Satisfying as this reception was, Fr Farrelly's welcome back was to be on a much grander scale.

At seven o'clock on the morning of 9 May 1889, the door of Wexford gaol opened and Fr Laurence Farrelly stepped out to a large assembly of well-wishers. Most were members of the Wexford town branch of the National League, but some had travelled from Arklow.[5] Like Clarke, his six weeks' imprisonment had not bowed him and he had retained his 'robust appearance.' A covered carriage awaited him and he was brought first to the local convent of the Sisters of Mercy where mass was celebrated. He was then taken to the house of friends before being conveyed to the town hall for a one o'clock reception and the presentation of addresses to him by Wexford corporation and the Wexford branch of the National League. From there, he made his way to the railway station, boarded a train for Arklow and arrived home at three-forty-three.

As might be expected, a huge crowd had gathered in anticipation of his arrival, and the composition of the head of that crowd gave it the appearance of a religious convention. There were four parish priests – Dunphy, O'Neill of Kilanerin, Germaine of Avoca, and Carberry of Rathdrum – and eleven curates – Manning of Arklow, O'Donnell formerly of Arklow and now of Glendalough, Ryan of Rathdrum, Manron of Wicklow, Barry of Avoca, Flavin of Barndarrig, Flavin of Fairview in Dublin, O'Gorman of the pro-Cathedral in Dublin, Hickey, diocesan examiner, Dixon, and of course Clarke of Avoca.

Amid this assemblage of clerics one man was conspicuous by his absence, Fr Michael Molony, parish priest of Barndarrig. Fr Molony's stance in relation to the nationalist movement is difficult to gauge. He had been prominent in the County Wicklow Tenants' Defence Association with Archdeacon Redmond in the early 1870s, and his name appeared from time to time at various meetings and demonstrations, but there were also occasions at which he might have been expected to appear but where his presence was not recorded. The coolness which had entered his relationship with Fr Dunphy might have stemmed from Fr Molony's disapproval of the direction in which the local National League was heading. Like his nephew, Fr Molony seems to have been a political moderate. His obituaries in both the *Wicklow News-Letter* and the *Wicklow People* support this.[6] The latter described him as a scholar, an antiquarian, devoted to his research and a regular contributor to historical and archaeological records. He appreciated art, had a valuable collection of paintings and manuscripts, and travelled to the finest galleries in Europe. Politically, the *People* said, 'he had moderate views through life, but was always to be found on the side of the people.' He was 'more a scholar than a politician ... preferring study to political controversy.' The *News-Letter* concurred; 'none will acknowledge his loss with greater sincerity than his Protestant neighbours.' So, perhaps he simply preferred to stay away from the celebrations surrounding Farrelly's release. He could, on the other hand, have been ill. He was seventy-seven years old, and his health had been failing for some time, suffering two strokes before his death just ten months after Farrelly's return to Arklow. His curate Fr Flavin was present to welcome Fr Farrelly home and he might well have been there in two capacities, his own and as a representative of Fr Molony, but there is no record of this being the case.

Farrelly's emergence from the train and his exiting the station was cheered by the crowd, who continued to cheer as he stepped onto a waiting wagonette to be driven to a field beside Fr Dunphy's house[7] - the very field in which Farrelly had made the statement which resulted in his imprisonment. A platform had been erected and Fr Dunphy presided at the meeting that was to take place. Addresses to Farrelly were given by the Arklow town commissioners, Wicklow town commissioners, Arklow Harbour Board, and the Arklow, Avoca, Aughrim, Castletown, Coolgreaney, Johnstown, Barndarrig, and Annacurrra branches of the National League. It should be mentioned that the harbour board was a newly constituted body of seven commissioners for the running and maintenance of the harbour which was handed over to them by the Board of Works.

The seven commissioners were Fr Dunphy, Daniel Condren, John Reynolds all representing the town of Arklow, Owen Fogarty representing the barony of Ballinacor South, John Storey representing the barony of Gorey, and Alexander Taylor representing the Treasury, and it was already being accused of political bias.[8]

Farrelly then took centre stage and spoke for over an hour, declaring his 'intention of continuing to denounce the enemies of the people.' A police reporter had been dispatched from Dublin to record the proceedings, lending a certain *déjà vu* quality to the event. Would Farrelly again overstep legal boundaries? Would he again face arrest for intemperate words? The fact that the event was taking place in a private field rather than on a public thoroughfare or open space pre-empted such a repetition; the reporter was simply refused access to private property on which a private function – albeit an extremely large one – was being held. Nor could the R.I.C. use rowdy behaviour as an excuse for gate-crashing. The conduct of the crowd was well-ordered and the fifty constables drafted into the town for the occasion were not needed. There would be other days when tempers would flare, but this was a celebration that was not marred by excess.

Fr Farrelly's return did not immediately spark off heightened antagonism between nationalists and unionists in the town, nor did it exacerbate the worsening relations between the moderate and militant nationalists. On the other hand, it did little to heal wounds. Sectarian and sectional politics continued to condemn Arklow to the economic doldrums. A letter written in response to the editor's remarks for the need of development in the county maritime industries was published in the *Wicklow News-Letter* of 6 July 1889. The author signed himself 'An Arklow Fisherman', and he agreed with what Molony and the independent ratepayers had been saying for some time.

> Your remarks on the want of maritime enterprise in Wicklow are honest and straight-forward. Arklow, in spite of every obstacle, is still an important fishing station. The poison of

narrow-mindedness, imbecile [sic] parochialism in the worst forms, and worst of all – ever since that grand old Churchman, gentleman and scholar Archdeacon Redmond was gathered to his fathers – ignorant religious bigotry have all been tried. No doubt, they have had some effect. Only for them Arklow would now probably be one of the most important fishing stations in Great Britain. But they have failed to quench the enterprise of Arklow, and consequently the old town is still able to take a creditable place amongst our Irish fishing centres. Our shipping is also looking up owing to the trade in paving setts which Mr Parnell's enterprising manager, Mr Kerr, has established both with England and the Continent. Even this valuable departure in local commerce was sought to be strangled in its birth by the introduction of an absurd display of sectarianism.

The summer months saw a continuing, if modest, rise in financial fortunes. In July more products from the quarries were being exported to England and Spain and the fishing season was also proving satisfactory. And yet political and social division were rife. The local landlord and magistrate, William Proby, earl of Carysfort, was persistently cat-called as he drove through the streets of Arklow.[9] Despite this, he had recently been working closely with Parnell on proposals to solve the on-going problems with the harbour.[10] It should be remembered that Parnell had taken a step back from the land reform movement and had never supported the Plan of Campaign. This distancing himself had caused disquiet among the more militant elements and his growing association with Carysfort confirmed their views that he had 'gone soft'. William M'Phail latched onto to this falling away of support for Parnell when he wrote

> What will the 'Laig' say to this? ... the great local sponsors are, of course, entirely left out in the cold, and it now only remains for them to hold a monster meeting around the pump on Parade ground [sic] and pass a vote of censure on Mr Parnell.[11]

He also remarked on the satisfying status of the fishing catches and advised

... if the Arklow fisherman would only keep his money safe and spend it as occasion required in a useful and sensible manner instead of giving it to everybody that asks him for it, we would hear very little of the poverty of Arklow next year.[12]

Once M'Phail had coined the word 'Laig' as a derisory approximation of the unlettered Arklow pronunciation of 'league', he was loathe to leave it unused. His editorial in the issue dated 5 October 1889 was headed 'Independents versus Terrorism' and he again urged voters to vote for whom they felt were the most capable candidates in the imminent municipal elections – as long as they were unionist or moderate nationalist, but he did not spell this out. What he did say was:

> Speculation is rife as to whether the interests of the town are to remain vested in the wire-pullers of that broken, discredited and bankrupt institution known as the 'Arklow laig', formerly, no doubt, a *bona fide* branch of the national Irish league, but long since repudiated and cut adrift by that body.

The repeated accusations by the *News-Letter* and Dr Molony that the Arklow branch of the National League was so militant that it had been 'cut adrift' from the national movement is not borne out by the evidence. There were tensions between them, but the Arklow branch was in good standing, as far as annual subscriptions to the central office was concerned, until at least May 1890;[13] nor does there seem to have been ill-feeling between the Arklow branch and most of the neighbouring branches. Unlike the *News-Letter*, the *Wicklow People* carried short reports on branch meetings held throughout the county and communication between the branches was regular and mutually supportive. Also, the appearance of representatives from almost all the surrounding branches at Farrelly's homecoming bears testimony to the fact that the Arklow branch was not the pariah M'Phail and Molony would have everyone believe. At a meeting of thirteen south Wicklow and north Wexford branches at Kilanerin 'to thwart further plantations,' Thomas Birthistle and James Doyle represented Arklow and apologies for inability to attend were sent by Fr Dunphy and Fr Farrelly.[14] Admittedly, the Arklow branch was not slow in using boycotting and other intimidatory action as has been seen. Further examples of this are reports at their meetings of naming 'some people in the town who persist in supplying the grabbers and emergency-men on the Brooke estate'; as well as boycotting blacksmiths shoeing horses belonging to 'objection-able traders that are supplying the grabbers'; and complaining to the Barndarrig branch that people from that area were deal-ing with 'objectional parties' in Arklow. But other branches were making similar reports.[15] The Arklow branch may have been out of step with central office in Dublin, but it seems to have been on good terms with its fellows in the region. In fact, the argument could be made that the central branch, with its city location and urban perspective, was out of step with the rural branches.

The battle between the local leaguers and Molony's inde-pendents intensified in November 1889, when Fr Dunphy wrote to the *Wicklow People* stating that a meeting of the National League branches in north Wexford and south Wicklow had been held to better organise against the landlords and, more ominously,

> to consider the attitudes of certain independents who have united with the Tories in the town in an endeavour to discred-it the local branch of the league and to lessen the influence of the respected priests of the parish.[16]

At that meeting, Dunphy declined taking the chair on health grounds, and his place was taken by Fr Farrelly. Before handing over to Farrelly, however, Dunphy reminded the delegates that 'the primary purpose of the National League was not home rule, but the protection of tenants.' This was a pivotal statement. It will be remembered that Parnell, the national executive, and the central branch of the National League had turned their energies towards establishing home rule as the primary objec-tive of the organisation, with tenants' rights a distant second.

Protection of tenants had been the aim of the Land League, outlawed in 1882. With these words, Fr Dunphy made it abundantly clear that the Arklow branch – and presumably the other branches at that meeting – still adhered to Land League rather than National League principles and so were defying the ethos of the central branch, the national executive and the national leader Charles Stewart Parnell.

Taking the reins, Fr Farrelly gave the assembly the clerical version of the split in Arklow. He told them that some years ago, the nationalists replaced the earl of Carysfort as chairman of the town commissioners and had been unbeaten ever since. The unionists then found 'some sore-head nationalists who were willing to barter their nationality for the honour of being supporters of an earl.' The electorate of Arklow, he said, was most limited, with only 125 people entitled to vote in a municipal election out of a population of 6,000. The unionists were supported by slightly less than half of those voters but in a coalition with moderate nationalists they could have the majority of the votes. This put Molony's independents in a position of holding the balance of power: 'twelve independents, with an aggregate valuation of £200, trying to govern the whole township.' In the three years they had been in existence, he claimed, 'they have opposed everything nationalist.' What was to be done about them? It was an important question, one that led to prolonged discussion, but disappointingly for this book, no decision was taken. Nevertheless, Farrelly's description of the situation leaves no room for doubt about the intensity of feeling between hardliners and moderates – or staunch nationalists and turncoats, take your pick.

CHAPTER 10:
Another zealous cleric

As 1890 dawned, the political divide in Arklow was three-way: there were unionists, moderate nationalists headed by Dr Molony, and the more militant nationalists headed by Fr Dunphy and his curate Fr Farrelly. Now another ingredient was

Revd Richard Carmichael Hallowes

added to the mix, evangelical street preaching. Although purportedly not intended to be political, it was not possible at that period in Arklow to separate religion and politics. It too was headed by a zealous cleric, the evangelical rector of Arklow, Revd Richard Carmichael Hallowes.

Hallowes had been appointed rector of Arklow in 1885.[1] He was then thirty-seven years old, the son of a Dublin solicitor, and had been educated in the London College of Divinity. He became deacon in 1878 and a priest in 1879. Before coming to Arklow he had served short terms as curate in Tramore, County Waterford, and in Cashel before being appointed curate to Dungarvan where he spent the years 1879 to 1884. He was then transferred to Abbeyleix for a year before he was appointed rector of Arklow. The new rector was married and had a son, also named Richard, who had been born in 1879. It is possible that Revd Hallowes met the Molony family during his brief stay in Cashel as the Molony home was just yards from the Protestant church, but any acquaintance with Michael would have been fleeting as Michael was a student in Cork at that time. Acquainted or not, Molony and Hallowes did have that Cashel link.

Records of the Church of Ireland parish are sparse,[2] but Preachers' Books from 1867 to 1904 show attendance figures of between 250 and 350 at church services. These figures were reasonably stable but seem rather low, especially when it is considered that in 1871, 704 parishioners petitioned the then rector, W.G. Ormsby, to remain in the parish,[3] and according to census figures for 1871, 1881 and 1891, there were respectively 748, 762 and 727 Church of Ireland people in Arklow, so a 'devotional revolution' similar to that experienced in the Catholic church does not appear to have taken place in the Church of Ireland.

These attendances fell far short of what Hallowes felt was satisfactory, and shortly after his arrival as rector he introduced Sunday evening and Wednesday evening services in addition to the existing Sunday morning service. It is difficult to say if the extra Sunday service attracted a greater aggregate weekend attendance, because it is not possible to assess how many people went both morning and evening. The Wednesday service seldom attracted more than a dozen or two.[4] Perhaps it was because of this lack of response that in late 1889 and early 1890 Hallowes decided that if the faithful would not attend the word of God in church, he would take the word of God to the streets. He may also have been eager to win converts from Catholicism. In January 1859, Archdeacon Redmond, the parish priest, had written; 'I sincerely thank God for the happy change that has taken place in my day, when Catholics and Protestants, instead of engaging in deadly feud and battle as of old, live together in mutual benevolence and peace,'[5] but by the 1880s, as demonstrated in preceding chapters, smoldering division had already been fanned to flames and the execution of Hallowes' plans

150

merely added fuel to the sectarian fire. If, as he later claimed, there was no political intent on his part, it shows a remarkable degree of naïvety.

The on-going matter of the Coolgreaney evictions was still being reported and debated in the columns of the local newspapers. One piece in the *Wicklow News-Letter* of 14 December 1889 made a point of stating that no Protestant on the Brooke estate had joined the Plan of Campaign and that all farms from which Catholic tenants had been evicted were re-let to Protestants. Seventy 'Brooke estate farms were distributed among 21 new tenants, all but two of whom were Protestant; seven came from Wexford, four from Cavan, and two each from Kildare, Wicklow and Dublin; the remainder hailed from Antrim, Carlow, Queens [Laois], and Aberdeenshire,' with the exception of the two Catholics the rents were lowered considerably, as well as other incentives offered to accept 31-year leases.[6] This anti-Catholic bias on the part of some landlords, and the participation of Catholic clergy in the push for home rule and land reform, as well as the close association between evangelical Protestantism with political unionist conservatism[7] had blurred the already nebulous borders of religion and politics. They were two sides of the same coin. However genuine Hallowes' intentions may have been, his apparent ignorance of – or indifference to - these realities of Arklow life was about to divide the different communities even more.

On Sunday, 6 April 1890, Revd Hallowes, accompanied by his curate Revd Harrison, Revd Hoffe of the neighbouring Kilbride parish, and the local Methodist minister Revd Harpur, held the first event on the streets of Arklow,[8] and the following week they had handbills printed and distributed to every house in the town, although the Catholic clergy were apparently excluded from this almost universal canvass.[9] In it they explained how they felt such open air preaching was good for the whole town. It would, they said, help heal the growing sectarianism between Protestants and Catholics in Ireland. In the light of subsequent events, the irony of this statement is unsurpassed.

Revd Hallowes begins preaching outside his church in Main Street,
opposite the graveyard that is now a public park.

If, as the circular stated, the aim was to bring Catholics and
Protestants together in reconciliation and prayer, it would have
been wise to make an approach to the Catholic clergy before-
hand to see if agreement might be reached on such a course of
action. If agreement could not be reached, then the opposition
of the Catholic clergy should have been taken into account
when planning the route of the proposed open air services.
There is no evidence of such contact having been made, and as
claimed in the *Wicklow News-Letter* of 12 July 1890, even the
circular had not been sent to Dunphy and Co. The opposition
of the priests to the services over the following months show
that even if their agreement had been sought they would not
have given it, and so the route chosen by Hallowes was bound
to exacerbate the already growing tension and division in the
town. From the outset, the police reported that these services
would inevitably lead to riot and disturbance. They based this
opinion partly on the fact that on a previous occasion in
Arklow some years earlier when religious services of an evangel-

ical nature were conducted in a tent near the town, sectarian feeling, leading to some disorder and rioting, was aroused.

Despite the stated aim of conciliation, the route and content of these events seemed tailored to spark off a violent reaction. On 17 April, the solicitor-general gave the opinion that the street preaching in itself was not illegal, but if the preachers caused obstruction on the public thoroughfare they could be indicted 'for a misdemeanour at common law.'[10] More serious perhaps was the possibility of arresting anyone who attended these services with the knowledge that they were 'likely to promote hostile demonstration and lead to breaches of the peace' for taking part in an unlawful assembly. The police were directed to caution the persons concerned, which they did.[11] The Protestant clergymen chose to ignore this warning and in May they announced that the street preaching would proceed as planned, despite being made aware that the Catholics of the town would attack them if they did so. On 25 May, Hallowes, Harrison, Harpur, and a Mr Keller, a lay preacher from Dublin, commenced singing hymns and preaching 'in the public street in Arklow'.

> They were immediately surrounded by a howling mob of Roman Catholics, who set up a most deafening noise by blowing foghorns, beating tin cans, shouting, hooting, and whistling. Only the ordinary police force of the town was available for duty, and they managed with some difficulty to escort the preachers in safety through the town. It is remarkable that on this occasion none of the Arklow Protestants took part in the services in the street, or accompanied their clergymen through the streets.[12]

This apparent lack of support for Hallowes from his own parishioners is interesting, and even as the weeks passed and the reaction became increasingly violent and divisive, the Catholic nationalist newspaper, *Wicklow People*, stated that the conduct of the four clergymen was 'nauseating to Protestant and Catholic alike' and that 'many of the respectable Protestants of Arklow disapprove of the action of the clergymen.'[13] Hallowes' superiors were not overly pleased either, and the Protestant archbishop of Dublin, William Conyngham Plunket, wrote to him in an effort to dissuade him from continuing with his plans, but again Hallowes chose to ignore such a request.[14] In May, the evangelical mission continued with predictable – and predicted – results. National newspapers latched on to the story. The unionist *Dublin Evening Mail* condemned the Catholic crowds and accused them of hitting one of the clergymen on the head with a stone.[15] The nationalist *Freeman's Journal* described the on-going affair as 'a scandal to the district' and referred to the Catholic objectors as a 'crowd composed of fishwives and their near relatives' who used 'abusive and blasphemous language.'[16]

Tensions and tempers seemed to calm for a week or two and Hallowes did not advertise further open-air gatherings. It was 'only by an accident' on the evening of Saturday 7 June that the head-constable at Arklow learned of Hallowes' intentions to street-preach the following day. The constable rushed to Wicklow to rally a force large enough to protect the preacher and his followers, and he arrived back in Arklow with twenty-two re-enforcements. As it happened, they were not needed, because Hallowes changed the venue of his services from Main Street to the 'Sand banks.'[17] There was a short prayer meeting, but nothing controversial seems to have been said to inflame the crowd of 600 who had assembled, so they went home quietly as the meeting came to an end. Despite the peaceful conclusion reported in the government memorandum, the *Wicklow News-Letter* still described the crowd as 'rowdies who were evidently prepared for a repetition of their disgraceful attacks upon the Protestant clergymen.'[18] The *Wicklow People* saw it differently, denouncing the erstwhile rowdy element as 'a few thoughtless women', and blamed 'the conservative newspapers such as the *Dublin Evening Mail* for stirring up the resentment.'[19]

By the middle of June, tensions had again become so strained that the matter was raised in the House of Commons,[20] when the conservative M.P. for East Belfast, Edward Samuel Wesley de Cobain, asked the chief secretary for Ireland about the disturbances and in particular if he were aware that a Mr. Hoffe and Mr. Harper [sic], together with many of the respectable residents of the town of Arklow, in their attempt at holding a religious service on the commons some quarter of a mile from the town were molested by a mob; that a District Inspector of the Royal Irish Constabulary and a constable, instead of securing for these gentlemen the right of holding the service, took their names, and in no way interfered with the action of the mob; that subsequently the Rev. Mr. Hallowes was hooted through the town, and some Protestant ladies were similarly treated; and would he take steps to secure for Her Majesty's subjects in that part of Ireland the free exercise of their privilege as citizens when they were infringing no laws, and instruct the officers and men of the Royal Irish Constabulary in their duty to afford protection to all citizens in the exercise of their undoubted civil and religious rights?

William Corbet, the East Wicklow M.P., stepped in and asked if de Cobain's attention had been called to the disturbance, as reported in the *Times* three days earlier, where three Protestant clergymen persisted in holding open-air meetings for preaching to Catholics in a district where the Catholics outnumbered the Protestants by three to one. He also asked if he were aware that a few years ago similar attempts were made to proselitise the Catholic inhabitants, which gave much offence to them and to their clergy. Pushing de Cobain further, Corbet asked him if he had seen a statement published in the papers to the effect that many of the most respectable Protestant inhabitants disapproved of the action taken by their clergy in this matter, and also that the resident magistrate and police authorities had advised them to desist from their action. The question therefore was not would the police protect the preachers, but what further steps should be taken in the interests of law and order to protect the Catholic people from what they regard as insulting to their religious convictions?

There followed several interjections: a) Thomas Edward Russell, the liberal-unionist for Tyrone South asked the chief secretary if a report in the previous Monday's *Daily Express* stating that the Episcopalian and Methodist ministers engaged in open-air preaching 'were stoned and assaulted by a hostile crowd, are true; and whether, so long as these services are conducted so as not to cause obstruction, he will protect these ministers in the exercise of a lawful right?'; b) the conservative member for Belfast South, William Johnston, asked a similar question. Johnston, it will be remembered, was the M.P. who suggested that Fr Farrelly had been the worse for drink the day he surrendered himself to the R.I.C. in March 1889; c)the nationalist member for Longford North was Tim Healy, who was well aware of the tensions in Arklow as he had been one of the barristers defending Frs Farrelly and Clarke, asked if Catholic priests applied for police protection to hold open-air services on the Shankhill Road and Sandy Row, Belfast would they be protected in the exercise of a lawful right?

Balfour dismissed Healy's question by saying that he had not received any report of such applications, and therefore could not give a detailed answer. Then he addressed the questions put by de Cobain, Russell and Johnston ('his hon. Friends behind' him); 'I have to say that some very discreditable scenes of violence directed against three Protestant clergymen at Arklow, and against one or two members of their congregation, took place on the morning and evening of last Sunday. Every protection will be given to these persons so long as they keep within the law.'

The local magistrates were understandably anxious about the whole situation and their anxiety increased as a very important date in the calendar of Irish Protestantism loomed large. The 12 July in Ireland is one of the year's most iconic dates. Commemorating the victory of Protestant William of Orange over the Catholic James II at the battle of the Boyne in 1690, it is the rallying call for assertion of Protestant political and religious rights. As the Arklow magistrates considered Revd Hallowes' street preaching activities, they were only too aware of the fact that 'The Glorious Twelfth' would have even greater significance than usual that year as it would mark the bi-centenary of Protestant ascendancy. Their first step was to augment the local R.I.C. force by fifty extra men. Despite this, disturbances continued every Sunday and on 17 July magistrate

M'Leod, and justices of the peace Taylor and Beresford, declared a ban on all such gatherings. The following Sunday, both factions seemed to have taken heed of the prohibition; the Catholic population remained indoors while the preachers and their congregation held a service in the yard attached to the Protestant school-house in the Fishery. Unfortunately, the school-house in question 'abutted on the main street of the town, so that the preaching &c., was audible for 100 yards around, and in the adjacent houses inhabited by Roman Catholics.'[21]

R.I.C. re-enforcements arrive at Arklow railway station.

The ban was, therefore, at least partly successful, but the preachers wrote to the chief secretary on 22 July outlining the reasons for the public gatherings. Significantly, their stated motives differed greatly from those of their circular of 12 April. In April they had claimed their intention to be one of healing division between Protestant and Roman Catholic, but now they proclaimed the purpose of the street preaching to be overtly proselytising. Four days later, on 26 July, the attorney-general deemed the magistrates to have acted beyond their powers and the ban was therefore illegal.

One of the weapons employed to great effect in the land-

Preaching in Tinahask, the predominantly Catholic are of the Fishery

lord-tenant war was boycotting and it was now used in this superficially religious conflict as Arklow Catholics withheld their custom from Protestant shops. Individuals of both sections of the community were attacked. Greater peacekeeping enforcement was needed and each Sunday throughout July and August, 1890 extra police and military were drafted in.[22] Fr Dunphy wrote to his archbishop saying that it was 'really shameful to see so much police here every Sunday guarding these fanatics.'[23] This high level of policing had the desired effect. The preachers were not allowed to cause an obstruction, and the Catholics, at the behest of the priests, stayed indoors. Small groups of women and girls and a few men continued to make noise each Sunday to drown out the preaching, but it was inconsequential and the authorities did not deem the disturbances serious enough to arrest those involved. This remission however was short-lived and tension levels grew as the weeks passed.

The *Wicklow News-Letter* pointed out that despite the presence of 200 police armed with rifles, revolvers, sword, bay-

onet and baton 'in this over-religioned seaside town' the disturbances were worse than ever.[24] It advocated that the preaching
should stop from a commonsense point of view. The article
incorporated a letter from Dr Molony, who pointed out that
there was a case for street preaching in cities such as
Manchester and Birmingham where 'there are unfortunately
thousands of people who never enter any place of worship.' But
that, he argued, was not the case in Arklow. Here everyone was
known to his priest or pastor and could expect a visit from him
should he abstain from attendance at church. He then pointed
out that many Protestants no longer attended the church in
Main Street, choosing instead to go elsewhere. This left the situation where Roman Catholics refused to hear Hallowes' outdoor sermons, the 'great body of Church of Ireland people did
not want to hear him', and because of his indistinctness, his followers couldn't hear him. This reference to Hallowes' poor diction was later echoed by another source.[25] Hallowes responded
to Molony's letter the following week, repudiating some of the
statements, but in further correspondence Molony's arguments
seem the more convincing.[26]

By September, the situation had become so bad that the
News-Letter editor wrote

> Arklow ... is now regarded throughout the United Kingdom as
> one of the most intolerant districts in Her Majesty's domin-
> ions. Ulster, it is considered, with all its extremities [sic] on the
> Glorious Twelfth and the Fifteenth of August, can hold its own
> for respectability and good 'neighbourship' when the fever of
> partisanship is assuaged.[27]

In the 16 August edition, the writer had accused Fr Farrelly of
stirring up the mob, but in the 30 August issue, he reported that
Farrelly and Fr Manning had tried to get all the men of the
Fishery to the sandhills, away from Hallowes and his followers.
Some of the women, however, refused to go, and created a noise
disturbance to annoy the preachers. The priests had gathered
an estimated 2,000[28] people and Farrelly thanked them for pre-

serving the peace. He went further, stating that 'anyone who would hit Hallowes was an arrant coward and a traitor to his country'.

The next six months were reasonably quiet, but neither Dunphy nor Archbishop Walsh was prepared to let things lie. On 29 November, Dunphy informed Walsh that a barrister-at-law would visit Arklow to see the locations where Hallowes was wont to preach, and to represent residents who wished to take civil actions against the preachers for 'the annoyance to themselves and their families.' He added: 'it is time to put a stop to him [Hallowes] as neither <u>wind</u> nor <u>weather</u> has any effect on him.'[29] In the same letter he condemns both 'Lord Carysfort and his clan [for giving] no charitable aid' to the fishermen in what was proving a miserable herring season, and the Protestant traders who 'won't look at us.' Fr Dunphy seems to have forgotten the abuse Carysfort had been subjected to and the fact that during the summer the Protestant traders had been boycotted by the people now seeking their charity.

On 22 January 1891, Revds Hallowes and Harrison were brought to court by S. Dixon, T. Kearon, D. Kavanagh, and D. Lambert on charges of 1) having taken part in an unlawful assembly, and 2) having obstructed the public highway. These charges obviously stemmed from the barrister's visit to the town in November. The magistrates, Colonel Miller, Colonel Forbes, Colonel Howard Brooke and Mr Alexander Taylor ruled that the clergymen were guilty of creating a road nuisance but that no unlawful assembly had taken place. Had they been brought before them on a road nuisance charge, they would have proceeded with the case, but as they had been brought before them on an unlawful assembly charge they could not proceed.[30]

The idea of bringing civil cases against the preachers had been the archbishop's, Dr Walsh,[31] and the diocese was not to be thwarted so easily. On 9 February, an application was made to the court of Queen's Bench for a writ of mandamus[32] directing the magistrates to take evidence against Hallowes and Harrison of obstruction and unlawful assembly. The *Freeman's Journal* of 17 February 1891 carried a report of the application.

When one of the justices of the court said it struck him as strange that a clergyman would preach in the public street when he had a church or even a field in which to preach, Mr Law, appearing for Hallowes and Harrison, replied that the practice was carried on extensively in England. The justice responded: 'Oh, England is a different country altogether from Ireland.'

The justice then asked, 'Is there not room in the parish church?'

'I presume there is,' replied Law, 'but Mr Hallowes believes he has a right to read the Bible in this country in public as well as in England.'

The question then moved on to the rights and wrongs of the situation. It was agreed that Hallowes had the legal right to do what he was doing as long as he didn't cause an obstruction of the public road, but moral right was something else. It was suggested by the court that if a Catholic priest did this in Belfast, the moral opinion at least would be against him as distinct from the legal. The justices felt that a clergyman should be aware of the possibility of causing breaches of the peace. Apart from the moral aspect there was the practical one – 'if every town in the country was to go this way the police force won't be sufficient', a remark which brought laughter. Law then said that nothing had been said about the crowd who attacked the ministers. Justice Holmes replied that he drew a distinction between educated men who should be able to reason and discuss matters and an uneducated people who 'fall on emotion and passion'. Despite these criticisms of Hallowes and Harrison the court felt it could not interfere with the decision of the magistrates and the appeal was refused, but the preachers were requested to exercise better judgement in future.

They didn't, and they were again before the Arklow petty sessions in March 1891 charged by four more individuals – James O'Neill, Andrew English, William Byrne, and Joseph Murray – for obstructing the highway.[33] O'Neill swore that he was a baker who wanted to get to his work at two o'clock on the afternoon of Sunday 1 March. He claimed he couldn't get past

the crowd and the lines of police and soldiers. For some time past, 100 Gordon Highlanders had been drafted in as well as 100 extra police every Sunday to keep the peace in Arklow. O'Neill's case was dismissed for it was proved that there was plenty of room for him to pass, and 'only half a minute' had elapsed before a passage was made for him. English, a jarvey, had several passengers on his car and could not get them to their destination, they had to get off and walk. Byrne proved that he was driving cattle and was turned back by the soldiers. Murray was also driving his horse-car when the soldiers stopped him, but his case was dismissed when it was shown that he was deliberately driving up and down the street. O'Neill, Byrne and Murray all had their cases dismissed because they suffered inconvenience at the hands of the police and soldiers who were there to protect the public peace. Only English's case was upheld as he was inconvenienced by the crowd. It was a subtle distinction. Hallowes and Harrison were found guilty of causing the obstruction and were each fined £1 or serve fourteen days in default. They refused to pay and were duly committed for a fortnight.[34]

Hallowes wrote a letter of complaint to Arthur Balfour, chief secretary of Ireland, on the grounds that not only had the magistrates treated them unfairly but that they had also stirred up the vitriol of the mobs once more. Balfour replied that he would not interfere with the magistrates' ruling, and also pointed out that large bodies of armed constabulary had for many months been drafted into Arklow for Hallowes' protection at great cost to the public purse. He said it was neither his duty nor his intention of deciding the rights and wrongs of the case, but he did say

> I presume that you are of the opinion that the utility of your exertions more than counterbalance the inconvenience and hardships suffered by the constabulary, their deprivation through long periods of the ordinary opportunities of religious worship, the weekly risk of a collision between them and the populace of Arklow, to say nothing of the cost to the Exchequer and the county of Wicklow. But whether you are right or wrong in this opinion, whether the facts I have recited should or should not induce you to reconsider the course you are pursuing, they should at all events preclude you from suggesting that you have not received adequate support from the officers of the Crown.[35]

Balfour then turned his attention to Hallowes' claim that he sought no more than what he would be able to do in England.

> I must remind you how different are the circumstances of the two countries.
> In Ireland the divisions between different sections of the community, caused by difference of creed, are so deep and far-reaching, religious convictions are so closely woven with political passions, that a course which would be innocent, and even praiseworthy, on one side of St George's Channel, may be morally, if not legally, indefensible on the other. That this is so must be a matter of the deepest regret, but it is a fact which cannot be ignored; and, though it affords not a shadow of excuse for the violence of a mob, it may possibly afford sufficient grounds for criticising those by whom that violence is knowingly provoked.

Another letter, this time from under-secretary West Ridgeway, was sent to Hallowes on 26 March advising him that further street services were prohibited, but open air services could be held outside the town in a suitable location where necessary protection would be afforded. The cost of the protection had already reached £2,587.[36] An inquiry was also held to see if Hallowes' allegation about ill-treatment at the hands of the police could be verified, but it was found that they had not used excessive force in moving him on to prevent an obstruction of the thoroughfare.

Fr Dunphy had written that 'neither <u>wind</u> nor <u>weather</u> has any effect on him';[37] it would appear that the Revd Mr Hallowes was also impervious to the law, for he continued preaching in the street. On 29 March he again led his followers to an open air service. Among the crowd was an evangelical lay preacher, Mr J Townsend Trench, who wrote an account of the event which was published in the *Freeman's Journal* of 1 April. Trench was no stranger to the area. In 1877 he not only carried out a valuation of properties of the town for the landlord, the earl of Carysfort, but he had drawn and water-coloured all the buildings on 217 pages, which were later bound in leather.[38]

He had travelled on the same train as 100 soldiers who had been despatched for their usual Sunday duty in Arklow, but the outdoor service had commenced at ten-thirty and was over by the time they arrived, and all seemed quiet and peaceful. There was, however, a service being conducted in the Protestant church in Main Street and Townsend Trench attended that, remarking that its 800 person capacity was about one-third full. When the service ended, the majority of the congregation went home, but Hallowes, Harrison and about thirty young girls aged between thirteen and fifteen assembled outside the door. Within a few minutes they were joined by a few dozen boys aged about ten years, and perhaps a dozen women and about the same number of men. Across the road were about fifty police.[39] Hallowes read a few bible passages, but despite his using a loud voice his diction was indistinct and Townsend Trench found it difficult to hear what he was saying.

When he finished, Hallowes led the group down Main Street. They sang hymns as they marched, and they were joined by others until there were about 200 in all. The fifty police walked behind them. They entered Lower Main Street and continued on into Tinahask until they reached the schoolhouse. Townsend Trench was struck by the fact that there was hardly anyone on the street and that all the doors were tightly shut, the residents following Fr Dunphy's advice not to get involved in any disturbance.

As the procession passed each house, the people inside beat the doors to drown out the singing. On reaching the school, Revd Hallowes and his followers turned around and walked back towards the town centre, but after only 200 yards they turned again and retraced their steps to the schoolhouse where he began his sermon, but again because of his poor articulation and the effect of the wind that was blowing, Hallowes' words could not be heard. 'Certainly if anyone wanted to find out the way to Heaven I defy them to make head or tail of it', wrote Townsend Trench. Of course, there is the possibility that Trench had hearing difficulties, but he assures his readers that he heard others uttering the same remark, and it should be remembered that Dr Molony had referred to Hallowes' indistinctness the previous year. It was, Townsend Trench felt, a waste of time.

The police asked Hallowes to move on, which he refused to do and challenged the police officer to arrest him. His followers all moved into the school, perhaps as a pre-arranged strategy so that none but the preachers would be arrested. The police moved in on Hallowes who dodged them and jumped on the low wall, then jumped down again, then ran behind the police. The police did not want to arrest him, fearing that by doing so they would make him into a martyr.

They formed a circle around him and walked back up Tinahask, forcing him to move with them. Hallowes' followers emerged from the school and followed him and the police back up the street. The doors of the houses remained shut, a feature which fascinated the writer of the account, himself a Methodist open air preacher in Dublin, but who disagreed with Revd Hallowes' methods.

> I stopped and asked permission to go into one of the houses (the houses are of a very poor sort, chiefly fishermen's cottages). I found five women and seven men in the house. I said, 'Well, boys, what are you all doing here?' They replied, 'We are shut up here because we do not like to create a disturbance by going outside, and we do not wish to hear Mr Hallowes' lecture.' I asked, 'Do you always spend your Sundays like this?' They replied, 'Yes, since we got the order from the priest to stop indoors, and this is the way we have to spend our Sunday afternoon, instead of being out to get the fresh air, in consequence of Mr Hallowes' procession.

The 'procession' then made its way back down to the Charter School again. This time the preachers and the congregation all entered the building. After a few minutes, Hallowes asked the congregation to stay in while he and his curate, Revd Harrison, went back outside to preach. He returned to them after a brief period and they all headed back up the street again, until they reached Parade Ground, which was already occupied by the military. Undeterred and unmolested, Revd Hallowes preached for half an hour, but his congregation was unable to hear him, for they had been forced to remain in Main Street by the police. At four o'clock the proceedings came to an end. Hallowes went home, the congregation scattered, the military and extra police headed back to Dublin and other bases, while the local police returned to barracks. The whole event bordered on the farcical.

There was a two week break in this repetitive trend. Because Hallowes had refused to pay his £1, he was arrested and served the sentence and during his absence the open-air services were conducted on the sandhills without any disturbance. On his return, however, he immediately began preaching on the street again and the noisy mob returned to disrupt the proceedings. As before, police and army kept the factions apart.[40]

As the summer progressed, the disturbances decreased to the extent that they were no longer deemed newsworthy, and it

Revd Hallowes arrested in the Fishery

was decided that the soldiers and extra police need no longer be drafted into the town. Nevertheless, there were occasional flashes of conflict, such as the incident of 19 July when Revd Harrison refused to move on when requested by the police. He locked one arm around a lamppost while holding his bible open in the other hand, from which he read aloud. In the struggle to prise him from the lamppost the bible was torn. Harrison made strong protests about police brutality, not against his person but

> against the Word of God, which he held in his hand, being rudely crushed and torn, some leaves being entirely pulled out and torn in pieces by police acting, as their inspector informed him, in accordance with strict orders from Dublin Castle.[41]

And so the slapstick comedy persisted month after month. More court cases followed, this time mostly claims brought by Hallowes' supporters against the police. At one of these, the local magistrate was the earl of Carysfort, William Proby. Proby spent some part of each year at Glenart castle, a mile and half

167

west of the town, and when he did so he sat on the bench as magistrate.[42] He said that in the early weeks of these disturbances, when the Catholic population turned out en masse to abuse the preachers, he would have vigorously defended Hallowes' rights, but since the people had shown that they were now willing to let the police handle it, he felt that Hallowes had lost the moral ground and should reconsider his actions. Again, Hallowes would not be swayed.

On 3 January 1892, at the conclusion of his sermon he pointed to the head constable and said: 'You had better put on your spectacles, and you will better be able to see ... That man is going to hell with sin; let him put that in his pipe and smoke it.' A week later, he punched two constables in the face with his clenched fist, but no charge of assault seems to have been pressed. On 17 January, both Harrison and Hallowes pushed the policemen so hard that the ranks were broken.[43] The following day the under-secretary informed the inspector general of constabulary that, in light of the preachers' violence towards the police, the preaching would be banned, not for obstruction, but on the grounds that they were likely to lead to a breach of the peace. When the police informed Hallowes of this the following week, Hallowes and Harrison ignored the warning. He again struck one of the constables in the face and Harrison grabbed another around the neck and tried to wrestle him to the ground. The Catholic population had been staying away, as advised by Fr Dunphy, but these weekly events brought them out onto the streets once more, not to take part but merely to watch the novelty of the forces of government do battle with the forces of evangelical Protestantism.

The government realised the situation could not continue. The chief secretary wrote that the police could not be expected to suffer that kind of treatment without retaliating indefinitely, and he was aware that the Catholic population were watching Hallowes and Harrison hit and kick the police with impunity and realised that they would have been severely punished for similar conduct. There were four courses of action:

1) to withdraw the police, and leave Messrs Hallowes and Harrison to the tender mercies of the mob;
2) to allow them to preach and continue protecting them;
3) to proclaim the meetings;
4) to prosecute the preachers for obstruction and assault.

The first was ruled out as a riot would take place and the local constabulary would have to baton charge or fire at the mob, and the government would be responsible for allowing the situation to develop. The second was also a non-runner as it would infer that the previous actions against the preachers had been wrong. The third would probably anger the Orange and Presbyterian population. The last option, arresting them, would probably cause a backlash in the northern counties. It was left to the local magistrate Alexander Tailyour to ask Hallowes if he would abide by the decision of a higher court as to the legality of the street preaching. Hallowes said that he would. Tailyour also felt that a prosecution for assault should have been brought against Hallowes in the knowledge that the magistrates would dismiss the case on the grounds of insufficient proof of his meetings being illegal. This would, at least, seem that action had been taken against the preacher, and the matter could then be brought to a superior court for a decision on the legality.

This was the course of action taken and a ruling was reached several weeks later. Henceforth, open-air services outside the town would be allowed and protected, but none were to be conducted on the streets.[44] But the preachers refused to abide by the ruling and continued to preach on the streets. In the December 1895 issue of the *Arklow Parish Magazine*, which Hallowes edited, he stated: 'There has not been one Sunday, or Fair Day, from 1894 to the date of writing, that the Gospel has not been preached in our streets.'[45] This was probably true, but the numbers of his followers had greatly decreased, as had the numbers who came out to hurl verbal abuse at them.[46] The chaos had receded and did not return.

CHAPTER 11:
Parnell's fall

It might have been noticed that Parnell did not play a particularly prominent role in the events described in the preceding chapters. At local level his low profile can be explained by his being based in London with more important affairs to deal with. That is not to say that he ignored what was happening politically in his home county. He did, for example, keep a close eye on the progress of his quarries at Arklow Rock, and according to the *News-Letter* he was in negotiation with Carysfort regarding the harbour development.[1] His lack of direct involvement in the Coolgreaney evictions, however, shows a marked contrast to his earlier 'hands on' approach to local events. The reason for this was Parnell's change of direction regarding national politics during his time in Kilmainham Gaol when he came to see land reform as only one aspect of the political dynamics taking place in Ireland at that time. With the demise of the Land League in 1881 and its transformation into the National League in 1882, the attainment of home rule became his primary aim. Other factors were at best of secondary importance, at worst a threat to that primary goal.

As the agrarian crisis intensified in 1886 he did not engage with it. In fact, he opposed the Plan of Campaign which had been organised by his lieutenants, Healy, O'Brien and Harrington. How much of this distancing was for show, a calculated masking of real feelings for political expediency, is uncertain. He had not forgotten how badly accusations of his support for the Phoenix Park murders had set back the cause of home rule, and the best way to avoid further accusations and 'contamination' was to publicly separate himself from purely agrarian matters, but such distancing was a luxury his enemies would not grant him. They were determined to remove him as leader of the parliamentary party.

In 1887 the *Times* published a series of articles written by

Richard Pigott, a County Meath born journalist, under the collective heading of 'Parnell and crime', the purpose of which was to associate the home rule leaders with agrarian outrage during the land war of the late 1870s and opening years of the 1880s. Pigott had worked for and had owned several nationalist newspapers and magazines. His extreme views and open support of fenianism landed him in prison several times. He was moderately successful financially, but was by nature improvident and in 1881 sold three publications he then owned to a publishing company owned by the Land League.[2] It was soon after this that Pigott appears to have become embittered against the league and those associated with it. Anonymously, he wrote a series of pamphlets in which he libelled his former associates. In 1886 he sold information to the National League's counter-organisation the Irish Loyal and Patriotic Union that accused Parnell of complicity in several major crimes during the land war. The *Times* secretly bought the papers from the ILPU and published its series based on them. The most damning of these, a letter purportedly written by Parnell in which he condoned the murders in Phoenix Park in 1882, was published on 18 April 1887. The case made by the *Times* was serious enough to prompt the government to appoint a commission to investigate the matter.

The commission of three judges was established in August 1888, and six months later, on 21 February 1889, Pigott was called to give testimony. Parnell's leading counsel was Newry-born Charles Russell, who was to become lord chief justice of England five years later.[3] Russell was famous for his powers as a cross-examiner and he tore Pigott's evidence to shreds. The case collapsed, Parnell was exonerated, and Pigott fled the country to Madrid where he shot himself before he could be arrested and returned to England to face charges of perjury. Parnell was fêted as a hero, a man of integrity who had not only been victorious in above-board politics, but had vanquished vile libellers, liars, and snakes-in-the-grass. His popularity soared to even greater heights, but like Icarus tragedy was about to befall him.

Ten years earlier, in July 1880, an attendant at the House

of Commons handed Parnell a note informing him that the wife of one of his parliamentary colleagues would like to see him outside. Waiting for him was Katherine, wife of Captain William O'Shea, the nationalist member for Clare. Parnell had never been known to have taken an interest in any woman. He did not even accept many dinner invitations and had declined several from Katherine up to that date.[4] Michael MacDonagh put this as follows:

> Until then, Parnell was untroubled about woman. An old priest who was at Arklow, near Avondale, in the years of Parnell's young manhood, told me that he had never heard even a whisper of sexual looseness in regard to him.[5]

But all that was about to change. Parnell and Katherine were about the same age, thirty-four when they first met, by which time she had been married to William O'Shea for thirteen years. The marriage was not a happy one, and the couple had been living separate lives for some time. Katherine lived in Eltham in Kent in a house given to her by her paternal aunt, Mrs Benjamin Wood, whom the family referred to as Aunt Ben. William took rooms in London in 1878 and visited his wife and children only occasionally.[6] The attraction between Parnell and Katherine would seem to have been immediate and mutual, and before long they were involved in an affair. Two months later, Parnell wrote to Katherine from Avondale, saying that for the first time in his life he had returned to Ireland with regret because 'of the absence of a certain kind and fair face.'[7] This was no sexual fling, but the beginning of a steady, long-term partnership. The first of their three children, a daughter named Sophie, was born in February 1882, when Parnell was in Kilmainham Gaol working on his ideas for the transformation of the Land League into the National League. Sadly, the infant lived for only two months, and was buried in the Catholic churchyard at Chislehurst near Eltham. Katherine was later to write that Parnell would often visit the cemetery and scatter wild flowers over the grave.[8] Parnell, for all his political ingenuity and worldliness, was rather naïve when it came to his relationship with Katherine. She later claimed that when she would warn him that their affair could ruin him, he would reply: 'My public life is my country's; my private life is my own.'[9]

Hypocrisy in sexual matters was a staple of late Victorian life, with prostitution as rife as prudery. The need for 'mistresses' and madams as outlets for 'male animal passions' was understood if never mentioned in polite society. Scandal was given only when something became public and sacrifice demanded only when it made the newspapers. The question has always been who knew about the Parnell-O'Shea affair? Who suspected it? The answer to both questions seems to have been; who cared as long as it was kept out of the media? Katherine always hinted that Gladstone knew of it.[10] There is also ample evidence to suggest that Parnell's lieutenants in the parliamentary party knew of it and strongly suspected that William O'Shea had more or less blackmailed Parnell into supporting his candidacy in a Galway by-election in February 1886.[11] In the closed, claustrophobic world of nineteenth century parliamentary politics, it seems inconceivable that the affair was not common knowledge. Michael MacDonagh, who was a journalist with the *Freeman's Journal* during those years, states that it was suspected and even known on both sides of the Irish Sea. While it was not openly discussed in England, it was tolerated. 'In Ireland, on the other hand, the matter was pushed into the back ground, as something ugly and disquieting, in the hope that it would never come into the light of day.'[12]

William O'Shea, of course, was not ignorant of the affair, but he seems to have tolerated it. This was not generosity of spirit on his part, but the fact that Katherine's Aunt Ben was a very well-to-do lady, and one who would never countenance divorce. He feared that if he divorced Katherine she would no longer be Aunt Ben's favourite relative and likely beneficiary. Even if Aunt Ben did not cut Katherine out of her will, William would have no claim on the inheritance if divorced from her. It was in his interests to say and do nothing to bring about a divorce while Aunt Ben still lived. When she eventually died in 1889 at the age of 95, William O'Shea lost no time in suing for divorce.

O'Shea had been born in Dublin in 1840, the son of a wealthy solicitor.[13] His father bought him a commission in the 18th Hussars. He met Katherine Wood and married her in 1867. He sold his commission in the army and moved to Madrid as a partner in a bank owned by his uncle, but the arrangement did not work out and William and Katherine returned to England. He started a stud farm, but it too failed, and it was only the financial support of Katherine's Aunt Ben that kept them solvent. He then became a manager in a sulphur mine in Spain but after eighteen months, this also came to nothing. In 1880, by which time he had ceased to live with Katherine except for rare visits, he joined the Irish Party and was elected M.P. for Clare. In the 1885 general election he stood as a liberal in Liverpool, but was defeated. Interestingly, Parnell pushed for his nomination for the home rule party in a by-election in Galway in February 1886, much to the surprise and disagreement of some of the party's leading figures, such as Joseph Biggar and Tim Healy. Just why Parnell should have done such a thing is difficult to understand. There was nothing in O'Shea's life to suggest that here was a man who could con-tribute to the home rule movement. He was a failed soldier, a failed businessman, a failed mine manager, and had a failed marriage behind him. Was Parnell motivated by guilt? Was he acting on a request from Katherine? Did O'Shea promise not to go public about Parnell's affair with his wife if Parnell helped him secure the seat? The third possibility seems the most plau-sible, and according to one source, Parnell is reported as saying that rejection of O'Shea would be a blow to his [Parnell's] power and would imperil home rule.[14] O'Shea was elected with a large majority, but once again his fickleness came to the fore and he resigned the seat the following year.

In 1889 William O'Shea filed for divorce, accusing his wife of adultery and citing Parnell as the co-respondent. The case opened on 11 November 1890 and the end of Parnell's political career was in sight. At that time, divorce cases were conducted by judge and jury and O'Shea played for their sympathy, claiming that he had been ignorant of the affair, but that is simply not creditable. The facts of the case, however, were beyond question and a *decree nisi* was granted. Not only did neither Katherine nor Parnell contest the case, but they never appeared in court to hear the evidence, much of which was sordid, almost music hall material. The press made the most of it, turning Parnell into a laughing stock. The court's decision was published on 17 November.

According to Katherine's biography, Parnell was delighted with the result. They were now free to marry. It did not occur to him that his political position would be compromised in any way, but in this he was greatly mistaken.

The reaction in England was shattering. Gladstone's liberals drew much of their support from non-conformists, many of whom saw home rule as a moral issue. How could these moralists continue giving their support to someone who was cited in the public press as living in sin with a married woman? Gladstone was quick to realise that Parnell had become a liability, if the Irish party wanted the continued support of the Liberal Party, they would have to jettison Parnell and elect a new leader. On 18 November, the day after the publication of the result of the divorce case, the member for Wexford, John Redmond, chaired the fortnightly meeting of the National League at which it was made clear that Parnell would not be thrown to the moralistic wolves.

> If the Irish people thought that Parnell entertained the idea of retiring they would come to him as one man, and entreat him not to desert them and their country. But, thank God, no such danger ever existed. With that indomitable courage which is, perhaps, his chief characteristic, Mr Parnell has declared his intention of standing by Ireland to the last, and we tell him here today, that never in his whole career was Ireland more determined to stand by him.[15]

Redmond, it seemed, had gauged the Irish reaction perfectly. The *Freeman's Journal* led the way in giving Parnell unqualified support. A mass meeting was held in Dublin's Leinster Hall, led by the lord mayor, at which it was stated that no one had the right to question Parnell's private life. Glowing tributes were paid to him, some, such as Justin McCarthy's words, were to sound hollow in the light of subsequent events. Even Tim Healy, whose personal relationship with Parnell was not good, expressed his loyalty to him.

In England, the mood was very different. Revd Hugh Price Hughes, writing in the *Methodist Times*, proposed that 'If the Irish people deliberately accept such a man as Parnell as their representative, they are morally unfit to enjoy the privilege of self-government.'[16] Another call for his resignation came from Michael Davitt, who had turned his attention from the Irish land question and home rule to British labour politics and he added his voice to the growing demand for Parnell to step down. It all came to a head on Tuesday 25 November in Committee Room 15 in the House of Commons. It was Parnell's first public appearance since the divorce proceedings. Jeremiah Jordan, a nationalist Ulster Protestant from Enniskillen but M.P. for Clare, proposed that Parnell should step down for the sake of the movement, but he received no seconder. Parnell was then re-elected as leader of the party and took the chair amid great cheering. It was here that he made his only public reference to the divorce case.[17]

> I am accused of breaking up a happy home, and of shattering a scene of domestic bliss and felicity. If the case had been gone into, a calculation had been made, and it would have been proved, that in the twenty-three years of Mr O'Shea's married life he spent only 400 days in his own home. This was the happy home which I am alleged to have destroyed.
>
> I am also accused of betraying a friend. Mr O'Shea was never my friend. Since I first met him in Ennis, in 1880, he was always my enemy – my bitter and relentless enemy. There is the further charge against me that I abused this man's hospitality. But I never partook at any time of Mr O'Shea's hospitality, for I never had bite or sup – never had a glass of wine – at his expense.
>
> I will not dwell any more on this subject except to say

that of the two principal witnesses in the case, one was a drunkard and the other a thief.

Now that I have lifted a corner of the curtain, I will only ask you, gentlemen, to keep your lips sealed, as mine are, on what you heard until the brief period of time will have elapsed when I can vindicate myself, and when you will find that your trust in me has not been misplaced.[18]

This speech was not made public until a year later, by which time Parnell was dead. It appeared in a series of articles published between 21 November and 5 December 1891 by the *National Press*, a Dublin-based anti-Parnell daily newspaper. The articles, published under the collective title of 'The Story of Room 15', were written by Donal Sullivan, one of the secretaries of the Irish party. He had taken a note of the speech as it was delivered.

Whatever those present in Room 15 might have felt about the moral aspects of the situation, not one uttered a word of condemnation. No matter how much they may have suspected or even knew of the affair, no matter what they had read in the press, here was an admission by Parnell himself that he had been conducting an adulterous affair. Many of the men present were devout Catholics, for whom the sanctity of marriage was one of the most important tenets by which they lived and yet they still refused to abandon Parnell. Who could have predicted at that moment that their 'undying' loyalty to him was to be cast aside within the hour?

The cause of that dramatic change of heart was Gladstone. News arrived that Gladstone had sent a letter to the newspapers stating that if Parnell did not step down, his [Gladstone's] position as leader of the Liberal Party would be rendered untenable. It was a dramatic choice – Gladstone (without whom the passing of home rule for Ireland into law would be impossible) or Parnell. At the time the news broke, Parnell was in one of the smoking rooms, and his erstwhile sycophantic supporters were trying to decide who should go to him and, in the light of this development, tell him that he should step down. Finally, Justin McCarthy and Thomas Sexton entered the room and explained the situation to Parnell who flatly refused to resign his leadership.

Three days later, a second meeting was held in Room 15, again with Parnell in the chair, and again he refused to step down and the meeting was adjourned for a further three days. Parnell had decided to put the matter in a manifesto, *To the people of Ireland*, in which he asked 'Will you consent to throw me to the English wolves now howling for my destruction?'

Seventy-three of the eighty-five members of the party were present. Six were in the United States, five of whom telegrammed their condemnation of Parnell's manifesto. Tim Harrington sent a note 'my heart is with Mr Parnell, but my judgement is against him.'[19] Despite his words of support in Leinster Hall, the real leader of the opposition to Parnell was Tim Healy who agreed with Sexton that the English liberals would have to be placated. At noon on Saturday 6 December 1890, the members again met in room 15. It was the last time they were to meet as a united party. Five and a half hours of heated discussion followed and the anti-Parnell faction placed themselves under Gladstone's leadership. Justin McCarthy stood up and invited those who wished to follow him from the room. Forty-five did so, twenty-eight remained with Parnell. His son, Justin Huntly McCarthy, M.P. for Newry, had voted for Parnell at the beginning of the week, but now he turned his back on him and joined the majority faction. He summed up the feelings of many when he said: '... many personal friendships that have endured ten years on the most intimate and warmest terms were dissolved and changed into bitterest animosities.'[20]

The breakaway majority went to another room where McCarthy was elected 'sessional chairman', pledging themselves independent of liberals and other parties and to work for home rule. When Gladstone heard the news he said: 'Thank God! Home rule is saved.'[21] Parnell still regarded himself as the leader, although two-thirds of the party had deserted him, and technically he was correct. The unanimous vote that had re-elected him leader just eleven days previously had not been reballotted. He was also sure that, unlike so many of his erstwhile colleagues, the people of Ireland would not desert him.

*

News of the O'Shea divorce case was carried by the *Wicklow News-Letter* on the second page, which was dedicated to national and international news, not on the fourth page which was the local news section.[22] It was the local page which usually carried the editorial column, so William M'Phail did not make any comment on the events unfolding in London. What was printed was William O'Shea's evidence that he first met Parnell after his election to parliament in 1880 and he first suspected that the party leader was having a liaison with his wife as early as 1881, upon which suspicion he challenged Parnell to a duel to be held 'in the north of France.' The duel did not take place and within a short period of time, O'Shea was satisfied that the affair had been nipped in the bud, even when Parnell had some of his horses shipped from Avondale and had them stabled in Katherine's premises. He again had suspicions in 1885, but apparently this did not stop him accepting Parnell's patronage in his bid to stand for the Galway seat in parliament. By 1887, the *News-Letter* report continued, Parnell and Katherine were sharing a house at 112 Tersillian Road, Brockley, where Parnell purportedly used the pseudonyms Preston and Fox.

The following week the *News-Letter* carried a full report of Gladstone's reaction to the divorce and his ultimatum that Parnell would have to step down as leader. It was headed 'Parnell crisis', but again it was in the national news page and there was no reference to it in the local columns. However, the support of M'Phail and the *News-Letter* for Parnell was unequivocal, and a supplement to the 6 December 1890 issue was dedicated to that cause. On 13 December, however, the *Wicklow People* editor summed up his reaction in a phrase – 'Parnell or Home Rule, which must go?' It condemned 'non-priest nationalists' and promised: 'When our people know the truth, they are not going to let Ireland sink so low as that the Island of Saints should be championed by a confirmed adulterer.' It was ironic that the unionist newspaper, conservative in its religious views and tory in its politics, should now champion Parnell, while the nationalist (albeit it even more religiously conservative) *Wicklow People* should bay for the blood of the man who had brought the cause of political self-determination for Ireland so far.

It is too simplistic to say that it was a case of being either for or against Parnell. No doubt there were those who did look on the matter in such black-and-white terms, but there was also a considerable faction who regarded it as a case of being for or against home rule, and that Parnell was now an obstacle in the way of that goal. The choices everyone faced were either the moral one of supporting or condemning Parnell's right to a private life, or the politically practical one of supporting or abandoning home rule.

Arklow Town Commissioners must have been shell-shocked, because the report of their December meeting made no mention of this crisis in national politics. Despite this lack of recorded reaction, there can be little doubt that the already fractured nature of nationalist politics in Arklow was to be prised apart even further. The local National League branch under Fr Dunphy would no longer support Parnell, while the 'non-priest nationalists' condemned by the *Wicklow People*, such as Molony and Troy, would remain loyal to him. The O'Shea divorce case was not the cause of the split in Arklow nationalist politics, but it did put it beyond any hope of healing.

The *News-Letter* of 13 December carried a column headed 'New Nationalists', describing the breakaway group headed by Justin McCarthy. There was also a report that John Redmond had been asked to accept an address from the Wicklow town commissioners for his work in defending men accused of boycotting replacement tenants on the Brooke estate at Ballyfad. The Wicklow commissioners also reiterated their 'unswerving confidence in Mr Charles Stewart Parnell.'

They wanted to go further, hoping to give Redmond a public reception, but he refused this saying that he was in the locality as a lawyer and he did not feel such a public display would be helpful in the prevailing circumstances. Instead a private function was held in the Green Tree Hotel, where he was staying. One thing was clear, the Wicklow town commissioners were fully behind Parnell whatever his private life may be. Two weeks later the comparatively silent Arklow town commissioners were to prove less loyal.

The 20 December edition of the *News-Letter* carried the startling report that Parnell had been attacked in County Kilkenny. He was in the constituency as part of the campaign to have the local Parnellite candidate elected in a by-election. Michael Davitt was also there, promoting the anti-Parnell, or McCarthyite, candidate. A scuffle broke out at one venue at which both factions had turned up together. This was continued after both factions reached Castlecomer where Parnell refused to enter into a public debate with Davitt. In the fracas, Parnell was hit in the face with a bag of lime and had to receive immediate medical attention. If the scene resembled something from the American wild west, it was rendered more so in that in an adjacent column was the report that the Sioux chief, Sitting Bull, had been killed in a shoot-out with U.S. cavalry.

Around Christmas, Parnell spent a few days at Avondale.[23] He had travelled to Boulogne to meet William O'Brien in a bid to heal the widening rift between his supporters and detractors in the Irish party. Reaching Dublin on his return, he took the train from Harcourt Street station, accompanied only by a press association reporter. Few seemed to recognise him, but that is understandable as he was dressed in 'a loose-fitting coat and cap', and his eye was heavily bandaged from the attack at Castlecomer. His arrival had not been announced and there were no crowds gathered at stations through which he passed. He looked fatigued, the strain of the past weeks telling on his whole demeanour and he slept 'unrefreshingly' in the first class compartment he shared with the newsman. They left the train at Glenealy, where they were met

181

by his quarry manager, William Kerr, who drove them to quarries newly opened in the Ballycapple-Ballard area. Iron had been searched for there over many years but without success, but Parnell's remarkable knowledge of the geology of his native county prompted him to re-open the old workings, and he seems to have met with some success. The reporter recorded Parnell's ease in discussing the mining operations with the men working there. They stayed over an hour and then moved on to Arklow. Only occasionally did anyone recognise the fallen leader.

At Arklow, they drove down Main Street on their way to his quarries at the Rock and it was only then did someone shout; 'Parnell!' and soon small groups gathered to cheer him and loudly denounce his enemies. As chance would have it, Revd Richard Hallowes was also making his way down the street and 'he had the honour of sharing with Mr Parnell the attention of the people, although in another form.' When Fr Dunphy learned of Parnell's presence in the town he invited him to lunch in his house, which Parnell did either before or after he had visited the quarry for over an hour. While they ate, a large enthusiastic crowd gathered outside to cheer and pledge their support for the man who had done so much for them. It must have heartened him, but as the *News-Letter* pointed out in its 3 January 1891 issue, the town commissioners were conspicuous by their absence. Under a heading, 'Ungrateful and Forgetful Arklow', M'Phail was scathing in his attack on them for their lack of an official welcome and asked if the success of the McCarthyite candidate in Kilkenny had made them reassess their chances of high office if they stayed loyal to Parnell?

Parnell was back in Arklow on Monday, 12 January, when a correspondent of the *Freeman's Journal* stated that although the visit was 'on business and entirely unannounced the town turned out en masse' to greet him. Among those to show their continuing support by welcoming him were town commissioner Kavanagh, Dr Molony (although spelt Moloney and Maloney in the *Wicklow People* version of the visit), Murray,

Garvey, and Robert Byrne, and poor law guardian Somers. It was a short report, no more than a couple of column inches, but the *Wicklow News-Letter* reprinted it changing it slightly to include names familiar to its readers, but sharing the *Freeman's* upbeat account of the occasion;

> [they] cheered the chief on his way to the station. While waiting for the train the platform and station were thronged with enthusiastic people who gave expression to the admiration and undying faith in the Irish leader. The names of Mr Healy and other seceders were received with groans and hisses.
>
> Mr Parnell was accompanied by Messrs Kerr and Strype [the engineer responsible for the harbour development] and was met on his arrival by Messrs Kavanagh, town commissioner, Dr Molony, Murray, Somers, poor law guardian, Robert Byrne, Garvey, etc. Just as the train was about to start Mr Parnell addressed the people. He referred to the fact that they were his old friends who knew him, and thanked them for their magnificent reception. As the train moved off vociferous cheers were given by the crowd for Mr Parnell and deep groans for his opponents.[24]

In the *Wicklow People* account, published on the same day, the reporter echoed the general tone of the event and added that T J Healy, a solicitor from Wexford and brother of the anti-Parnell M.P. T M Healy, was a passenger on the train and when this became known he became 'the recipient of a demonstration of a very hostile character.'

When Fr Farrelly read the *Freeman's* account he was not happy, and wrote to the editor to dispute its accuracy.

> Sir,
> … First, the people of Arklow did not turn out *en masse*. On the contrary, the majority of Mr Parnell's admirers was composed of children returning from school, and women drawn there by curiosity. The crowd at any time did not amount to three hundred. This you must allow is a small representation of a town of six thousand inhabitants. In the next place, Mr Parnell was not unexpected as he was in and around Arklow for over three hours. I think it is very bad taste of Mr Parnell's

friends to try and make political capital out of his business visit to the town.

Yours faithfully,
L.J. Farrelly, C.C. Arklow
13 January 1891.

(We print Fr Farrelly's letter as a matter of courtesy but we are of opinion that 'contradictions' of so trifling a kind are not worth the space they occupy. – Ed. *FJ*)

The *Wicklow People* of 17 January also printed Farrelly's letter, but immediately beneath it was another contradicting Farrelly, stating that the people had turned out *en masse* (about 1200) and that the enthusiasm of the crowd was unmistakeable.

Farrelly was quite evidently no longer in Parnell's camp. Archbishop Walsh was not pleased by what he read of Parnell's reception in Arklow either, and he demanded to know why Dunphy had entertained him and why Parnell was still so admired in the parish. Dunphy replied

> I can assure your Grace I gave no countenance in any way to what took place ... As for the fishermen they usually follow me when left alone and I am not a bit afraid that when the occasion comes they will be found on the side of virtue ... I gave Parnell more hard knocks than he got from any of his opponents – which I must say he bore with great patience from which I expect better results than if I took a different course. I have up to this in my public life I hope gave no reason to my fellow priests to be scandalised with me.[25]

It is difficult to gauge to what extent Dunphy had turned against Parnell at this stage. It is beyond question that he did entertain him to lunch, and this at a time when many erstwhile Parnellite clergy had turned their backs on him and condemned him from the pulpit. Also, it is interesting that in his response to Walsh's demand of an explanation he says 'I gave Parnell more hard knocks than he got from any of his opponents', which suggests that he did not count himself among those opponents. Whatever Dunphy's personal relationship with Parnell was after the split, it was clear that Fr Farrelly was strongly opposed to any reconciliation with the fallen leader. On 4 June 1891 he wrote to Archbishhop Walsh assuring him of the town's disaffection with Parnell:

> Your Grace may have heard a report that is making the rounds, namely that east Wicklow is certainly lost to the cause. I write to assure your Grace that as far as I can learn, such is not the case. One cannot form a correct judgement from the Wicklow meeting as it was mainly made up of outsiders and non-voters. I think we have six months before an election. East Wicklow will be sound. I believe with some little management, the fish-ermen of Arklow will be found where they have always been – on the side of their Archbishop & priests.[26]

CHAPTER 12:
Division within division

Workers' rights

The Land League had been established to promote and defend the rights of tenants. The National League continued this crusade, albeit as only one plank in the overall aim of establishing home rule. But what of the rights of urban workers?

Unions for skilled tradesmen were well established by the last quarter of the nineteenth century, but craftsmen were jealous of their standing in the extremely hierarchical world of labour and many were as opposed to non-skilled labour unions as were employers. Parnell, the champion of the tenant farmer, was implacably opposed to any trade union. In 1891, he told Michael Davitt that if he [Parnell] led an Irish government he would not tolerate unions, describing them as the 'landlords of labour'. Aware that liberal capitalists, priests, and farmers would baulk at socialist movements such as trade unions, he feared that they would prove harmful to home rule. 'Whatever has to be for the protection of the working class should be the duty of government'.[1]

By the 1880s, however, non-skilled workers were also beginning to unionise and make demands for better wages and conditions. Industrial unrest became more frequent and organisers were eager to visit small towns and villages when called upon to help establish new branches of their particular unions, societies, federations, associations or combinations. Arklow was a rich hunting ground for such organisers, and grievances were not always confined to conditions or money. For example, there was a strike at Parnell Quarries in August 1890 which stemmed from 'insulting remarks' a Protestant overseer named McAllister had made one Saturday night regarding the street-preaching, or rather remarks regarding the Catholic residents' objections to it. The following Monday morning at work, a delegation of Catholic workers demanded an apology, but instead

McAllister repeated whatever the offending comments had been and there was an immediate down-tools by all 140 workers. Parnell himself was called upon to intervene, and on his promise of an investigation being carried out, the men returned to work.[2]

In September, the dockers (those employed in loading and discharging the ships) in the port of Wexford, all of whom were union members, refused to discharge or load vessels unless all the men employed were fellow members. Sailors in the same port had organised and had been offered a five shillings a month increase in their wages by the local shipowners, but the men refused this offer, demanding a ten shillings increase on monthly wages of £3-10-0 for able-seamen, and ten shillings a month extra on a mate's monthly wage of £3-16-0.[3] The Arklow vessel *Livonia* was in Wexford harbour at the time and the crew refused to man her unless they too received the union rate. In Limerick, another Arklow vessel, the *Satellite*, was likewise strike-bound.[4] In October, moves were afoot to establish a labourers' union in Arklow. It was time for the employers to safeguard their interests and the shipowners formed a federation of their own; the irony of forming a union to protest against the formation of unions seems to have been lost on them.[5]

Employers became increasingly watchful for any signs of possible agitation and the 15 November 1890 edition of the *Wicklow News-Letter* carried a report of a scuffle between George Kearon, junior, an Arklow shipowner, and Patrick Comerford, a representative of the National and Amalgamated Firemen's and Sailors' Society of Great Britain and Ireland. It was a minor incident in itself, but it signified a new dynamic in the social and political unrest in Arklow at that time. A group of local sailors contacted the Firemen's and Sailors' Society in the hope of forming a branch in Arklow. Some of these men worked on the local brigantine the *Spray*. The vessel was small, eighty-seven tons, and had been built in the Canadian maritime province of Prince Edward Island in 1864. She had been bought by Arklow shipowner William Philpot in 1880, but by 1890 had been acquired by unionist town commissioner

Richard Kearon.[6] Arklow was a busy port, with over 200 fishing boats employing 1,000 men and boys and sixty-eight trading vessels.[7] This meant that berthing space was in short supply and vessels often had to tie-up two or even three deep alongside the quay walls, necessitating those boarding and disembarking having to cross the inner vessel to reach the outer one. Such was the case when Patrick Comerford arrived from Dublin to speak with the men on board Richard Kearon's *Spray*. As mentioned, the scuffle itself was of no great importance, nevertheless the union brought a case of assault against Kearon and it was dragged through the courts, receiving plenty of local press coverage while the more interesting story, that of the workers against the employers, got relatively few column inches. Further industrial unrest was seen at the harbour a week or two later when the dockers went on strike after a Catholic shipowner and dispensary committee member, Owen Fogarty, employed non-union dockers to discharge the *Eva*, another small vessel built in Prince Edward Island in the 1860s.[8]

M'Phail of the *News-Letter*, ever vigilant against insipient communism, was pleased that the number of strikers was small,[9] but it was a growing trend with a labourers' union started in Wicklow town in January 1891 and another strike at the Rock quarries in February when a non-union carter was employed.[10] There was yet another strike there four months later for a week-ly wage increase of three shillings. Parnell offered two shillings, but this was rejected. This industrial action may well have been orchestrated for political reasons, as some of the strikers were brought to a political rally in Carlow to speak against Parnell as an unfair employer. To counteract this, Dr Molony organised a pro-Parnell meeting in the sandhills in the Fishery area of Arklow at which other quarry labourers spoke in favour of Parnell.[11]

Women's rights
Another factor to emerge from the socio-political milieu was the extension of suffrage to some women in the Arklow munic-ipal elections. Arklow township had been incorporated under the provisions of the Towns Improvement Act (1847).[12] Two wards were established, the Arklow ward which was allocated twelve representatives, and the Ferrybank ward which had three. One third of the members had to stand for re-election each year. The theory was that in this way each year saw new commissioners taking their seats with new ideas and fresh vigour, while the experience of two thirds of the members was retained. In practice, most of the outgoing commissioners were re-elected, so there was little scope for either new ideas or fresh vigour. Arklow municipal elections were to be held on 15 October each year. A review of registered voters could be called for annually and the eligibility of each voter challenged.

In 1889, there were thirty-one women in Arklow on the register for municipal elections. For some reason, Richard Kearon of the Arklow Independent Ratepayers' Association requested through his solicitor that a list of eligible voters be published, omitting 'from the same the names of certain female voters.'[13] Just why he wanted 'certain' females excluded was not made clear, but the town commission chairman, Daniel

Condren (one of Fr Dunphy's close allies in the local branch of the league), Mr Fitzhenry the town clerk, and the commission solicitor Mr M'Innerney refused to revise the register. The matter was brought to arbitration, but the arbiters made no decision on the matter. Kearon's determination to have particular voters omitted from the register suggests that he believed they would vote according to Fr Dunphy's wishes, and not for the conservative unionist candidates or others of the Arklow Independent Ratepayers' Association. This, of course, would not in itself constitute justification for having the women excluded from the register, some legitimate reason for exclusion would have to be found.

The four retiring commissioners in 1889 for the Arklow ward were Job Hall (unionist), John Reynolds, Joseph Doyle, and Henry Delahunt (all three of whom were members of the Arklow branch of the National League). Candidates for election had to be nominated. Fr Dunphy, as chairman of the local National League, put forward four nominees: the outgoing John Reynolds, Henry Delahunt, and Joseph Doyle, and John Bradford. Alexander Taylor (or Tailyour, depending on how the journalists were feeling at the time), estate agent of the earl of Carysfort and prominent local unionist, also nominated four candidates; Job Hall, Thomas J Troy, Dr M J Molony, and John Tyrrell, owner of John Tyrrell & Sons boatyard.[14] There was some confusion over Tyrrell's nomination. His son wrote to Mr Fitzhenry, the town clerk, saying that his father's name had been put forward without his consent and that he wished to withdraw from the election. Fitzhenry at first took this at face value and a batch of ballot papers were printed without Tyrrell's name appearing, but he then decided to confirm the matter with John Tyrrell himself. Tyrrell said that his son had no right to write the letter and that he had no intention of withdrawing. Because of this rather strange occurrence some batches of ballot papers included Tyrrell's name and some omitted it, leading to official complaints by members of the National League that Tyrrell's candidacy was rendered void, but the nomination was allowed to stand.

The election was to prove a most divisive event, with the local National League heaping scorn on the Ratepayers' Association. Troy, Molony and Tyrrell regarded themselves as nationalists, but the local leaguers saw them as nothing more than traitors. For days before the polls opened, the National League faction put up posters throughout the town:

PEOPLE OF ARKLOW

Will you support the eight* nominated by Father Dunphy, pres-ident of the League, or will you support the emergency** candi-dates nominated by Mr Taylor, fresh from the ruthless eviction of Denis Murphy and his helpless family?
Here are the League candidates nominated by Father Dunphy: John Reynolds, Henry Delahunt, John Bradford, and Joseph Doyle.
Here are the nominees of Mr Taylor: Thomas J Troy, Dr M J Molony, and John Tyrrell, shipwright.
We confidently appeal to the nationalists of Arklow to dis-charge their duty at the hall with credit to themselves, and to the vantage of their country's cause.

GOD SAVE IRELAND
[* 'eight' is incorrect as Dunphy seems to have nominated only four. **'emergency' referred to those employed by landlords to forcibly evict tenants in arrears, thereby branding Troy, Molony and Tyrrell as enemies of the people.]

It will be noticed that the unionist Job Hall's name was not list-ed in this poster as one of Taylor's nominees. Those intending to vote, however, would not be confused as to his unionist pol-itics, but the naming of Troy, Molony and Tyrrell was to make sure that, although they described themselves as nationalist, they had been nominated by a unionist 'fresh from a ruthless eviction' and not by the local National League.

The league was also determined that Richard Kearon's attempt to exclude female voters from the election should not be forgotten, and on polling day they handed voters green slips of paper on which were printed the following lines:

Thackaberry* went to town, with vengeance all aloney
Swearing he'd break the women's votes as they wouldn't
back Maloney.
Judge Andrews took the matter cool, like the Old
O'Gradys
He had sufficient gallantry to not attack the ladies.

[* 'Thackaberry' was Richard Kearon, unionist member of
Molony's Independent Ratepayers' Association.]

The voting was brisk at first, but died off after a while, and
when the tallies were complete it was clear that the National
League campaign, spearheaded by the local clergy, was victorious. Topping the poll was Henry Delahunt with 60 votes, followed by John Reynolds (59), Doyle (55), Bradford (54),
Molony (53), Troy (47), Hall (45), and Tyrrell (35). Dunphy
was delighted that his four nominees were the first past the post
making it a landslide success.

He addressed the crowd outside the courthouse saying
that he knew the voters of Arklow would do their duty. He
could, he said, 'respect a good Tory – an honest Protestant who
would do his duty consistently by his party, but [we] have not
had only to contend with the Conservatives of the town but
also to stand against members of [our] own party – snakes and
grabbers who sought to put themselves before the world that
they are National Leaguers, and that the members of the local
branch are not leaguers at all.' He was, of course, referring to
Molony without naming him, saying that the sooner his name
was erased from the central branch register the better. He was
an 'upstart who owed his position to the vote of the National
League (hear, hear). They had now defied him and kicked him
into oblivion. This would be a lesson for him and all those who
would attempt in future to run in opposition to the decision of
the priests and people of Arklow.'

Molony was incensed by these remarks. At first he had no
intention of explaining or justifying his beliefs or his actions to

anyone, but a friend, 'for whose opinion I have the greatest respect', convinced him that he would have to put his opinions and his reasons before the people.[15] This unnamed friend explained to Molony that if the National League, through the *Wicklow People*, were given free rein to blacken Molony's name and politics he would never win enough support to change the entrenched attitudes that prevailed. He had no option but to defend his position and hope that the logic of his arguments would win support, or at least defuse some growing opposition to him. With this in mind, Molony first wrote to the editor of the *Freeman's Journal*,[16] pointing out that he was surprised to find himself described as 'unionist' in one of their reports, but added, '... if you restrict the term "Nationalist" and define it as meaning "a flunkey of the parish priest of Arklow", then I am no Nationalist and your correspondent may call me a Unionist or anything else he pleases'. But he reminded them that for ten years he had done all he could for the advancement of his country in both England and Ireland. He also told the *Freeman's* that he had been nominated not by Taylor but by the ratepayers' association. He wrote a longer letter to the editor of the *Wicklow People*, explaining that he felt it necessary because of the slander levelled at him by 'a person of a class hardly likely to be readily suspected of disseminating malignant falsehood and [was] consequently all the more dangerous'. Fr Dunphy, it would seem, was not the only one who could point the finger without naming names.

Molony reiterated that the Arklow Independent Ratepayers' Association crossed party lines, but that all its members agreed to work together on purely local matters. He again stated that neither Carysfort nor his agent Alexander Taylor had anything to do with the association, and that Taylor had not nominated the association's candidates. He then turned his attention to the personal aspects of the attack on him and the association:

> I am told that the head and front of my offending is that I 'go against the clergy'. Well, sir, in ecclesiastical and spiritual mat-

ters I need hardly say that I bow most respectfully to the opinions of the clergy, but not being a professional flunkey who wants to scrape up a few patients by hanging on and toadying to the local clergy, I decline to be dictated to in purely temporal, and above all on local municipal questions by the clergy or anybody else.[17]

He signed this, M J Molony, Central Branch, Irish National League.

The editor of the *Wicklow People* was unimpressed by this letter and was even more scathing in his attack on those who called themselves nationalists yet put themselves in opposition to the local branch of the National League. He categorised the Ratepayers' Association candidates as 'the anti-nationalist faction', referring to Hall as 'an avowed Tory'. It was, he wrote, not enough that they had to go against the local branch of the league, but that they were nominated by Lord Carysfort's agent, Alexander Taylor, 'the emergency agent, fresh from the eviction of Denis Murphy of Killahurler'. As for Molony, the editor wrote, he had aligned himself with coercionists and if that was how he served Ireland while in England it was time he was exposed for what he was.

The following week, in the issue dated 26 October 1889, the editor had even more reason to gloat, as he published two further letters from Molony. The first must have been particularly galling for Molony to write because it was an admission that he had been mistaken in thinking that Taylor had not nominated him and the others. Taylor *had* proposed their candidacy, but Molony denies he knew that this had been the case. The *Wicklow People* was not gracious in victory. It asked if Molony, Troy and Tyrrell were truly nationalist, would Sandy Taylor (as they referred to Alexander Tailyour) have nominated them? Would he, for example, have nominated any of the candidates put forward by Fr Dunphy? Surely, this association of a landlord's agent belied Molony's claims to nationalism. In the second letter Molony repeats that he honestly believed that he and the others had been nominated by Richard Hudson,

Richard Kearon and Dr Howard, all members of the association. He also denied that the association was anything other than 'a purely non-political, non-sectarian combination.' Finally, he refuted the statement made by the editor that he was under an obligation to the parish priest or anyone else for his position as medical officer for Arklow. In the eyes of the editor, however, 'non-political and non-sectarian combinations have no place in the death struggle of the Irish people today.'

There was no going back from this. Too much had been said and written, too many insults had been thrown, too many bridges burned.

*

The passing of a year did nothing to heal the growing rift. As October 1890 came around Fr Dunphy, parish priest, and Daniel Condren, chairman of the town commissioners, nominated Bernard Kearney, publican and grocer, John Hannigan, publican and grocer, John Cullen, shopkeeper, and Richard Howard, apothecary, as their party's candidates. Howard was the Dr Howard who had been a member of the Ratepayers' Association, but in recent months had severed his connection with it to align himself with the local branch of the National League. Why he had this change of heart is not recorded, perhaps he felt he could no longer support Parnell. Job Hall, James Tyrrell and Richard Kearon nominated each other, all members of the Arklow Independent Ratepayers' Association.[18]

Under the system of the time, the names of registered voters were ticked as the voters entered the polling station to cast their votes just as they are now, but in a small town such as Arklow, the political allegiance of each was a relatively easy matter to determine and predictions of the outcome of the election based on who had voted were very accurate. It is not too much to say that each vote was known before it was cast, particularly as in 1890 there were only 127 registered voters in this town of over 4,000 inhabitants.[19]

The election took place in the courthouse. Daniel

Condren presided and the nationalist observers were headed by Fr Dunphy. With him were Patrick Kavanagh, Henry Delahunt, Thomas Birthistle, John Reynolds, John Hannigan junior, James Canterbury, and James Doyle. Keeping an eye on proceedings for the independent ratepayers were Samuel Marshall, George Kearon junior (who would attack the union representative within a couple of weeks), Charles T Evans, and Richard Myers. The polls opened at eight o'clock and would remain open for twelve hours. The weather was inclement so both parties put covered wagons and horse-drawn cars at the disposal of registered voters in a bid to get as much support as possible. One nationalist voter left his sick bed and hobbled into the booth on crutches to make sure that he would have his say. Despite this and other measures, at the end of the day only 106 of the 127 registered voters had made their choice.[20]

Once again, the inclusion of women on the register was a bone of contention. The previous month a long and inconclusive legal argument had taken place in the commissioners' offices as to whether the word 'person' in the act governing voting rights had been intended to include women.[21] Nothing had been decided and the arrival at the polling booths of twenty women to cast their votes caused a stir. Records are vague as to whether they arrived *en bloc*, in small groups or separately, but arrive they did. Sixteen of them were known to be nationalist and four turned up in support of the independent ratepayers. The nationalist observers saw immediately the advantage they would gain by allowing the women to cast their votes; likewise the independent ratepayers saw that they would be at a disadvantage if they were allowed to do so. The decision fell to the supposedly impartial town commission chairman, Daniel Condren, who was of course second-in-command of the local nationalist party after Fr Dunphy. Not surprisingly, Condren ruled that the women should be allowed to vote. Those against agreed to let the election proceed, but were determined to contest the decision in court if the result went against them.

The ease of categorising how electors would vote might seem surprising to modern eyes, but even today tallymen are remarkably accurate in their predictions. With the tiny electorate in Arklow municipal elections in the late nineteenth century a crystal ball would not have been needed. Such was the close scrutiny of who turned up to vote that the *Wicklow News-Letter* editor, William M'Phail, could confidently announce that of the twenty-one missing voters fourteen were independent ratepayer supporters and seven were nationalists. Not only that, he was able to show exactly how the women's votes affected the individual tallies of the candidates. The numbers beside the candidates' names below are the total votes for each, those in parenthesis are male votes only.

Nationalists	*Independent Ratepayers*
Richard Howard 67 (51)	Richard Kearon 48 (44)
John Hannigan 60 (44)	Job Hall 46 (42)
Bernard Kearney 60 (44)	John Tyrrell 43 (39)
John Cullen 53 (37)	

Once again, the National League candidates swept the board. M'Phail wrote that Richard Howard had received votes from several independent ratepayer supporters because

> he cannot be considered an Extremist in one sense, and up to this election was one of the independent ratepayers representatives. Mr Hannigan when a town commissioner some few years past was not an Extremist. Undoubtedly, had the independent electors of the township responded to the call [to vote] in the same manner as those on the opposite side the result would have been very different.

Expediency often gives rise to uncharacteristic moves by political groups. The support of the Catholic clergy-led faction of the nationalists in Arklow in 1890 for women's suffrage should not be taken as a party belief in the moral right of women to vote. It was merely politically expedient. The woman's place was in the home and participation in the public sphere was not to be encouraged. So Daniel Condren's support of the women who turned up to vote, backed no doubt by Fr Dunphy, was not based on the principle of a woman's right to vote, but in the knowledge that four-fifths of the votes cast by women in that election would be for his party. In a town of increasingly confusing allegiances, no vote could be ignored. Had the majority of women voters been independent ratepayers voters, it is extremely doubtful that Condren would have allowed them their right to cast their preference, and the Ratepayers' Association would have championed their cause.

As expected, Richard Kearon on behalf of the Ratepayers' Association brought a case to have the election declared void. This was heard by the Queen's Bench in January 1891. The decision was, as scrutiny was 'rendered impossible because Daniel Condren, the returning officer, had not marked on the counterfoil of the ballot papers the numbers of the voters as they appeared on the register,' the election was declared invalid. Not only that, Richard Kearon's costs, as petitioner, were to be paid by Condren for his negligence. As there was no dispute about the first three successful candidates, a by-election was to be held for the fourth seat which had been won by John Cullen.

Dunphy was not convinced that Cullen could secure it a second time and nominated Peter Garvey instead to contest the by-election. On the other side, Richard Kearon was nominated by John Tyrrell. Crucially, the Queen's Bench ordered that the names of the women who had been eligible to vote should be struck off the register. This meant an expected reduction of sixteen nationalist votes. Only seventy-five voters turned up at the polling station to vote in the by-election, forty-two of whom voted for Garvey and only thirty-three for Kearon.[22] Little seems to have been said by either side about the fact that at least twenty erstwhile eligible voters had been deprived of their franchise simply because they were women.

*

Despite the rising tensions between employers and workers, and between male domination of the electoral system and women's suffrage, the two foremost aspects of public life in Arklow continued to be party politics and evangelical street-preaching.

In September 1890, the former took a very sinister turn when on the night of the fifteenth or early morning of the sixteenth of the month, Fr Farrelly's horse had both fore-legs broken at his home. No one was arrested for the crime and in December, Farrelly brought a claim for malicious damage against the ratepayers of the district.[23] The horse had been valued at £50 and Farrelly wanted to be compensated under the malicious damage laws which provided funds from public coffers in cases where culprits could not be identified. It should have been a straightforward matter, but legal obstacles were raised at various stages of the proceedings to thwart Fr Farrelly's claim.

For such a claim to be heard several procedures had to be adhered to, such as formally informing officers of the court of the plaintiff's intention to claim and also in having the claim included in the printed list of impending cases. Farrelly's solicitor, Mr Hanmore (who had also represented Mr Comerford, the union representative, in his case against George Kearon), made the formal submissions but was too late in having the case included in the printed list. Both sides argued whether the proper procedures had been observed, the plaintiff's counsel saying that they were and that it was not the plaintiff's fault that the case had not been entered in the list, the magistrates stating that the fact remained that it could not be heard as it was not in the list. When Hanmore pointed out that a case not on the printed list had been heard in the last session, the magistrates denied any knowledge of such a case. It would appear from this that Farrelly had justification in seeing himself as being victimised for his political activities. When Hanmore suggested that they re-enter the case for the next session, Farrelly declined saying that the bench was opposed to him. Once again, the hardening belief in 'them-and-us' was to the fore, causing further alienation, distrust and general polarisation.

The street-preaching continued to be a major cause of

antagonism. Not only were Catholics and Protestants divided by it, but divisions within these divisions were created and widened. Some Catholics believed the open-air preaching should be allowed as long as it was conducted in a well-ordered manner respectful of the religious beliefs of the majority of the population. Many Catholics, however, were less accommodating and felt that no open-air preaching should be allowed. The more tolerant Catholics were ashamed of the actions of their more agitated co-religionists. There was a similar division forming in the Protestant community. Dr Molony's letter to the staunchly Protestant unionist *Wicklow News-Letter* pointed out that many of 'the more respectable' Protestants were no longer attending Revd Hallowes' church in Main Street, an allegation Hallowes denied, but other sources support Molony's assertion. Even the local magnate and magistrate, William Proby, could no longer support Hallowes' actions.[24] Hallowes was increasingly marginalised within his own community, and his zeal was becoming tinged with the paranoia often associated with the zealot. His fourteen days' imprisonment in March 1891 for refusing to pay a fine of £1 for causing an obstruction on the public thoroughfare made him a martyr in the eyes of many in other parts of the country, but to the majority of Protestants in Arklow, it was further embarrassment. It marked a new stage in his unreasonableness and brought the Church of Ireland into disrepute.

His departure for Wexford goal had been remarkably similar to that of Farrelly several months previously. For a start, there were two clergymen on their way to serve prison sentences, in this instance Hallowes and his curate Harrison, in the other Farrelly and Clarke. On both occasions, the convicted men were escorted to the station by well-wishers. The magistrates had acceded to Hallowes' and Harrison's request for several hours' stay on executing the order so they could make arrangements for the parish. This done, both men then walked to the station to catch the last train of the day. It was shortly after eight o'clock in the evening and a crowd of about 300 had assembled at Marlborough Terrace. A procession was formed and hymns were sung. The police were out in force – not in so large a number as on street-preaching days, but enough to deter Catholics from interfering, 'but strange to say, the latter did not put in an appearance.'[25] At the station Hallowes, Harrison and Hoffe, the curate at Kilbride, took up a position at the end of the platform and several more hymns were sung, after which the whole gathering knelt down and prayed. At this point District-Inspector Sharpe came forward, respectfully touched Revd Hallowes on the shoulder and formally took him in custody. Some of the gathering invited Sharpe to take part in the prayers but he walked away, duty done and content to let matters proceed until the arrival of the train. Minutes before it was due, he took the clergymen into the waiting room. When the train finally arrived, 'an hour late' during which time Hallowes addressed the crowd and yet more hymns were sung, they were placed in a first class carriage with four policemen. On their arrival in Wexford, they were met by the local rector and his curate.

The presence of 300 people would suggest that there was widespread support for the preachers among the local Protestant community, but several factors should be remembered. The population of Arklow in 1891 was 4,172, of whom 727 were members of the Church of Ireland.[26] Also, the impending imprisonment of the clergymen would have attracted evangelical support for them from outside the locality. As well as that, it is reasonable to assume that a section of the 300 would have turned up as a show of respect for the men if not for their actions. Taking these elements into the equation, 300 was not an indication of widespread support.

Imprisonment did not phase Hallowes or Harrison in the slightest, and some months after his release Hallowes wrote to the News-Letter to complain that the home of a leading Protestant named Tyrrell had been vandalised, and that access to it had been gained through next door premises which was owned by Mrs Anne Troy, Thomas Troy's mother.[27] Hallowes stated that the house had been entered through the roof and that the rooms were splattered with human excrement. The following week, Thomas Troy answered these allegations on his mother's behalf. He said that the vandalised house was undergoing renovation at the time and so was vacant, with the result that access could have been easily gained in ways other than through his mother's premises. He also stated that he had spoken with Mr Tyrrell who said that no such vandalism had taken place, although there was excrement thrown at the back window which seems to have come from Mrs Troy's premises. On hearing this, Troy had inspected the damage and conceded that it was possible that the filth had come from a sky-light in Mrs Troy's house, and he promised to investigate the matter. On being questioned, a servant of Mrs Troy admitted that he had emptied a chamber pot through the sky-light rather than carrying it down through the house and the contents may have gone over the wall and smeared Mr Tyrrell's back window. Thomas Troy was satisfied with this explanation and believed that Mr Tyrrell also accepted that there had been no malicious intent. Within a few days, however, Tyrrell decided that he could not accept this explanation and supported Revd Hallowes' opinion of it being a wanton act of vandalism. Troy asked what pressure had been brought to bear on him to recant and follow his minister's line of attack?

This shows how ridiculous the whole situation had become. A dispute over the right to preach the gospel had become an argument regarding the intent or otherwise of discarded shit. The siege mentality was well-and-truly to the fore.

It has to be admitted, however, that Hallowes had plenty of excuse to feel besieged. Not only were his street sermons shouted down and vilified, but even when he was about his everyday business he met with abuse in the streets. As he made his way from his house at Lamberton to the town centre, he would have to pass the national school on Coolgreaney Road. Seldom, if ever, could he pass by without being cat-called and ridiculed by the children. His sisters Juliana, Emily, and Marianna, then aged fifty-one, forty-seven and thirty-seven respectively[28] and who lived with him, suffered the same treatment. It became unbearable and he contacted the district inspector of the national education board to put a stop to it. The inspector called a meeting in December 1890.[29]

The school manager was the parish priest, Fr Dunphy, and he was represented by Fr Manning. At the meeting Manning asked Hallowes to repeat the language he claimed he was being subjected to. Hallowes, of course, refused to 'pollute his mouth with it' but said that 'no child could be found anywhere but in Arklow to make use of expressions so reprehensible.' He further claimed that they abused him in the presence of their teachers and even used the same language in the hearing of their priests, Dunphy, Manning and Farrelly. Manning did not deny this, but said that in his opinion the children showed 'moderation' in their dealings with Hallowes, because 'he had sent their parents to jail.' This was a ridiculous statement. People had been jailed for disturbances arising from the street-preaching but that is hardly the same as Hallowes sending them to jail. A few days later the inspector issued his report, which Hallowes had printed in the *News-Letter*. It was found that the school authorities, both management and staff, were guilty of allowing bad behaviour to go unchecked in the school and that improvements must be made in controlling the children. It was a moral victory for Hallowes, but the events of the past year or two, which had given rise to this meeting, brought honour to no one.

CHAPTER 13:
'... no divorce between religion and politics ...'

The gloves were now off and battle lines drawn. While the *News-Letter* expounded its new-found support for Parnell (helping to confirm suspicions that Parnell was somehow no longer, or perhaps never had been, a 'real' nationalist), the *People* reminded its readers of its unassailable credentials as the journal of true Irishness and patriotism. It carried a letter to the editor reminding readers that the first issue of the *People* had appeared on 18 March (the day after St Patrick's Day) 1882:

> ... down to 1882 Catholics of Wicklow town or county had no local organ to defend their interests or voice their aspirations ... the local Tory sheet [was] always one-sided ... The committee of the Catholic club of Wicklow town, having communicated with the leaders of public opinion throughout the county resolved to establish a weekly Catholic newspaper. Of course, it goes without saying that the organ of the Catholics of Wicklow, born heirs to national principles, should be nationalist, but its emblems should the <u>Cross and the Shamrock</u> intertwined.[1]

The writer, Fr Francis MacEnery, curate of Dunlavin in west Wicklow, was calling for full solidarity behind the Catholic hierarchy and for all to 'scourge and scorn anti-clerical nationality.'

In the same issue, the Donard branch of the National League, also in the west of the county, issued a statement that Parnell was unfit to lead the Irish people and was endangering the cause of home rule. The Irish National League of Great Britain at its meeting in Leeds also condemned Parnell and sided with the Justin McCarthy faction of pro-clericism. The Catholic bishop of Raphoe, later to be Cardinal Michael Logue, declared that Parnell was now doing the work of his enemies and that 'the cause had fallen through one man's sin.' In a barbed choice of words he re-iterated 'there should be no

divorce between religion and politics.'² This echoed the statement issued after a meeting of the Catholic hierarchy in
December which declared Parnell unfit to lead the Irish peo-
ple.³ The Protestant Home Rule Association also felt compelled
to state that they no longer supported Parnell and the great
majority of their members were behind McCarthy. Such was
the swing of branches against Parnell that the Inspector of the
R.I.C. instructed county inspectors to ascertain how many
National League branches were in favour of Parnell and how
many were opposed to him.⁴

The situation in Arklow was very confusing. Some members of the clergy, such as Fr Farrelly, were now undoubtedly
against Parnell and claimed they spoke for the people of the
town. Yet when Parnell visited Arklow in the last week of
January he was awarded a 'magnificent reception.'⁵ A *Wicklow
People* report states that Fr Dunphy met him off the train – and
it should be remembered that the *People* was now anti-Parnell –
and they adjourned to the priest's house where they stayed for
half-an-hour, before Parnell went south to visit his quarries at
the Rock. While he was thus engaged, the crowd erected arches and hung banners with slogans such as 'We have no king but
Charlie', 'Viva la Parnell', and 'God Save Ireland' to greet him
on his return. At Bridge Street, the crowd unhitched the horses and pulled the carriage to the courthouse. Parnell was visibly
moved by this show of support by the ordinary townspeople. It
was, he said, 'a source of the greatest satisfaction to me to know
that the people of Arklow do not think less of me than formerly.' Dr Molony was again to the fore in welcoming Parnell to the
town and proposed a vote of thanks for all he had done for the
area. He was also anxious to assure him of their 'unswerving
loyalty and faithfulness to him as leader of the Irish people.' He
referred to the false impression recently given in the *Freeman's
Journal* of Arklow's desertion of Parnell and that this turn-out
had clearly shown that the people of Arklow were still behind
him. An address was presented to Parnell by the recently-
formed Arklow branch of the Sailors' and Firemen's union.
They condemned those town commissioners who had aban-

doned him, but assured him that the people had not. 'As the commissioners,' they said, 'were not freely elected by the people, but merely nominated by individual dictation, their action, or rather their inaction, can in no way be attributed to any lack of enthusiasm and fidelity on the part of the people.' Members of the Arklow Young Irelanders Society told him that they refused to hand over their destinies 'to an invertebrate committee – our motto is we have no king but Charlie.' The fishermen added their collective voice of support, and the bakers' union were represented by Patrick Bradford who, as registration agent for the National League in Arklow since 1885, assured Parnell that 'three-fourths of them are entirely behind you.' Two-thirds of the remaining fourth he said were undecided but will be true in the long run. Another address was given by the shipwrights' union.

So what was the truth of the situation? Was support or condemnation of the 'fallen Chief' a class issue rather than a national or religious question? Were the majority of the Arklow Catholic middle class toeing the clerical line while craftworkers, fishermen, sailors, and bakers remained strongly pro-Parnell? The fact that this display of support was published in the anti-Parnell *Wicklow People* lends it a credibility that would be suspect in a pro-Parnell newspaper such as the *News-Letter*. Perhaps Dunphy's and Farrelly's confidence in controlling the people was not as well-founded as they would have liked.

Whatever about Arklow, there can be no doubt that the anti-Parnell faction was making great strides elsewhere and the majority of National League branches were eager to re-organise themselves to reflect the new political realities. A new organisation to cater for these discontents was formed, the Irish National Federation, and a new journal to reflect their opinions was established, the *National Press*. Throughout March, the *Freeman's Journal* published short reports from around the country of National League branches which were remaining loyal to Parnell. For some reason Wicklow town commissioners had been omitted from this list of the faithful and they were far from pleased by the omission. They were among the most loyal to

Parnell and in March 1891 they set up a Parnell Leadership Committee 'to support Parnell in his fight for Irish Independence against treachery, Whiggery, and dictation.'[6] The Coolgreaney and Johnston branch of the National League, on the other hand, sided with the clergy and repudiated Parnell's leadership. And so it was throughout the county and the country, some pockets remained with Parnell while others rejected him.

In April, the Arklow branch of the league met to consider severing its affiliation with the central branch, because of the latter's instance on recognising Parnell as the leader of the movement. At that gathering were Frs Dunphy, Farrelly, O'Donnell and Manning, Daniel Condren, John Reynolds, James Canterbury, James Doyle, Thomas Birthistle, John Cullen, Cornelius Allen, Stephen Kane, Patrick Byrne, William Murray, Patrick Rourke, Laurence Hanagan, Thomas Byrne and James Neill. Fr Dunphy presided and Fr Farrelly formally proposed that the Arklow branch of the Irish National League be dissolved and that a public meeting be convened the following Sunday to form a branch of the Irish National Federation. In his usual flowery style, Farrelly said that they could no longer wait and that he hoped the people would be found 'where they were always found in the past, namely on the side of Faith and Fatherland.' He laid out his reasons, accusing the central branch of shameful conduct in the previous six months and the entire country was sick of 'Harrington [the national secretary] and his league.' There was, he said, no accounts kept but autocratic letters and they allowed anyone in at £1 per year – it was 'taxation without representation'; the central branch were 'the Parlour Patriots of Upper O'Connell Street ...'; '... Harrington was to the league what Parnell was to the Irish Party – a dictator'; 'the league now belonged to one man and not to the people who fund it'; 'it is trying to separate the priests from the people.'

Not to be outdone, and confirming the continuing dominant role of the Roman Catholic clergy in the new organisation, Fr Manning proposed that as the *Freeman's Journal* could no longer be trusted – [it still supported Parnell, but this was soon to change] – this new Arklow branch of the National Federation would pledge itself to the new *National Press*.[7]

A collection was held at the chapel gates the following Sunday to get the new federation branch up and running, and that evening a meeting was called to elect officers. All that changed was the name of the organisation to which they were affiliated as Fr Dunphy was elected president and Daniel Condren was branch chairman. The annual subscription of £5 was sent to the central branch of the federation.[8] The same issue of the paper recorded that a federation branch was also formed at Castletown, with Fr Farrelly as president. Another was established at Aughrim, and from that time on the weekly *Wicklow People* column headed 'This Week's Meetings' showed that most towns and villages in the county now had branches of both National League and National Federation, with the clergy dominating the committees of the latter. A resolution of the federation branch in Kilmore, County Wexford, summed up this role of priests in politics:

> We firmly believe that in the present distressing crisis of our country the influence and active co-operation of the clergy in the national movement is more than ever necessary and we believe it will be a fatal mistake if the clergy give way to the present Tory and Parnellite cry of clerical dictation.[9]

If this were not enough, on the same page was a letter from a 'Wexford man in America' calling on the people of Ireland to reject Parnell, 'the question should be settled not on his undoubted past service, but on his future usefulness.'

Three weeks after the formation of the Arklow branch of the federation, Dr Molony and others called a meeting to establish an Arklow Parnell Leadership Committee along the same lines as that in Wicklow town. Those present were Molony, Patrick Kavanagh, RTC Johnson, Michael Clarke, John Hanagan, John M'Loughlin, Patrick Bolger, P W Doyle, James J Bolger, Andrew Byrne, James Clarke, H J O'Neill, W Murray,

William Kavanagh and R Murphy. Letters of apology were received from John Byrne, Hugh Byrne and Dr Howard. Howard's position is again difficult to gauge. He had been a member of the Independent Ratepayers' Association, but at the municipal elections in October 1890 he had changed allegiance to Fr Dunphy's National League and seven months later, in May 1891, he again aligned himself with Molony and company. The *Wicklow News-Letter* had said at the time of the election that Howard was not 'an extremist' so perhaps we can take it that while he felt more nationalistic than his membership of the ratepayers' association might infer, Dunphy's strongly anti-Parnell National Federation branch was a step too far for him. Molony was elected chairman and it was resolved that, at the request of the Wicklow branch, they attend a county meeting in Wicklow on 31 May, and to invite everyone, including clergy, to attend.[10]

The invitation to clergy to attend a meeting in support of Parnell had to be tongue-in-cheek. No one really expected it to be accepted, and in the long, long list of those present no clerical title is recorded. However, delegates and followers from all over the county, north Wexford and Dublin did attend, but there was an obvious exception, no mention of Arklow representation was made in the *People* report, despite the naming of all other centres. The *News-Letter* however did name thirteen Arklow delegates, but neither Troy nor Molony was among them.[11] This was a very poor showing on the part of Arklow Parnellites. Overall, though, it was an impressive turn-out in favour of the beleaguered erstwhile 'uncrowned king'. Perhaps it was the large numbers and strength of feeling that prompted the *People* the following week to attack Parnell even more rabidly than heretofore. It argued that those who still believed Parnell was leader could not deny his links with tories because

for those of us who have observed Mr Parnell's career over the past few years must have become convinced that he is the Conservative of Conservatives. This is rather his misfortune than his fault, for the Tory is born, not made ... He is an Englishman in sympathy and a landlord in fact. That he should gravitate to Toryism, as he did in 1885, is therefore not by any means surprising.

There were many who agreed with this view, and hardly a week went by without the editor recording branches of the new federation being formed in places such as Ballinglen, Annacurra, Bray, Dunlavin and Roundwood. These were encouraged by a statement of the Catholic hierarchy in late June when it was resolved at a meeting in Maynooth that Parnell was unworthy of the confidence of Catholics, 'we call on our people to repudiate his leadership.'[12]

As far as Parnell himself was concerned, he continued to look upon himself as the leader of the home rule movement, although the breakaway anti-Parnell faction was bigger than the pro-Parnell faction. Neither did the attack on him in Kilkenny make him rethink his position. He believed the Irish people were fully behind him. While this was true in the larger urban areas, his support in rural districts was rapidly dwindling. As soon as Katherine's divorce was finalised, the couple made preparations to marry. The marriage should have brought an end to the 'disgrace' of their 'living in sin' and so heal divisions, but it didn't. No sooner had the wedding taken place on 25 June than more of his erstwhile supporters turned against him, including the owner of the *Freeman's Journal*. Members of the Catholic hierarchy declared that marrying Katherine had only aggravated the original 'offence'. Parnell, who for so long could not put a foot wrong, could now do nothing to appease his attackers.

He last spoke to the House of Commons on 3 August 1891,[13] but he still travelled every weekend to address public meetings in Ireland, trying to convince the people that it was Ireland's future that was of the utmost importance, not his private life. The grip of the Catholic church in Ireland, however, was too great and Parnell was now beyond the pale. His party lost three by-elections in quick succession and the strain was taking a heavy toll on him physically and emotionally. The travelling alone was gruelling. He would leave his house in

Hove in Sussex, travel by train to London, then another train to Holyhead to catch the mail boat to Kingstown (now Dun Laoghaire) and then on to wherever he was needed. His physical appearance deteriorated and concerns for his health were widespread. His rhetoric gave no hint of a flagging spirit, the words and power with which they were delivered remained unaltered and unrepentant, but away from public gaze it was clear that his health was failing rapidly.[14] At yet another public meeting at Creggs in the west of Ireland on 27 September he was suffering from an acute bout of rheumatism and he carried his left arm in a sling. He told the gathering:

> If I had taken the advice of my doctor I should have gone to bed when I arrived in Dublin, but if I had done that my enemies would be throwing up their hats and announcing that I was dead before I was buried ... I know that you look to Ireland's future as a nation – if we gain it. We may not be able to gain it, but if not it will be left for those who come after us to win. But we will do our best.[15]

He left Ireland three days later, returning to his wife and children and their home in Hove, promising to be back the following weekend. Just after midnight on 6 October 1891, Parnell died of rheumatic fever. He had, quite simply, been hounded to his grave.

*

News of his death spread across the world. In his native county the sense of shock is still palpable when reading the newspapers of the time. The *Wicklow People* of 10 October stated that when the news reached Arklow at two o'clock on the afternoon of Wednesday, the day after Parnell's demise, it was not believed at first, and there was a tremendous rush when the evening newspapers arrived to confirm what they most feared. For a while, all differences were left aside in genuine grief and nearly every shop was partly or wholly shuttered.

On the part of the nationalists the tendency is to forget the feuds and unhappy incidents of the past ten months, and to remember only the Parnell, who by his indomitable courage, self-sacrifice and brilliant services, was very largely instrumental in securing for Ireland her present proud position on being on the eve of having her just claim to National autonomy finally and satisfactorily adjusted.

In the light of the *People*'s increasingly vicious attacks on Parnell, this smacks of crocodile tears, and as will be seen, the 'feuds and unhappy incidents of the past ten months' were not to be forgotten for long.

William M'Phail of the *Wicklow News-Letter* seems to have had a somewhat schizophrenic regard for Parnell. M'Phail was a staunch unionist who saw home rule as the thin end of the wedge that would sunder the British empire. Politically, he was opposed to everything Parnell held most dear. On a personal level, he admired Parnell's energy, his entrepreneurial spirit, his achievements in industry, his eloquence. Most of all, he admired Parnell's love for his home county, a love M'Phail shared. They both wanted what they believed was in the best interests of Wicklow, even if those beliefs were diametrically opposed. M'Phail would always be a unionist, would always vote unionist, but he could not deny what Parnell had done for the county, and could not understand how a large section of people for whom Parnell had sacrificed everything had effectively killed him. His anger towards them was focused primarily on the clergy-led nationalists in Arklow. It will be remembered that in January 1891, under the heading 'Ungrateful and Forgetful Arklow', he had attacked the town commissioners for turning their backs on Parnell when he visited the town. His anger was greater now that Parnell was dead. In the 17 October issue, he published an account of the reaction to Parnell's death which had been submitted by 'a correspondent'. As will be noticed in the piece, the terms 'Federationist', 'Healyite', and 'McCarthyite' are interchangeable, each denoting the anti-Parnellite home rulers led by the local Catholic clergy.

When news of Mr Parnell's untimely death reached Arklow, a

feeling of intense sorrow was expressed amongst all classes, and the shutters on many business establishments remained up until Monday. Of course, a small fraction of the Federationists or 'shoneen' Nationalists felt jubilant over the Chief's death and failed to pay common respect to the memory of a great man by partially closing their establishments and consequently their puny and selfish patriotism was exposed in all its rottenness. They refused to honour a man whom, a few months ago, they fawned upon as a dog would his master, and now they find themselves treated by their townsmen as contemptible, miserable 'shoneens', who are unworthy of the respect or support of the people.

The writer went on to say that 'probably they had a hand in' an attack on Parnell in Carlow. If this is a reference to the lime-throwing incident in Castlecomer, which is in County Kilkenny not Carlow, the previous December, it is totally without foundation. However, it might refer to the attack made on Parnell's character by some of his disillusioned quarry workers in Carlow in June. It was an emotionally charged piece, the historical accuracy of which should be treated with caution, but it nonetheless paints a picture of the high tensions of the time. Thankfully, its vitriolic outpouring is confined to the first paragraph, after which he (assuming that it was a 'he') turns his attention to those nationalists who had stayed loyal to Parnell.

> However, a meeting of the Parnellite Leadership Committee was convened by circular at their rooms in Main-street, to express their deep regret with the family of Mr Parnell and to pledge allegiance more strongly in future to that policy of independent opposition which the lamented patriot so gallantly espoused.

It was a large meeting and Dr Molony was elected to the chair. In the course of a 'very able speech', he outlined Parnell's public career, his achievements at national level and his adherence to independent thinking and action. He called on all those present to continue in this cause. 'Ireland had lost a valuable son', he concluded, 'who had been, [I] would say fearless of contradiction, foully murdered by his countrymen.' The meeting closed with several resolutions, perhaps the most telling of which was

> That we desire to record our sense of the loss sustained to the Irish nation generally, and Arklow particularly, by the death of C S Parnell, who, while fighting Ireland's battle, educated prejudiced English public to understand our national sentiment, and to alleviate the suffering caused by centuries of misrule, and who yet found time to set an example in his private capacity of what one capable and genuine Irishman could do towards further native industry, and developing the latent resources of our country to improve the condition and earning the everlasting gratitude of the labouring classes.

Arrangements were then made to send a large contingent to represent Arklow at Parnell's funeral in Dublin. The following Sunday, 110 tickets were purchased at the railway station to join the cortege to Glasnevin. Thomas Troy, who had also been at the meeting recorded above, was also present at the funeral, but Dr Molony was not, his absence probably due to pressure of work.

With regard to Parnell's contribution to the development of native industry, M'Phail had a small piece on the same page, in which he announced that even at the time of his death, Parnell had been engaged in forming a steamship company which would further enhance the numbers employed at his quarries at Arklow Rock. While primarily engaged in shipping stone to England and elsewhere, the steamers would also take on other local produce as cargo for distribution. 'All that was wanted to enable the steamer to trade successfully with Arklow was the completion of the harbour,' which another article on the same page assured the reader that stone for this purpose was being donated by Parnell. M'Phail pleaded, 'Mr Parnell is now dead, but if these ideas be ever carried into effect, it is well that it should be known with whom they originated.'

There was one other item on that page, the editorial which M'Phail used to vent his enraged satisfaction to the fullest: 'Bravo, Arklow!' he wrote, in connection with the annual municipal elections in the town which had taken place on 15 October, just nine days after Parnell's demise.

As mentioned above, Parnell died on 6 October and just nine days later the annual election to fill the five rotational seats on Arklow town commission was held. Political boundaries were no longer so sharply defined. It was not a race between unionist and nationalist, but a contest between the Federationist home rulers and Parnellite home rulers. The hardened attitudes of these factions made cross-voting an unlikely scenario. The Parnellites accused the federationists of allowing the Catholic church to dictate how votes should be cast; the federationists accused the Parnellites of entering into a pact with unionist conservatives in the Independent Ratepayers' Association. Only time would tell who had the greater support among the small, and hardly representative, electorate.

As usual in these municipal elections, five seats had to be vacated and contested. Four of these were in the Arklow Ward; Daniel Condren (Federationist), Thomas Birthistle (Federationist), Michael Clarke (Federationist) and Patrick Kavanagh (Parnellite) retired by rotation. The first three sought re-election, Kavanagh did not. The only one of the three Ferrybank Ward seats to be up for grabs was occupied by Samuel Marshall (Conservative) who had been elected and re-elected several times unopposed. Now, he again sought re-election and was again returned unopposed. On Monday, 12 October Michael J Molony, physician, and Thomas J Troy, merchant, were nominated by John Tyrrell, Hugh Byrne and Patrick Bolger of the Arklow independent ratepayers; Michael Clarke, victualler, Thomas Birthistle, publican, David Bradford, undertaker, and Daniel Condren, publican, were nominated by Fr James Dunphy. Richard Kearon, shipowner, was nominated by James Tyrrell, W H Fitzhenry and James Bolger and Job Hall, merchant, was nominated by Edward Cole and James Tyrrell to represent the conservatives.

In one of the few understatements written in either of the local newspapers in relation to local politics, the *News-Letter* correspondent said: 'Great interest was manifested in the contest throughout the day.' The banter, good-natured and otherwise, can be easily imagined. Tensions may have been high and perhaps disagreements may even have spilled beyond the verbal, but there was also a lighter-hearted element in which 'bets were freely made for and against the different candidates.' As the time for declaring the poll drew close, the courthouse and vicinity became thronged with people. Upwards of fity extra police had been drafted into the town to preserve the peace. At the end of polling and as the counting of votes got under way, Molony proposed a vote of thanks to the presiding officer, Mr Gormley, Town Clerk, seconded by Condren. It was, by that stage, probably the only thing on which they could agree.

The results were published in both the local newspapers two days later, and M'Phail did not forego his chance to gloat:

BRAVO, ARKLOW!

The nominees of the Federation were routed – horse, foot, and artillery – at the Municipal election in Arklow on Thursday ... The Rev Mr Dunphy, parish priest, scanned almost every man that visited the polling booth in Arklow. He hovered in the vicinity of the court-house throughout the day, but his party, despite his efforts, were predestined to meet with ignominious disaster. We are informed that he even brought down a reporter from the journal to which we have already made allusion [*National Press*] in order that the intrigue between the Tories and the adherents of the late "fallen leader" might be duly chronicled in the paper in which nobody will advertise. We deny that there was any compact between the Parnellites and the Unionists. The ex-Chairman of the Arklow Town Commissioners [Daniel Condren], when he became the exponent of Municipal law, acted so indulgently that he crammed the register with bogus votes. He even took the ladies under his patronage, and admitted them to a share of the election of civic representatives.

Invested with the dignity of judge and elated with the august position he filled, he dispensed the franchise with unsparing generosity. Happily, however, there was a tribunal higher than the one over which Mr Condren presided, and some of his judgements were thus overruled

... Their defeat, however, was a galling one. It stung them to the quick, and now it has induced them to disseminate nonsense to explain away the success of their opponents. The Arklow Parnellites are in high feather at their decided victory, while the Conservatives are also well pleased at the return of both their candidates. The Healyites, on the other hand, are utterly woe-begone. Certainly, considering all that Mr Parnell did for Arklow, it seems passing strange that even a trace of Healyism should be found there. However, the great majority of the inhabitants have now marked, in the most forcible manner, their disapproval of any attempt to brand Arklow as a Federation stronghold. The people of Arklow have taken over the management of their own affairs. They have emphatically declared that in the conduct of their Municipal business they will neither accept dictation nor brook intimidation from any person, no matter who or what he may be. Bullying and boycotting are of no avail against independence and honest courage.

M'Phail's reference to 'the great majority of the inhabitants' conveniently ignores the fact that very few of the inhabitants had been given the opportunity to voice their opinion one way or the other because of the very restrictive franchise. This was simply an emotional rant which, once vented, gave way to a factual account of the election. The result, of which M'Phail made such a song-and-dance, while clear-cut was not the emphatic declaration he portrayed it to be. Molony topped the poll with sixty-eight votes, Troy came second with sixty-three, third was Richard Kearon with fity-two, fourth Job Hall with fifty, fifth Daniel Condren thirty-nine, joint-sixth Thomas Birthistle and Michael Clarke with thirty-two, and eighth David Bradford with thirty-one votes. As the Ferrybank Ward seat had been filled by Marshall once again, only the four Arklow Ward seats had to be allocated so the top four candidates were duly elected, two Parnellites and two tories, with all four of Fr Dunphy's federationists being beaten. Such was Molony's personal vote that 'he is mentioned as the future chairman.'

The predictions of Molony's chairmanship proved well-founded. It was a remarkable achievement. He was thirty years old and had been in Arklow only six years. But what an impact he had made. In that relatively short space of time, he had engaged with all classes of the general public, both in his professional capacity as a doctor with a private practice and as the public health physician and surgeon. He had taken part in organising sports days and musical and variety entertainment to raise money for the poor and those stricken by sudden disaster. He had avoided becoming entangled in what he saw as the narrow politics of the local clergy – Catholic and Protestant – and continually sought a middle road along which the entire town might advance.

This was particularly interesting in light of the fact that it was the machinations of Fr Dunphy, whether Molony cared to admit it to himself or not, which had secured him the post of medical officer for the district. Such was his aversion to the polarisation of local politics and religion that he had either founded, helped to found, or at the very least became the first chairman of the middle ground party, the Arklow Independent Ratepayers' Association. It must be said that the membership of this association was middle class, consisting of publicans, shopowners, shipowners and doctors, but the same accusation could be made against the National Federation candidates. The tiny percentage of the population on the electoral register points to the legal exclusion of the majority of the people from the political process, and the marked dominance of the professional classes in such organisations indicate a customary class restriction. Ordinary workers were not encouraged by any faction to take leading roles in community politics. They were simply expected to turn out *en masse* when required, to cheer when prompted and jeer when cued. Mention of election candidates and the names of committee members organising social events were usually followed by their role in life, none is classified as labourer, fisherman, deck-hand, or carpenter. This is not to say there were active exclusion policies based on social standing in place, but it is difficult to discern any proactive inclusion policy by any party.

Not surprisingly, the federationists again accused the ratepayers' association of being in bed with local tories. Molony wrote to the *Wicklow People* denying this claim and pointed out that Fr Dunphy might also be accused of an alliance with tories when, at a meeting of the harbour commissioners a few weeks earlier, he had proposed Alexander Taiyleur (Tailyour or Taylor) for a postion, 'a gentleman heretofore described by his new friends as an arch-coercionist and a ruthless evictor.'[16] The following week, however, the editor convincingly blew Molony's assertions out of the water, citing the *News-Letter's* joy at his party's success as adequate proof that Molony and company were closet tories. The same edition carried a letter from Fr Dunphy showing how the ratepayers and the tories were hand-in-glove. He reminded Molony and all the readers that in the ratepayers' first election in 1888 they had nominated 'two unionists and one tory and left a vacancy for Lord Carysfort', then [1889] three unionists and one tory, then [1890] two unionists and two conservatives, and this year two Parnellites and two tories.' It is interesting to see who Fr Dunphy labelled 'tory' or 'conservative', because in 1888 the ratepayers' nominees were Richard Hudson, Patrick Maher and John Tyrrell, all three of whom described themselves as Catholic nationalists. Their nominees in 1889 were Molony, Troy, John Tyrrell and Job Hall; the first three would also have described themselves as nationalist, but Fr Dunphy obviously regarded them all as unionists; everyone would have agreed that Hall was tory. Their nominees in 1890 were Job Hall (tory conservative), Richard Kearon (tory conservative), and John Tyrrell (who would still describe himself as nationalist, but must be one of the two 'unionists' identified by Dunphy). There was no fourth nominee so therefore no second 'unionist'. Notwithstanding his self-righteous labelling, Dunphy had crunched some numbers to add weight to his accusation. He said that

> 97 went to the polls, (38 Tories, 30+ nationalists, 19 Parnellites). In counting, 46 voted solidly for the two Tory candidates and Messrs Molony and Troy, therefore everyone who

voted Tory also voted for Molony and Troy, and consequently 38 Tories and the renegade nationalists, led on by Messrs Hugh Byrne and John Tyrrell, must have combined to do the dirty work and send the factionists to the municipal chamber of Arklow.

Molony argued with this interpretation, stating that of the ninety-seven votes cast, thirty-eight were for conservatives and fifty-nine nationalist. He posed this question; he had polled sixty-eight votes, even assuming that all tories voted for him, where did the other 30 votes come from?

> While the full strength of the obedient Federationists following was 32, polled by Messrs Clarke, Birthistle and Bradford, Mr Condren polled 39, thus outstripping his brothers by 7. It is now a matter of public notoriety that these extra seven votes were recorded by specially solicited conservatives. 'A deal with the Tories,' forsooth! Verily, those who live in glass houses should not throw stones. The majority of the Catholic nationalist ratepayers voted for me and, as a matter of course, my colleague Mr Troy.[17]

The belief that Molony and Troy were closet tories was further strengthened shortly after the election when Revd Hallowes called on their support. He appealed to the Parnellites of Arklow not to stand by and see him abused and 'the Word of God torn and trampled upon.' The *Wicklow People* was quick to regard this as putting the matter beyond doubt. 'It is said of [Daniel] O'Connell that whenever he found the *Times* writing of him in a kindly or commendatory manner, he forthwith examined his conscience to discover in what way he might have sinned against Ireland. In regard to the patronage of Mr Hallowes, the Arklow Parnellites might very well follow suit.'[18]

Whatever the truth about who voted for whom, and the subsequent arguments regarding the election, Fr Dunphy's arch-rival had headed the poll and at the first meeting of commissioners after polling day it was proposed that Molony, as poll-topper, become chairman. Unusually, all fifteen attended with

Dr Howard, who had occupied the chair for the previous year, presiding until the new chairman was elected. The vote was split, seven for Dr Howard to retain the chairmanship, seven for Molony to replace him, and the casting vote fell to Howard who quipped: 'Of course, I vote for myself. Love your neighbour as yourself, but there is no reason why you should love him better.' And so, Howard held the chair for the coming year.

CHAPTER 14:
Two elections; two outcomes

Molony's duties as town commissioner were not onerous. There was a monthly meeting, but his attendance record over the ten months up to October 1892 was not all that it should have been. His professional duties as public medical officer as well as treatment of his private patients were perhaps mainly responsible for this, but even if these were the reasons for his frequent absences from commission meetings the question remains should he have taken on the responsibility if he did not have the time to devote to it?

As medical officer, his relationship with the Rathdrum Board of Guardians had not improved, and most correspondence between them was through the governing body, the Local Government Board. As mentioned previously, Molony's public health dispensary was accommodated in the fever hospital a short distance from his house. While most of the running costs of the hospital were funded by the Wicklow grand jury, rent for the dispensary office and surgery was paid by the Arklow dispensary committee to the fever hospital committee. In the summer of 1892, the grand jury funding was withheld from the hospital for reasons unspecified, so the hospital committee raised the rent for the dispensary rooms to help make up the shortfall. The local government board told the Rathdrum board of guardians to contact Molony for a report as they wished to look for new premises for the dispensary as they were 'no longer happy with the dispensary being in the hospital.' Molony did not furnish the report and a few weeks later he was told again to do so.[1] Molony responded saying that he saw nothing wrong with the dispensary being in the hospital and that he had 'never heard of its being attended with bad results during the many years it has been so used.'[2] Whether Molony refused to supply the requested report or simply failed to do so is unclear. One way or another, there is no evidence that he acceded to the demand. His non-compliance might be attributed to many causes, one of which was the fact that the medical officers of Ireland were, like the labourers, craftsmen, sailors and dockers, beginning to voice dissatisfaction with their duties and remuneration.[3]

The withholding of the grant by the grand jury was a serious matter. On 11 April, Molony was present at a meeting of the governors of the hospital in the Marlborough Hall to assess the threat of closure. The composition of this gathering showed that when the chips were down factional differences were set aside. Carysfort's agent, Alexander Tailyour, took the chair, but Fr Dunphy and two of his curates, O'Donnell and Manning, were also present, as were Dr Molony (pro-Parnell nationalist), Dr Howard and John Reynolds (anti-Parnell nationalists), Dr Richard Halpin and Edward Kearon (unionists), J H Long, John Storey and R Philpot (political affiliations unknown). There were no patients in the hospital at that time, but it was important to maintain it because epidemics such as cholera and typhus were regular visitors to the congested parts of the town, and the governors were determined to present a united front in its defence.[4]

Despite these demands on his energies, Molony did find time to participate in two concerts held in the Marlborough Hall at which he sang 'topical songs' making 'a couple of local hits in an effusion entitled "A pity to waste it", presumably of his own composition.'[5] What a pity these 'local-hitting' songs have been lost to posterity, they could have told us as much about the author as about their topics and targets. Tom Troy was again to the fore in these entertainments, playing the flute while his wife again played a solo on the pianoforte. Molony's wife, in one of the few references to her existence, played the banjo, but neither she nor Mrs Troy was referred to by their first names.

If Molony was working as hard as ever in several capacities, it must be said that the sixty-three-year-old Fr Dunphy showed no signs of slacking either. In February, the foundation stone was laid for a new convent school that would accommodate 500 girls, and once again he had been instrumental in bringing this about.[6] Also, in the previous November he had been working behind the scenes to secure contracts for seven Arklow fishing boat crews to teach the Aran islanders how to fish. This was done under the aegis of the Congested Districts Board, a government body recently established to alleviate poverty on the western seaboard and other congested areas. Surprisingly, the islanders had little knowledge of, or skills in, fishing on a commercial basis; 'most of the Inishmore men could be described as farmers who did a little fishing'[7] and it was decided to establish a training scheme to rectify that situation. Seven Arklow boats which had been mackerel fishing for years on the Cork and Kerry coasts were subsidised to go to the Aran Islands. Five other boats from Connemara and Aran joined the group to make an experimental fleet of twelve.[8] But how could Fr Dunphy claim credit for this government initiative? As always when it came to the economic development of the town, Fr Dunphy was involved. The parish priest of Baltimore, Fr Davis, was a member of the CDB. He knew the Arklow fishermen well as they spent several weeks of each year mackerel fishing in that area. The parish priest of the Aran Islands, Fr O'Donoghue was, like Fr Dunphy, always working to improve the lot of his parishioners. It is easy to see these three like-minded parish priests working together for the benefit of all concerned.

Nor were the fishermen of Arklow the only ones from the town to benefit from this new development. John Tyrrell & Sons had built most, if not all, of the Arklow fishing boats involved in this enterprise and they proved so well suited to the task on the west coast that orders were placed with Tyrrell for more boats to be built for the islanders. One of these was a nobby named *Father O'Donoghue*, after the island parish priest. The fact that John Tyrrell was a member of Molony's ratepayers' association and a turncoat in Dunphy's eyes would not have mattered to Dunphy. The scheme would benefit Tyrrell's employees, and Fr Dunphy did not allow politics to interfere in such matters of common benefit.

But the wider world of politics could not be ignored in general matters, and the anti-Parnell federationists continued making strong gains around the county and country, although some instances of pro-Parnell power could be seen from time to time. An example of this was when the Catholic poor law guardians in Rathdrum refrained from voting Fr Manning (the parish priest of Glendalough and not to be confused with Fr John Manning, the Arklow curate) on to the local dispensary committee, even though parish priests in most areas had been elected to seats on dispensary committees.

The newspaper which had so closely aligned itself with home rule from the beginning and with Parnell in his rise to power, now turned against him. The *Freeman's Journal* had stood by him in the immediate aftermath of the split, but his marriage to Katherine was deemed a step too far. In March 1892, it merged with the one-year-old organ of the anti-Parnellites, the *National Press*.[9] It was all shaping up for a final showdown, and it came in the form of a general election.

Over six years had passed since Parnell's home rule party had reached the zenith of its political strength in 1885. They were then focused and united, but what had been true in the 1885 general election was no longer true. When a general election was called in 1892, it was immediately recognised that it was going to be one of the most important elections in Irish history.

In Wicklow, for the first time in two decades, the result would not be a foregone conclusion. The home rule party was split right down the middle exposing a great gap through which the unionists, if they could get the right candidate, just might squeeze. To prevent this, and even more important, to ensure that their respective candidates would emerge victorious, both nationalist camps would have to pull out all the stops. Little wonder that Molony, leader of the Parnellites in Arklow, had little time for writing reports and seeking out new premises for his dispensary. Irish nationalist politics was haemorrhaging through the gaping wound of internecine feuding. Since 1829 there had been six liberal and two conservative members of parliament for the Wicklow constituency. Since 1880, both representatives had been home rulers. When the constituency was divided into East and West Wicklow in 1885, the returned candidate for each was a home ruler.[10] Now the balance of power had shifted and the unionist population, particularly in East Wicklow, were confident that they had a good chance of winning the seat from the divided nationalists, and the man they asked to represent them was Captain Robert Charles Halpin.

Halpin was a remarkable individual.[11] A Wicklow town native who first crossed the Atlantic as an apprentice ship's officer at the age of eleven in 1847, master mariner by the age of twenty-one, shipwrecked twice by twenty-two, blockade-runner into confederate ports in the American civil war, first officer and chief navigator on the 1865 and 1866 transatlantic telegraph cable-laying ships, commander of the largest ship on earth, the ss *Great Eastern* by thirty-five and in that position was mainly responsible for the successful linking of Britain with Canada, France with Canada, Portugal with Brazil, Britain with India, India with Singapore, and Singapore with Australia by telegraph cable. Successful, famous and rich by his forties he built a luxurious house at Tinnakilly between Rathnew and Wicklow and entered into a period of his life which might be best described as phased retirement. Throughout his career he had always been proud of being a Wicklowman and he now took an active role in local matters such as becoming a member of Wicklow harbour board, the annual Wicklow regatta committee, of which he served as chairman for several years, and generally supporting any move that would develop the county in general and his native town in particular. As a staunch unionist, he was welcomed into the most loyalist of homes and political circles, as a seaman of the first order he had the respect and admiration of the county's seafarers and fishermen. He had, in short, many of the qualities of Parnell, but he lacked Parnell's charisma. Nevertheless, he had wide appeal, and he was undoubtedly the best candidate the unionists could put forward. When he agreed to accept the nomination, William M'Phail was ecstatic:

The announcement that he had consented to stand for the parliamentary representation of the division must have afforded genuine pleasure to members of every creed, class and even politics in the constituency.[12]

There was probably an element of truth in that. Halpin, a prominent member of the local Church of Ireland, does seem to have been free of religious rancour – his finding work for Wicklowmen on board various ships irrespective of their religious leanings would point to this.[13] He could also cross class boundaries because of his hands-on approach to seafaring, and there was even a glimmer of hope that his commonsense and stability might appeal to disillusioned nationalists.

The Parnellites had an experienced candidate in William Corbet, one of the minority of home rulers who had stayed loyal to Parnell throughout his ordeal and after his death. Corbet, too, was a local resident having his home at Spring Farm, Delgany. He had first been elected to parliament in the 1880 election as one of the two members for Wicklow. After the splitting of the constituency in two in 1885, he was returned as the sole member for East Wicklow. His position had been unassailable, polling more than twice the number of votes of his nearest rival. Had the O'Shea case not taken place, had Parnell not been thrown to the wolves, the seat would undoubtedly have been Corbet's again. But the O'Shea case *had* taken place, and Parnell *had* been sacrificed to the gods of Victorian hypocrisy. Corbet's election could no longer be taken for granted.

The anti-Parnellites (McCarthyites, Healyites or federationists as they were variously known) also had a candidate, but he had several disadvantages to overcome. His name was John Sweetman, a forty-seven-year-old resident of Drumbaragh near Kells, County Meath. He had been born into the business class, his father a Dublin brewer, his mother the daughter of a Dublin merchant, and was educated at Downside School in Somerset. His nationalist leanings brought him to some prominence and it was he who proposed the election of Parnell as president of the Land League in 1879. He had various business interests, including the unusual one of organising Irish groups to emigrate to Minnesota where they could form colonies. It was not entirely successful, but it did help a number of people to obtain a better life in America. He was also a major investor in the *National Press* newspaper, the federationists' journal, which had recently merged with the *Freeman's Journal*. On 3 June 1892, the *Times* of London mentioned that, at a convention to select nationalist candidates for the two parliamentary constituencies in County Wicklow, 'Mr John Sweetman of County Meath, who had contributed £1,000 as a donation to the fund for starting the *National Press*, had been unanimously selected for the Eastern Division.' Was this suggesting that he had bought his candidature?

Throughout the campaign the *Wicklow News-Letter* was neither subtle nor shy in promoting Halpin. M'Phail blazoned his virtues and sang his praises at every opportunity. The only other newspaper in the county, the nationalist *Wicklow People*, was equally vociferous in its support of Sweetman. This made canvassing for Corbet a very difficult task, despite the fact that he was the only one of the three candidates to have parliamentary experience. His supporters would have to get out and spread the word as best they could. This was particularly difficult in Arklow, which had the only anti-Parnell organisation in County Wicklow.[14] By June, Fr Dunphy's anti-Parnell federationists were confident of defeating 'old and new enemies' and of getting the stranger Sweetman elected.[15]

Polling dates of 7 July in East Wicklow and 13 July for the western constituency were set and the race began in earnest. On 28 June Halpin addressed a large crowd in Bray, where he freely agreed that he was, as his opponents labelled him, a 'coercionist and Balfourian.' In home rule, he said, he saw not only nothing but ruin for Ireland, but also the beginning of the destruction of the empire. Three days later, on 1 July, the people of Arklow were given two opportunities to hear what Halpin had to offer them. The first took place at two o'clock in the afternoon at the quayside and was tailored for the fishermen and boatowners. He spoke of the harbour, the needs of people who relied on the sea for their livelihoods, he spoke in terms they knew. Three hours later, he made a second speech at the courthouse. This was more wide-ranging and seemed to go down well.[16] Even the *Wicklow People* suggested that 'in Captain Halpin the Conservatives have certainly a strong candidate, but [he] will not head the poll.'[17]

Sweetman, on the other hand, was finding it very difficult to garner the support. He had attended a meeting in Wicklow and was on his way to the station when he was met by 'a crowd of rowdies' who threw missiles at him. This was the second attack on him in three days. The first took place at Rathnew railway station where he was waiting for a train. His attackers had been to a 'factionist [i.e. Parnellite] meeting.'[18] This was in stark contrast to his fellow anti-Parnell candidate in West Wicklow, James O'Connor, who was expected to beat the Parnellite candidate there, John Henry Parnell (Charles' brother) by at least a ratio of four-to-one, showing that the 'grand old county of the O'Byrnes and the O'Tooles is still solid on the side of mother Ireland.'[19]

Sweetman's first public meeting in Arklow proved that the federationists under Fr Dunphy could rally a crowd to the cause of the clerics' candidate. That he was the clerics' choice was left in no doubt by the number of priests recorded at the gathering. Fr Farrelly took the chair and immediately attacked the Parnellites in their use of the phrase 'clerical dictation.' It was, he said, nothing more than 'priestly duty', and recited all that the Catholic clergy had done for the down-trodden Irish people. He then introduced Sweetman to the crowd, which the *Wicklow People* estimated to be about 3,000. Sweetman was, he said, well known to his brother [i.e. Farrelly's] in Meath and he could vouch for his soundness. In contrast, he then turned on Corbet's poor attendance record in the House of Commons. He said that Corbet had attended only two sessions in the previous two years,[20] that he was a landlord, and not a very good one, and had refused National League intervention in a dispute with his tenants on his estate in County Limerick. There were a couple

229

of heckling mumbles from the crowd, but Farrelly challenged the dissenters to come to the platform to voice their opinion. There were no takers, and so Fr Farrelly introduced Tim Healy, one of the main precipitators of the division in Committee Room 15 in December.

Healy, in his support of Sweetman, began wooing the crowd by saying how he had long wished to see Arklow, obviously forgetting that he had unsuccessfully defended Farrelly in September 1888 in the courthouse two hundred yards from where he now stood; he had read of it, he said, and its hardy men; how good it was to see such a fine fleet of boats in the harbour. He promised that he would not say anything against the 'politically dead' Corbet, but then proceeded to rip him to shreds. He explained the political realities that faced the electorate in terms men of the sea would understand:

> If sailors had a falling out as to how their boat should be directed or steered, they might be all equally good sailors, but if one of them was on for pulling down the sheet, or heaving it, or going on a wrong tack, what chances would there be for the captain to keep that boat right? In the parliamentary ship which we are steering, we were a united crew until a couple of years ago ... [I am] not going to say a word against the captain of that vessel. He has gone to a judge before whom he would get justice and to whom he would have to render an account of his actions. Therefore, let him sleep, God rest his soul. But we have to do with the present and the future, not the past.

It was a reasonably good analogy, but he went on to belabour it to the point of condescension, speaking of 'trim ballast', and party agreements as 'the crew signed articles' on which Parnell had reneged. Again he turned to Corbet's record in parliament, voting only once in 1891, and again Healy donned his verbal seaboots: 'A fisherman who went out once a year might as well pack it in.' A heckler shouted and, unable to respond intelligently, Healy became abusive: 'There is a fool in every crowd ... it is very creditable to Arklow that [in] a big town like it there is only one fool.'

He summoned up another local issue to win support for the candidate. Referring to the calls of the Parnell faction to keep priests out of politics, and linking Molony and company with the street preachers, Healy said: 'I would rather have the priests on my side than Mr Hallowes. I read the other day that that gentleman had made an appeal to the Parnellites to help him against the priests. Any man ought to know what they were when they had a "curreann" like that on their side.' This brought laughter from the crowd, which encouraged him to really attack Hallowes. Just what 'curreann' meant is not known, but it is reasonable to assume that it was far from complimentary. The priests, on the other hand, 'have influence not because of their Roman collars or black coats, but because of their good hearts,' and he cited Fr Farrelly's record of standing by tenants as an example. Turning again on Corbet, Healy said that of the eighty-six nationalist M.Ps. in the Commons, fifty-six were federationists and only thirty were Parnellite. Michael Davitt was one of the former and while he was a prisoner [for his fight for tenants' rights] William Corbet 'was drawing a salary from Dublin Castle' for his work regarding 'lunatic asylums.' John Redmond, Parnell's successor as leader of the parliamentary National Leaguers, 'was a clerk in the House of Commons and his brother William an officer in the yeomanry or militia while [I] stood in the dock in Cork in 1880. Yet these two gentlemen now come forward as patriots.'

At last, after Farrelly's and Healy's harangues, the floor was given over to the candidate John Sweetman, who had little to add, admitting that the others had stolen the limelight, making his contribution rather insignificant. Neveretheless, the Fife & Drum Band accompanied him to the station, followed by 1,000 well-wishers.

While Halpin and Sweetman trod the boards in a bid to win votes in every corner of the constituency, Corbet was conspicuous more by his absence than by his oratory. He was accused by Healy of staying in Spring Farm, where nobody could get near him, where he 'should stay at home with his baby'. Farrelly also made reference to their leaving Corbet 'with his cradle,' which brought laughter from the crowd. Whatever his domestic commitments, Corbet was undeniably lying low, or at least his appearances were not being reported as fully as those of his rival candidates, but then how could they be as the *News-Letter* backed Halpin and the *People* backed Sweetman?

As polling day neared, there was no obvious favourite. A high poll and close count were the only certainties. In fact, the first of these 'certainties' was to prove false as the turnout was lower than expected, being slightly less than in previous elections. A total of 3,773 voters cast their votes, compared with 4,085 in 1886, a decrease of 312 or 7.5 per cent. While this is not a significant difference in itself, the way those votes were cast is of immense importance. The count took place in Wicklow town, which had remained staunchy loyal to Parnell and the result, when it was announced, did not please those who had gathered to hear it. The total nationalist vote (Parnellite and anti-Parnellite) had fallen from 3,101 to 2,548, a decrease of more than 17.8 per cent. The unionist vote was up by almost 24.5 per cent, netting Halpin 1,225 votes compared with 984 for Colonel Tottenham in 1886. The real interest lay in the comparative pulling-power of Corbet and Sweetman. Corbet's vote fell from 3,101 in 1886 to only1,115, a decrease of just over sixty-four per cent. Sweetman, the non-resident newcomer, polled 1,433, beating the unionist Halpin by just 208 votes and was duly declared elected.

According to the *Wicklow News-Letter*, a howl of disbelief and anger rose from the crowd. Sweetman and his followers were in danger of being attacked and the new M.P. had to be escorted through the street by the R.I.C. to, appropriately, the local Catholic curate's house. Sweetman was hooted at and cat-called all the way up Kilmantin Hill while his followers were left to their own devices. M'Phail was incensed and he immediately blamed the Arklow fishermen for 'blindly following the dictates of their clergy to vote for a stranger in the county ... Arklow is undoubtedly a stronghold of the clerical party.'[21] It was a far cry from his praising them a year earlier in the wake of the municipal elections when he declared 'they will neither accept dictation nor brook intimidation from any person, no matter who or what he may be. Bullying and boycotting are of no avail against independence and honest courage.'[22] The 'clerical party' obviously had put their act together in the interim. It was a tremendous blow to the Parnellite nationalists in the county, particularly to those in Arklow. Stock would have to be taken of the defeat, and plans made for the future.

The *Wicklow People*, not surprisingly, took a very different view. 'Factionalism [the name it now used to refer to Parnellism] in Wicklow is now a thing of the past.' It singled out three priests in the county who 'counselled and assisted [the voters] like true shepherds' and cited Wicklow town as a 'place of dupes' where 'the Catholic(?) Club expelled the *Wicklow People* and the *Irish Catholic* to make way for the local Orange paper' – the question mark after Catholic is as it appeared in the newspaper.[23] There was, therefore, neither magnanimity in victory nor graciousness in defeat. The *People* reported great celebrations in Arklow, with large crowds in the streets and bonfires on the hills, bands playing and addresses given in the field beside Fr Dunphy's house. Dunphy himself thanked the fishermen for their support 'to which was largely attributable the return of the nationalist candidate.' Farrelly likewise thanked them for

> proving wrong that "Arklow was straight and strong Factionist" ... it was their proudest boast that the people of Arklow could hand down to their posterity that they could make and unmake members of Parliament [cheers and laughter], for it was by their vote and their vote alone that yesterday's victory had been carried ... Two years ago [we] were united, landlords and landlordism were trembling; they were giving reductions in rent. Was there one word about reductions last year or the year before? No, they [the landlords] were now hand-in-hand, as they saw them in the courtyard the other morning arm-in-arm with the Factionists of the town and elsewhere ... what did the *Independent* – that rotten rag of Factionism – say that day? "If Sweetman is returned, Arklow may be thanked for it." [Cheers][24]

The last speaker recorded was Fr Whitty, a curate from Avoca, who also credited the Arklow fishermen with Sweetman's victory. The deservers of the credit or condemnation, depending on the viewpoint, were by universal opinion the Arklow electorate, and it is a jibe which Wicklow town people can still level at Arklow people with justification.[25]

The following week the *Wicklow People* further gloried in James O'Connor's victory over the Conservative candidate Colonel Saunders in West Wicklow, pointing out that O'Connor's majority was 1,798 (2,582 to 784), coincidentally reminding all of the rebellion year in which 'Saunders' grandfather commanded the shooting of thirty people dead, one of whom was the grandfather of Daniel O'Connell.'

In August, the same paper reported earthquake shocks felt from Greystones to Wexford. There was no equipment then as there is now to measure its intensity, but it can hardly have been greater than the political upheavals Wicklow had faced throughout the previous year.[26]

'Factionism in Wicklow' did indeed seem to be dead. A meeting of Parnellites in Aughrim in August attracted a mere 300 people, despite the presence of the Redmond brothers, John and William.[27] In Arklow, the two Parnellite town commissioners, Molony and Troy, seemed to be keeping very low profiles, seldom attending the monthly meetings. In fact, Molony did not attend a meeting until the end of September, just weeks before the annual municipal election.

Despite the victory of the anti-Parnellites in the general election in July, the Arklow municipal contest would be a much closer race, and it was expected that the ratepayers' candidates of Parnellite/Tory mix would again win the day. As Troy and Molony had only served one year, their seats were safe for another two years. The outgoing members were Henry Delahunt, John Reynolds, Joseph Doyle and John Bradford, all anti-Parnellite nationalists and all four were proposed for re-election. The opposition they faced were George Kearon and James Tyrrell, both tories, and John Tyrrell and Denis Kavanagh, both described as 'Redmondites' (the new name for

Parnellites or factionists). As prescribed by law, polling took place on 15 October, and as predicted the Arklow Independent Ratepayers' Association candidates proved victorious.

The *Wicklow People* recorded the results with what reads like resigned recognition of the inevitable, once again accusing the Parnellite candidates of entering into an unholy alliance with local tories. It had warned that there were 117 voters on the register, of which fifty were recognised conservatives, 'so if all these and nine Redmondites vote, the coalition will win.'[28] It was a matter of simple mathematics. As it turned out, the leading 'coalition' – still being denied by the Parnellites – candidates got one more than the required nine and the results were: Denis Kavanagh (Redmondite) 60; John Tyrrell (Redmondite) 60; George Kearon (Tory) 56; James Tyrrell (Tory) 54; Henry Delahunt (anti-Parnell Nationalist) 39; John Bradford (anti-Parnell Nationalist) 36; Joseph Doyle (anti-Parnell Nationalist) 35; and John Reynolds (anti-Parnell Nationalist) 34.

So, the anti-Parnellite faction, that is Fr Dunphy's National Federation group, had their M.P. at Westminster, but the local Parnellites and conservatives now had a majority of the Arklow town commissioners with four Parnellites (a.k.a. Redmondites, factionists in the *Wicklow People*, nationalists in the *News-Letter*): Dr Michael Molony, Thomas Troy, Denis Kavanagh, and John Tyrrell and seven conservatives (a.k.a. tories, unionists): George Kearon, James Tyrrell, Samuel Marshall, John Storey, Richard Hudson, Richard Kearon and Job Hall; as opposed to four anti-Parnellites (a.k.a. federationists, nationalists in the *Wicklow People*): Dr Howard, John Hanagan, Peter Garvey, and Bernard Kearney.

With such a strong hold, it now seemed inevitable that the chair must go to either a Parnellite or a conservative and, as had been the situation twelve months earlier, it seemed that Dr Molony would be the occupant. This time, with tory backing, he would have the votes to carry it. Fate, however, was to step in and deliver a shock as great to the people of Arklow as Parnell's death had been to Ireland in general in October 1891.

CHAPTER 15:
The death of Dr Molony

Much has been made of Dr Molony's workload. His dispensary district was a large one; with 6,390 people it was the second most populous in the Rathdrum union. Only the dispensary district in and around Wicklow town had a greater population, 6,939, but they were more geographically concentrated.[1] It was the hilly terrain of the hinterland that made the Arklow district such a taxing one. Molony also had his private practice, which included the position of surgeon to Parnell's Arklow quarries,[2] and he contributed articles to medical journals. Apart from these professional commitments, from the time of his arrival in Arklow in April 1885 he had involved himself in the social fabric of the local community, taking part in organising the annual sports day, performing in fundraising entertainments in the Marlborough Hall, getting involved in local politics with the Independent Arklow Ratepayers' Association, and was president of the Commercial Club. He was a member of the central branch of the Irish National League and a staunch supporter of Parnell. He was young, obviously fit, physically strong and psychologically able to handle all the demands on his time. But he was not invulnerable, even though he and all who watched his amazing work rate might be tempted at times to think that he was.

It was while visiting a patient in one of the outlying districts that Molony was caught in bad weather, receiving a severe wetting from which he developed pneumonia. From the outset it was a severe case, but his medical attendants felt confident that he would recover. They were wrong. On Friday, 21 October, his condition deteriorated and it was soon evident that he was in his final hours of life. He died about noon the following day, exactly one week after his success in the municipal elections.[3]

With remarkable efficiency, the *Wicklow News-Letter* carried news of his demise in that day's edition, which was in the shops just two hours after the event. It was a very brief notification, without editorialising, and no more than a single column inch in length, but it was nonetheless admirably prompt. The following week, William M'Phail, a long-time admirer of Molony, made up for the short, unadorned piece. It opened with an expression of deep regret and no one who had followed the *News-Letter*'s coverage of Arklow politics in the preceding years could have doubted the sincerity of that regret. It then went on to give a brief overview of his education and his medical career prior to his arrival in Arklow, before dealing with his impact on the town …

> … he was but a short time practising till his remarkable skill and ability became apparent, and as a consequence his services were more widely requisitioned. Something of his private, apart from his professional, character became known, and his real worth daily more and more appreciated. Enthusiastic in the pursuit of his profession, and a charity upon which only his income placed a limit, ever on the alert to relieve suffering and want, his unremitting care and skill were bestowed equally on the poor and lowly as on his more wealthy patients … Totally oblivious of self during times of public affliction – notably during the influenza epidemic[4] – the work cheerfully performed by him would have taxed the energies and capabilities of three ordinary individuals.

He went on to write of Molony's writing activities, his published work in medical journals and the fact that his paper on 'Hygiene' was read at a meeting of the British Medical Association, and 'attracted great attention from the savants there assembled.' But it was for his political views and his determination to hold true to them that most exercised M'Phail's emotional outpouring:

> In public matters his independent, strict adherence to principle and straightforward conduct, while it made him hosts of firm friends, aroused the hatred and enmity of some who followed him even to his death with their malice and meanness. Beyond the grave he is free from their persecution, and can

reap in peace the reward of his kindness and charity. The Great Supreme Judge, who reads our inmost thoughts, and to whom the secrets of our hearts are bare, will decide between the doctor and his enemies. In His hands we leave both. At His tribunal all must render an account of their stewardship; neither malice, nor lying, nor hypocrisy will avail; and from His decision there is no appeal. Under a slight outward appearance of brusqueness was a hidden kindness of heart ... Everyone of worth in Arklow and districts around, irrespective of creed, mourns the death of an honest Irishman, a gentleman, and a scholar. To his bereaved widow, aged father, and the members of his family, we tender our deep and sincere sympathy.

This was stirring, gloves-off stuff, with its references to 'malice ... meanness ... enemies ... persecution even to death.' M'Phail's mention of Molony's 'slight outward appearance of brusqueness' is the only direct indication of a man who did not suffer fools gladly.

One more remark is intriguing and frustrating in equal measure, the reference to his 'bereaved widow'. This is one of the few references to Molony having been married. The 1880s and 1890s were, of course, a period of sharp division between the public sphere of the male and the domestic sphere of the female, so it is hardly surprising that she did not figure in his public life, but she was mentioned as having taken part in a concert held in the Marlborough Hall under the aegis of her husband's Commercial Club in late January 1892: 'Mrs Molony, accompanied by the orchestra, played a couple of banjo solos in a pleasing manner, and her efforts were warmly encored.'[5] Not exactly a rave review, but it is one of only a few references to her existence and the only reference to give a hint to her personality. Evidence of who she was, where and when they met, even if they had children have been lost to history. Exhaustive research in general register records in Ireland, Scotland, England and Wales has yielded no likely candidates.[6] Also, she had left what had been the family home at 8 Marlborough Terrace before the 1901 census was taken. In fact, it would appear from evidence to be given shortly that she remained in the house only a very short period after her husband's death. Mrs 'Michael' Molony, in short, remains a mystery.

Immediately beneath the obituary is an account of the funeral which makes the existence of the elusive Mrs Molony even more vague. According to M'Phail, from the time of death to interment, an estimated 3,000 people visited 'the chamber of death.' At three o'clock on Monday afternoon, the coffin was taken from the house and began the mile-long route to the cemetery. Crowds lined the streets and fell in behind the hearse as it made its way down Marlborough Terrace, left into Upper Main Street, past Wexford Road and Vale Road, up Coolgreaney Road until the cemetery was reached. An estimated 5,000 people turned out to pay their respects, 'and no creed nor class was absent.' Revds Hallowes and Harrison were present. The members of the Commercial Club were there in force, wearing crepe armlets, and carrying the remains from the hearse to the grave. The chief mourners were his sixty-three-year-old father Daniel who had travelled from Tipperary to be with his son as his health deteriorated, and his brother Joseph. A list of the most prominent figures in the district followed these two names. No mention is made of his widow. This might be explained by the fact that those listed were 'following immediately behind the hearse.' It is only in relatively recent decades, in Arklow at least, that women walk behind the hearse. That was the role of male mourners. The principal women mourners travelled by car behind the on-foot cortege.[7] Perhaps the young widow was conveyed to her husband's interment in this fashion, but it is strange that she is not even mentioned in the account.

Less strange perhaps is the absence of any of the local Catholic clergy. Neither Dunphy nor any of his curates felt it appropriate to attend, and the Catholic funeral service was read by Fr Monahan of Barndarrig. It will be remembered that Fr Monahan's predecessor as parish priest at Barndarrig had been Fr Michael Molony, Dr Michael's uncle. He had died the previous year and it would have been interesting to see, had he been alive, if he would officiated at his nephew's funeral. M'Phail ended his account of the funeral with the words a long time will pass ere his place can be filled. The people of Arklow may, indeed, well say in their hearts today: - "He was a man, take him for all and all; we shall never look upon his like again".

The *Wicklow People* account was much shorter and more matter-of-fact, admitting that he was 'greatly esteemed by the community, irrespective of creed or class.' Among the wreaths was one from his widow, who seems to have conspired with the newspapers to have her name lost to history for it was inscribed simply, 'His poor little wife.'[8]

Four days after the funeral, on Friday 28 October, a committee was formed to take steps to commemorate Molony's life and work in Arklow. The names of those present again reflect Molony's cross-community popularity. There were Catholics and Protestants, nationalists and unionists, businessmen and seafarers. It is significant that at that meeting Dr Richard Halpin, whom Molony had beaten in the election as medical officer and whom Molony had cited as being in breach of health regulations by having a stinking sewer on his property, was elected chairman of the committee. Other members were John Donnelly and T J Troy (elected joint secretaries), E Kearon, Hugh Byrne, Richard Kearon TC, John Tyrrell TC, John Storey TC, P Bolger, R Mowatt, P Kavanagh, J F Evans, S Marshall TC, D Kavanagh TC. The following resolutions were unanimously adopted:

> Proposed by Mr R Mowatt, seconded by Mr J Donnelly – that this meeting, in response to the earnest wish of the friends of the late Dr Michael J Molony, undertake the duty of Erecting a Suitable Memorial to perpetuate the memory of one whose unselfish devotion to his professional duties endeared him to all classes of the community; and also as a tribute to his inviolable integrity, his simple honesty, his unswerving independence and his genuine zeal and regard for the sick poor committed to his care.
>
> Proposed by Mr Evans, seconded by Mr P Bolger – for the purpose of carrying out the foregoing resolution, a Subscription List be now opened. To keep this movement free

from the aspersion of a begging appeal, the Committee has decided to confine its operations exclusively to the true friends and admirers of the deceased. In acting thus they are fully conscious that such a course would have the sanction of the lamented friend whose memory it is proposed to honour.

Being aware of the mutual feelings of regard which existed between you and our deceased friend, we confidently request your kind and valuable co-operation and support.

Subscriptions will be received by the Treasurer, or any Member of the Committee.

Arklow, October 28th, 1892.[9]

When Molony first fell ill, Dr Halpin stepped into the breach, and at a special meeting of the Arklow dispensary committee on 3 November, chaired by the earl of Carysfort, a vote of sympathy was passed to 'Mrs Molony'.[10] It was also agreed that Dr Halpin be appointed *locum tenens* at £3-3-0 per week, his appointment to date from 17 October to 28 November 1892. It was also agreed that the election of a medical officer to replace the late Dr Molony be held on 21 November. To avoid the awkward embarrassment experienced when Molony took over the position six years earlier, committee members Philpot and Condren were to take inventory of the dispensary and compare the items with invoices.[11] As soon as Molony died, the local apothecary Dr Howard sent a bill to the dispensary committee for medical supplies supposedly ordered by Molony. The committee said they knew nothing of such an order and that the bill should be sent to the executors of the late Dr Molony.[12] This may seem a trifling matter and hardly worthy of inclusion here, but it illustrates the short-lived nature of eulogy, particularly as the majority of the dispensary committee were still Fr Dunphy's men. Life goes on.

A few weeks later, Dr Charles Edward Roche Gardiner was elected the new medical officer for the district, getting seven votes. His rivals were a Dr O'Gorman, who polled four, and Dr Richard Halpin, who scored only one – what was it about him that generated so little support? Whatever the reason, he was not destined to succeed to what had been his father's position for many years. The dispensary committee was still firmly in the hands of the pro-clerical anti-Parnellite party and it was clear that no supporter of Dr Molony or unionist (which to them amounted to the same thing) would be elected.[13] Gardiner was to be paid £100 a year (£20 less than Molony) and £10 as medical officer of health (£5 less than Molony).

Molony's friends were not so quick to forget him and the fund for a memorial stood at over £55 by 19 November.[14] The committee were already warning intending contributors that an early closing date was envisaged. In the same edition, it was reported that the town commissioners had generally agreed that Molony, as poll-topper would take the chair. Now it was agreed that the position should go to Thomas Troy, his 'friend who had fought shoulder to shoulder with him in trying to uphold those principles which he believed to be the best for mankind.' It went on to praise Troy's qualities, much of which had been said and repeated many times in relation to Molony. In accepting the position, Troy fired a salvo that plunged Arklow into a spiral of allegation and counter-allegation that marked some of the most disgraceful months in the town's long history.

The monthly meeting of the town commissioners on Monday, 7 November was adjourned as a mark of respect to Molony's memory, but before separating Troy was elected chairman, despite a half-hearted attempted by John Hannagan to have Dr Howard re-elected to the position.[15] Troy hit the ground running, first thanking the commissioners for the honour bestowed on him, but immediately launched into an attack on remarks passed, he believed, as a slur on his dead friend:

> I regret that my first duty – a very grave and serious duty, which I owe to my deceased friend and member of the board – is to contradict some statements publicly made by a rev gentleman on Sunday week, at twelve o'clock prayers in the Roman Catholic Church, in language I can only characterise as unchristian. After alluding to him as a certain individual who died recently, he went on to say – "Everyone knows what becomes of the persons who neglect their religious duties.

Their friends are few at the last moment. God Almighty help them in the end. The slimy serpent followed him into the chamber of sickness. They sent their emissaries there. He was not able to repeat his prayers at the last moment." Gentlemen, it is to me a painful duty to have to make these remarks, but I will not shirk my duty to the dead. On behalf of Dr Molony's father, who was present from the moment his illness became serious – I was also there till his death – and in justice to his wife and medical attendants I say that each and all of the foregoing statements are absolutely without foundation and untrue. During his life he was subject to the same treatment from the same source on account of his principles, ill befitting ministers of the doctrine of peace and goodwill. If feelings of common decency, however, do not make them respect the dead, we must only shame them into letting him rest in peace.

Although Troy did not identify the priest responsible, his (Troy's) godfather, Fr Dunphy, was recognised as the man in question. Troy was not the only person to take exception to Dunphy's words. The following week, a meeting of the central branch of the National League was reported at which John Redmond proposed that a roll of honour called 'Ireland's army of independence' should be drafted and that each subscriber would be issued with a silver badge as a sign of membership. It was heartily endorsed, but more significant was a short speech given by another M.P., Dr Kenny, who wished to address the league about the death of Dr Molony who had been 'a strong and strenuous soldier in the cause.' They 'were aware of the terrible and vindictive persecution which their friends throughout the country were exposed to, and which occasionally was made to pursue them into the grave … He wanted to call attention to the language which appeared in the *Wicklow People*, which 'was a friend of the Seceders. In this paper Fr Dunphy's – [Kenny had no hesitation in naming the priest involved] – language was described at a meeting … of the town commissioners.' He then goes on to quote what Troy had said. He finished by calling on Archbishop Walsh to take note of the language used and to decide if such language should be permitted among his clergymen.

It was obvious that this was going to be a storm of significant proportions, and Molony's unnamed widow was not about to subject herself to it. She instructed W Greene to sell by auction the furniture of the Molony household at 8 Marlborough Terrace on Tuesday, 22 November 1892.[16] It is to be hoped that she had left the town soon after the auction and did not have to hear or read of the fall-out of the allegations and counter-allegations that grew steadily degrading and degraded.

Under the heading 'Mr Thomas J Troy and the Arklow priests,' there was a report of a meeting in the field at the rear of the Catholic church.[17] It had been called to express indignation at Troy's remarks respecting Fr Dunphy. Dunphy was not present himself, but he was represented by Frs Manning and Farrelly. Daniel Condren proposed that John Hanagan take the chair, and Richard Howard, the local apothecary who had been replaced by Troy as chairman of the town commissioners, was the first to speak. He said that he was present in the church when the remarks allegedly against Dr Molony had been made and he (Howard) could not make out that the words conveyed anything like what had been attributed to them. The words were simply a general warning against leaving conversion until it was too late. They were made in the context of a recent visit to the parish by the archbishop and the remarks were part of a general discourse on the benefits of confirmation in equipping children with the strengths to face the trials and tribulations of life. Howard saw no personal attack on anyone in the words used. It was merely a warning not to put off conversion until such time as when the body and mind would be too weak to reconcile the penitent to God. He added that some reference had been made to the street preaching and the great dissatisfaction the practice had aroused among the Roman Catholics of the town. What was the purpose of the street-preaching? It was not for the benefit of the Protestant community, for they had their own church in which to attend their services. It was not to instruct young Protestants in the tenets of their religion. Its only purpose could be to proselytise. Howard, although having begun by saying that he would not speak for long as he was 'not what was called a good speaker', turned to sarcasm. The reverend gentlemen, he said, who are engaged at this do not think that the Catholics are sufficiently instructed [laughter] ... that Messrs Hallowes and Harrison think that the Catholics were poor, unenlightened people, who had no chance of going to heaven at all. [Renewed laughter] Howard continued in this vein, ridiculing Hallowes and his curate in their efforts 'to show the way to heaven' because the parish priest was unable to do so. But, said Howard, the Catholic people of Arklow knew that their own clergy were quite capable of showing the way to heaven better than anyone else. This, Howard argued, was the context in which Dunphy's words had been spoken, a general warning against loss of faith and that Fr Dunphy should not be accused 'of using words that he never said.'

Fr Farrelly, who was received with loud cheers, was the next to speak. He started by reminding them that the last time he had had the pleasure of speaking to them was to congratulate them on 'crushing factionism in the county Wicklow, and today we are going to make an effort to crush toadyism in the town of Arklow.' This brought cries of 'Put them down!'

> We are here today to wipe out an insult – a gross insult, a slander – that has been cast upon the people of Arklow through their respected parish priest by the newly-elected Chairman of the Commissioners of Arklow – of the Tory Commissioners of Arklow. Now, I will read to you the insult that was offered to you, through Fr Dunphy, by this gentleman. Listen to it. It is as follows – 'I regret my first duty, a very serious duty', [laughter]. Remember that it was a serious duty that devolved upon him. This statesman [laughter] when he opened the proceedings did not begin by telling us that he was going to give us gas light for lamp light. It is usual for statesmen like him to give us an outline of their programme when they are elected to any high position. But this one did not ... he did not care about the drainage of the town, or the housing of the poor, or the fishing interests. No! Something else troubled him. I will tell you what it was. It was to contradict – that is to give the lie – a statement publicly made by a reverend gentleman on Sunday week at the twelve o'clock prayers. Twelve o'clock prayers, mind you that! Eh, did you ever hear of twelve o'clock prayers on a Sunday?

245

That smells of Protestantism and Hallowism. Now listen to the remainder of that statesman's remarks – [here he quoted what Troy had said in the commission chamber] –

Well, my friends, I have the best authority for stating to you – and to anyone whom it may concern – that this is a false and perverted version of what Fr Dunphy said on the occasion. He never alluded to the individual who died recently. I have authority for saying that, and he never said a word about him not being able to say his prayers either. I have Fr Dunphy's authority and other men's authority for saying that. But let us take away these two additions – these two maliciously perverted additions – of the Chairman of the Town Commissioners.

Let us take away that from this version that I have read, and tell me is there anything you could condemn in the words. Fr Dunphy, as parish priest, was bound in conscience to warn his parishioners against a danger that was in their midst – [hear, hear] – and if he did not do that, he would not deserve to be your parish priest. He was bound to warn you of two proselytisers who are disturbing the peace of this town for the last two years. He was bound to tell you to keep away from them; to have nothing whatever to do with them; and he added 'On a recent occasion these two, like serpents, tried to creep into the death chamber of one of my parishioners.' Was there any harm in that, I would like to know? He was bound to tell you the fact; aye, and if this Roman Catholic Town Commissioner had a spark of manhood in him, he would have revolted against the insult that was offered to his dying friend by these two gentlemen who tried to get up to his death-bed chamber. But this eloquent Chairman of the Tory Town Commissioners bottled his wrath to keep it warm until he had a good opportunity of letting it forth. He did not write to the papers about it. No! He waited until he had a Tory audience – until he was elected Chairman by the Tory Commissioners – and then what did he do? He repaid them quickly for their confidence in him. They knew him perfectly well. A respectable Protestant stated, indeed, the other day, that they would not have elected Troy if he had not been against the priests. And he proved himself well entitled to that qualification. The very moment he got into the chair he commented on matters outside the business entirely. The first duty he had to do was to vilify his own parish priest. [Cries of 'Down with him!'] And where did he do it? Before the very men who are paying Hallowes and Harrison for vilifying your religion on the streets of Arklow every Sunday. I think he went a little too far ... He wanted to repay the Tories for putting him where a respectable man should be. Well, my friends, and whom did he attack? A priest who has lived in your midst, labouring and working night and day for your interests, first as curate and then as parish priest. This is the man whom your newly-elected Tory Chairman attacked. If you want to know what Fr Dunphy has done for the parish of Arklow and for the parishioners, look around you. Look at the convent; look at the church; look at your pier there below; look at the convent schools erected here the other day. And this man, after years of toil and labour and self-sacrifice, has now been insulted by a thing like that Chairman of the Town Commissioners. Yes, this thing actually dares to insult him. Since this newly-elected Chairman was in petticoats, and as far as I know from the time he left them off up to the present, he has never done any good for either town or country. Fr Dunphy has been working for you. During the last six years, when we have been fighting for our lives, Fr Dunphy was in the forefront of the struggle. He has never ceased to work for the people here and in the country. This is the man this Chairman looks upon as a serious duty to vilify.

My friends, I will not detain you much longer, but I want to tell you about Quixote. You have all heard of Don Quixote; but afraid that you haven't, I will tell you a little about him. Don Quixote was a Spanish peasant but he became a knight by some chance or another ... Now, like a great many of us, he had a little learning, and you know a little learning is a dangerous thing; but Don read his books again, and at last he overdreamt himself and became a hero. He thought he had a mission too; and do you know what that mission was? It was to relieve all distress in the world – distressful damsels and everything else that way [laughter]. He also clad himself in armour. It was an old rusty set, but it did not matter. It did not diminish his ambition. Having put that armour on one day, he got a rustier horse and mounted his steed. With armour on and lance in rest, he sallied forth in quest of distress, so that he might relieve it. But what did he come in contact with first, do you think? Nothing more or less than a wind-mill [laughter]. Now you can picture to yourselves what he was like as he steadied himself in his saddle, with his lance in rest, preparing to hurl himself against it. Those of you who have read the story know the result of the conflict ... the wind-mill did not come off second best [laughter].

I allude to this old romance because I think we have got a Don Quixote too in Arklow – a modern Don Quixote. He has a peculiar mission too, and that is to crush the priests if he can [cries of 'he will never do it.'] He has got to relieve the distress of the world. Nothing can be done but under his direction; but what happened to Don Quixote when he went tilting against the wind-mill will happen our Don Quixote too. He will be reduced. He will not succeed against the priests of Arklow. He will not succeed or be able to bespatter or stain the fame or respected reputation of the parish priest of Arklow – Fr Dunphy [cheers.]

The report of his speech ends with remarks from the crowd such as 'He would never get tired', 'He is the best of the lot', and 'Arrah, did you ever hear anything like him?', and the reason for reprinting it verbatim is to show not only its content, but also the skilled way in which it was delivered, using sarcasm, laughter, indignation, literary allusion, and other rhetorical devices. There was something of the rant about it, but it was a controlled rant. Farrelly knew how to woo, cajole, and stir up emotion. He knew how to form a bond between speaker and listener, and his style of delivery says as much about the prevailing political and religious animosities as does the content. He had stripped Thomas Troy bare, exposed him to ridicule, but he was careful never once to remind the people of the close personal connection between Troy and Dunphy, that of godson and godfather. Perhaps some of the jibes were cheap and would have no place in more dignified debating arenas, but he knew who he was speaking to, and in such circumstances Laurence Farrelly was a hard act to follow.

But someone had to follow him and it fell to the inarticulate Avoca curate, Fr Whitty, who had been on hand to support Sweetman at the general election just a few months earlier. He played the unbiased, disinterested observer, but still managed to refer to the chair of the Arklow town commissioners as 'that little god Troy.' He also called Troy 'a combination of a sugar cask and a whiskey barrel,' and a 'dirty little whipper-snapper.' He admitted that he did not have Farrelly's ease with words, and it was soon obvious that neither did he have his stamina as his steam ran out as quickly as his schoolyard name-calling.

Fr John Manning was the last to speak and he, as the other speakers had done, reminded the audience that they were not there to make an apology for the parish priest. He had nothing to apologise for. 'His character was as far above those who were snarling at him as the moon was above the dogs.'

It was all stirring stuff and in a pre-Sunday afternoon television age this was an entertainment as well as a political and religious rally. But even more was in store as the crowds left the field. It was Sunday, and irrespective of such gatherings, it was the day when the 'serpent-like' Revds Hallowes and Harrison were about their lord's business. As the crowd left the field and entered Parade Ground, there was Hallowes, standing at the public pump, Harrison preaching at his side. His voice and words were clearly heard by all those who filed past, but under the watchful eye of Fr Farrelly, the crowd did not heed him. Most did not pause to comment or condemn, but as usual 'a good deal of scoffing and jeering [was] indulged in by the women, but they were soon out of sight along with the male companions, and the square was left entirely in the possession of Mr Hallowes who continued to stay in the locality for a considerable time afterwards.'

The tragic death of the young doctor left a gaping hole in the fabric of Arklow's social and political life. The vitriol that had filled the columns of the local newspapers as to what Fr Dunphy said or didn't say petered out within a matter of weeks, but Revd Hallowes would not let it go. He had for some time distributed the *Arklow Parish Magazine*, an impressive publication[18] that was really a general Church of Ireland magazine with several pages dedicated to the parishes in which it was distributed. In the January 1893 issue[19] he wrote of the general sense of loss among all sections of the community, pointing out that 'the only discordant sound – to use no stronger word – proceeds from the clergy of his own Church.' He praised Troy's courage in defending his friend's reputation and memory against the might of the parish priest. He accused Dunphy of having no such courage because he relied on the power of his position. Instead of castigating Molony, Dunphy, as his pastor, should have visited the dying man. He then denied that he or Harrison had played 'the slimy serpent [which] followed him into the chamber of sickness' as depicted by Dunphy:

> It is a gross untruth for anyone to say that either the Rector or the Curate of Arklow ever made any attempt to enter Dr Molony's house much less his bed-chamber, when he was sick or dying.

That was the last word I have found on the subject.

*

Plans to erect a fitting monument to Molony were proceeding, and in February the *News-Letter* announced that a meeting of the committee decided that it would take the form of a cross with an anchor and chain. 'Some of the designs which were submitted for consideration were exceedingly handsome.'[20] Three weeks later, however, the anchor and chain were jettisoned for a much grander design, probably on the strength of increased funds. The company of Fitzpatrick & Sons of Dublin was commissioned to erect a twelve foot 'exceedingly graceful and magnificently carved' monument of solid Sicilian marble with limestone base. It was to be surmounted by a very elegant Celtic cross artistically worked in front with ivy. The cap was to be of richly moulded gablets at the sides and in the centre was to be a wreath of flowers handsomely carved and well relieved. Six months were to pass before it was ready to be unveiled.

On Thursday, 3 August 1893, crowds again assembled in the street with the Marlborough Hall on one side and Molony's house on the other. Both the unionist *Wicklow News-Letter* and the nationalist *Wicklow People*[2] carried extensive accounts of the event and the speeches. As the former gave a more detailed account of the procession, it is quoted here in full:

The procession that wended its way through the streets of Arklow, on Thursday, to the grave of the late Dr Molony, although associated with a very sad and solemn occasion had one gratifying feature, and that was the remarkable way in which it brought together many people of widely divergent views. It was, in fact, a unique incident in the history of Arklow. Dr Molony had that one peculiar characteristic of attracting around him a circle of friends that were strongly opposed to his own views; thus the *personnel* of that body that visited the cemetery to unveil his monument admits of an easy explanation. But, in that respect, it had still a further significance. Those who took a prominent part in the proceedings on Thursday were genuine friends, which in the light of some events which are fresh in the memory of our readers, compels us to look back on the procession with feelings of unmixed satisfaction. It was an object lesson, indeed, to those who waver in their fidelity, to prove what unanimity of men of probity and honour can display in the sacred cause of loyalty to a man that died while helping his fellow-man to struggle through life, it is sufficient to mention that the two men who led the way to the grave of Dr Molony were Mr Corbet and Mr E Kearon. There followed behind others no less prominent in their steadfastness of purpose and their total want of hypocrisy; the tribute that was therefore paid to the memory of the departed gentleman was one that was distinguished for its wholehearted sincerity. Such incidents as these deserve to be specifically mentioned, particularly when one bears in mind that it is not so long ago since Arklow received Parnell one day with shouts of welcome and the next day opened its arms to the man who boasted that he had brought him to his Waterloo.

The proceedings attending the unveiling ceremony were thoroughly well carried out. At half past two the members of the committee of the Commercial Club met at the Marlborough Hall, and having donned armlets of crape, headed a large procession to the cemetery, where the monument stood ready to be unveiled. All the business establishments were closed with the exception of a few. Of this fact it is perhaps unnecessary to make mention; the tribute was joined in by all that was respectable and all that was of any worth in the town, so those who singled themselves out from it cannot certainly be congratulated on their tactics. Mr William Redmond M.P., as representing the Independent Party, attended as a substitute for his brother, Mr John Redmond M.P., who was unfortunately prevented from being present owing to indisposition. Mr William J Corbet, ex-M.P., also travelled down to Arklow to unveil the monument. Most of those who walked to the cemetery wore Sunday attire, and the entire proceedings were characterised by a solemnity consistent with the solemn function which was to be performed. When the procession reached the cemetery there were already great numbers of people assembled, and when the ceremony began the attendance must have been close to two thousand.

The report then names 160 of those present. The usual names, those which have appeared regularly in the course of this story, are listed first: Dr Halpin, the town commissioners, and so on. Hallowes and Harrison were there, but no Catholic clergy are listed. Molony's widow is named, but again with an amazing disregard for her position as his wife. She is listed 134th in the litany of names. Immediately following her name is that of Tom Troy's wife and family. What is the story behind this exclusion? Is there a story? Was it conscious or unconscious? Surely, it would have been automatic to place her name at the top of the list. If she preferred discreet anonymity, then it would have been best not to mention her at all. As it is, she takes her place behind the names of

friends and acquaintances. The *Wicklow People* did not mention her at all, although it did give pride of place to Molony's father, Daniel, who had made the trip from Cashel – the *News-Letter*, on the other hand, did not include him in its extensive list.

Dr Richard Halpin, as chairman of the memorial committee opened the proceedings by recalling how he and Molony
had not only been professional colleagues but friends. He had,
he said, never 'met a more able, a more brilliant, or a more
kindly medical man.' Words are easily spoken, but actions are
often truer indicators of feelings and it is clear from Halpin's
central role in erecting the monument that he held no animosity towards Molony despite the fact that Molony had become
medical officer, a position Halpin understandably might have
felt was his, and despite Molony's reporting him for defective
drains. It says a great deal about Halpin's willingness to forgive
and Molony's ability to attract friends. Corbet then spoke a few
words about his 'lamented friend' and removed the veil. It was
at this juncture that Molony's closest ally, Thomas Troy,
stepped forward and delivered the main speech of the day.

> I see around this monument today, ladies and gentlemen, rep-
> resenting different religious beliefs and shades of political
> thought. This is as it should be; for no matter how we may dif-
> fer in creed and politics yet there is one platform on which we
> can stand in common and unite, and that is in doing justice
> and honour to the memory of the dead, whose lives while
> amongst us have been spent in the noble endeavour to do their
> duty to their fellow-man. Few amongst you have had as many
> opportunities as I can claim to have had of observing and
> knowing how truly good and noble and generous was the heart
> of the man who lies beneath. Living in a small, remote town
> like Arklow, deprived of the society of advanced men of sci-
> ence of his own and other professions, a life's stream has ebbed
> out amongst us at the early age of thirty-one years which, had
> Providence otherwise ordained and under other circumstances
> where his great latent talents would have been called into
> action by his surroundings, would have reflected credit not
> only on the immediate district in which he lived, but even to
> the country which gave him birth. Animated with that true
> and all-embracing spirit of Christian charity which stops not to
> enquire what is the creed of the fellow creature who seeks
> relief, at what shrine he worships, or how often he kneels to
> pray – he went through the daily routine of his duties amongst
> the poor, far exceeding the actual limits those duties required.

By many a poor cabin hearth has he sat hour after hour during a winter's night, watching with solicitude the changes of a critical case, giving words of hope where hope was possible, and kindly comfort – aye, and even pecuniary assistance from his own limited resources – to the sorrowing and anxious wife or mother or daughter, as the case might be, who watched by the bed of sickness. I have, and shall always hold, a vivid recollection of the morning of his death. He had got relief from pain – the pain of the previous day – that ease which in most cases is the forerunner of dissolution, and as the night passed away and the daylight streamed in through the partially opened shutters, raising his eyes he exclaimed: 'Oh, the beautiful daylight that I shall never, never see again,' and then the words that he uttered were characteristic of the man, and showed that even on the verge of Eternity, the feelings that had actuated him during life were still dominant. Speaking in a tone of deep regret, he said: 'Oh, if only I had something to give the poor, the poor, the poor!' He is gone forever from amongst us – gone beyond earthly power of recall – he has passed that border land which divides the finite from the infinite: to him the secrets of the great hereafter are now as an open book.

Personally, I recognise in the death of Dr Molony the loss of a friend, who was to me almost more than a brother; whose genial kindly nature, whose honesty of purpose, whose general worth of character impressed me from the first moment of our acquaintance, an acquaintance which ripened into the firm unaltered friendship of years – which I shall look back to till I reach that Eternity to which he has passed, as containing for me some of the transient gleams of sunshine which are allowed us in our passage through this world, where all is waste and decay.

Fellow town commissioner John Storey was next to speak, consoling Molony's family with the thought that 'Dr Molony has left behind him an unblemished record and a stainless name ... [his immediate family] should assuage and mitigate their sorrow for he has left such a bright halo behind him.' The last to speak was William Redmond M.P., who spoke on behalf of those not from the town or county, but who knew of Molony's qualities. It was an able speech, but the day belonged to Troy.

The spoken word is ephemeral, but the sentiments

expressed that day in 1893, are preserved on the monument which still stands in Arklow cemetery:

North side, upper panel:
This / monument is raised / to perpetuate the memory of / Doctor Michael J. Molony / for several years Medical Officer / of Arklow Dispensary District / whose unselfish devotion / to his professional duties / endeared him / to all classes of the community / and also as a tribute to / his inviolable integrity / his simple honesty / his unswerving independence / and his genuine zeal for the sick poor / committed to his care / Born 1st January 1861 / Died 22nd October 1892 / R.I.P.

North side, lower panel:
An upright honest man lies buried here
Gentle he was, and courteous, good and brave
A faithful friend, unselfish and sincere
He trod the path of honour to the grave
His record 'Good', his name without a stain
This marble monument shall long endure
To tell he lived and laboured not in vain
True to his God, his country and the poor

CHAPTER 16:
A slow healing

Throughout Ireland and Britain the different reactions to the Parnell-O'Shea affair had shattered all chances of home rule for the foreseeable future. In Britain, the religious right, which had supported a limited measure of self-determination for Ireland, could not countenance a man whose private life was not lived by their tenets. In Ireland, the Catholic church played the same role as the religious fundamentalists across the Irish Sea. The home rule movement was fragmented beyond repair. Despite these catastrophic developments, the British prime minister, William Ewart Gladstone remained confident of pushing it through parliament. He was now in his fourth term as premier, having previously served as such between 1868 and 1874, when home rule was first mooted; between 1880 and 1885 when the Land League and National League were bringing the whole question to a head; in the February to July period of 1886 when the first attempt to pass it into law was made; and he regained the position for the last time after the general election of 1892. It was he who forced the issue regarding Parnell's replacement as leader of the Irish party. In February 1893, when Gladstone was in his eighty-fourth year, he again brought home rule before the Commons.

This time, as Gladstone had suspected, it was passed by the lower house after the second reading on 21 April by a majority of forty-three votes and at the third reading on 1 September by thirty-four votes. Before it could become law, however, it would have to go through the House of Lords. Equally as expected, the Lords voted against it by 419 votes to forty-one on 8 September. The lords were always going to be the main stumbling block, and whatever chance there might have been of a united nationalist party pushing it through, the fragmented and spent force that now threw insults at each other in the streets and in newspaper columns would convince no one that Ireland was ready and able to manage its own affairs. When realisation finally struck Parnellites and anti-Parnellites, they must have wondered what had happened. How had defeat been clutched from the jaws of victory? Like two children fighting over a toy, it now lay broken between them. How could such people be deemed mature enough for self-government?

Political aspirations were left impotently aside and concentration was turned to other aspects of what it meant to be 'Irish'. Cultural movements such as the Gaelic Athletic Association (sport), Conradh na Gaeilge (language), Comhaltas Ceoltóirí (music), the Celtic Twilight (poetry and theatre), the collection of folklore and ancient tales, all came to the fore in this period. But there was also something else. New shoots of self-belief and determination were spreading among a new generation, a generation that would no longer be prepared to accept the half-measure of home rule. Young men and women throughout the island who had grown up in the euphoria of the late 1880s and early 1890s and witnessed that Irish desire for freedom had been thwarted yet again, not simply by the apparent self-destructive tendencies of the Irish nation, but by the machinations of the British political system. This new generation, like the generation which had preceded Parnellite constitutionalism, had adequate reason to believe that British parliamentarianism was a system that could not be trusted. Even though they knew that armed rebellion had been tried and had failed on numerous occasions, they saw that the constitutional approach had also failed. Aware of this growing trend, some of the older heads, those who had been engaged in the political fight for home rule, realised that a healing would have to take place and a united constitutional front would again have to show that the ballot was preferable to the bullet.

In Arklow, the division between the main nationalist camps remained unbridgeable throughout the 1890s. Things had been said and done that could not easily be forgotten or forgiven by either faction. But nothing lasts forever. A slow and suspicious healing began to take place. It is difficult to say when the first signs of tentative reconciliation appeared. Sometimes it was as nebulous as the names of different people being found sharing platforms or sitting on committees believing, as Michael Molony had always advocated, that some matters were greater than petty rivalries and blinkered politics. It is worthwhile to record a few instances:

In 1894, it became known that the major explosive manufacturer, Kynoch Limited of Birmingham, wished to open a factory in Ireland.[1] It had not decided on a location, but favoured the east coast. Arklow met most of the criteria, but it was the persistence with which the town leaders put their case that persuaded the company to establish its Irish factory in Arklow. To the fore in that campaign were Thomas Troy and Fr Dunphy. Troy was town commission chairman again and he made several trips to England to convince the directors of the wisdom of the move, but he was ably assisted in getting almost full backing in Arklow for the venture through the influence of his godfather and political enemy Fr Dunphy. When the well-to-do residents of Ferrybank objected to the factory being located on their side of the river, worries were raised that the company would pull out even before it arrived. A public meeting was held at the courthouse to resolve the problem. In what was probably the greatest show of cross-community solidarity ever witnessed in Arklow up to that time, the townspeople incontrovertibly displayed that they were capable and willing to set aside sectional and sectarian differences for the general good. The unionist chairman of the town commissioners, Richard Kearon (who had taken the chair from Troy after a recent election) presided, and among those present were Fr Dunphy, Fr Manning, Revd Harrison, Thomas Troy and the rest of the town commissioners of all political shades.[2] This was the type of unity that could have put the lie to those who opposed home rule on the grounds that the Irish were too fractious to govern themselves. Had Dr Molony been alive to witness it, he would, no doubt, have remembered his letter to the *Wicklow News-Letter* in December 1887:

... people of all parties here can unite and pull together for a good project, independent alike of religious and political 'lines of cleavage'. This is a step in the right direction and indicates that even in Arklow modern progress is beginning to make itself felt.

Further evidence of healing rifts was seen in 1896, on the fifth anniversary of Parnell's death. In each October since his massive funeral, large crowds had converged on Dublin's Glasnevin cemetery to commemorate his passing. The *Wicklow News-Letter* issue of 12 October 1896 praised the County Wicklow contingent for its grand turnout, believing it to be the greatest since Parnell's death, and possibly indicating that hard lines of division were beginning to soften. It recorded

> from all corners of the county came the tried men and true who have stood many a severe test in the past and come through unscathed, men who, in far darker days than the present, faced a persecution as terrible as it was subtle, and whose independence and courage have gained the respect of friend and foe alike.

The most interesting phrase in this is 'in far darker days than the present', indicating that an easing of tension was taking place. It then went on to name the centres in Wicklow which were represented within the county contingent; Wicklow town (the largest), Rathnew and Ashford, Roundwood, Rathdrum, Aughrim, Annacurra, Avoca, Tinahely, Shillelagh, Carnew, Barndarrig, Bray, Delgany, Greystones, Kilmacanogue, Dunlavin, Blessington and Ballyknockan. But it was the 'unusual, and even unexpectedly, large' Arklow contingent which was given special mention.

> In this town where the adherents of Independence had such a hard battle to fight for their political existence, the reaction in favour of Parnellism has been most marked, and this was demonstrated beyond all doubt by the strength and enthusiasm of the contingent which it sent to Dublin.

With remarkable attention to detail, the newspaper then listed many of those present in the various contingents. Of the 153 people from Arklow named, however, none is immediately recognisable as federationist. Certainly none of the local clergy – Roman Catholic or Church of Ireland – made the journey. In fact, of the literally thousands of names recorded from the county not one was a clergyman.

On 26 December 1896, the *Wicklow Star* carried a short article in memory of Dr Molony. It was an odd piece in that it was not timed to mark an anniversary, Molony having died on 22 October 1892, but it is an important piece to historians as it included a sketch which is the only image known to have survived of the man. It also serves to show that his memory was still alive four years after his untimely death. The writing was politically neutral, concentrating on his professional life and work rather  than the more polemical stance of the *Wicklow News-Letter*. It might be deemed a unifying rather than a divisive piece.

By 1900, the divisions within constitutional nationalism were ready to be bridged. Under the leadership of John Redmond, the National League and the National Federation (the Parnellite and anti-Parnellite factions) regrouped under the name of the United Irish League, and the Irish Party regained some of its political clout. As the first decade of the new century closed, new legislation divested the House of Lords of blocking bills for more than two years. This meant that any bill passed by the Commons would become law after twenty-four months even without the consent of the Lords.

The way was open for a new Home Rule for Ireland bill. It was passed by the Commons in 1912 and it became law in 1914. The outbreak of World War 1 and the Easter Rising of 1916, and the resistance of northern unionists allowed the British government to renege on its parliamentary duties and home rule was consigned to history – but that is another story for another day.

*

What of the main protagonists in the turmoil (or various strands of turmoil) recorded in these pages? What follows is a brief account of the subsequent careers of each. Some are very brief, others, such as Thomas Troy, need longer summaries.

William Corbet (1824-1909)

After Corbet lost the 1892 election to John Sweetman, he continued to remain faithful to Parnell's policies, and he regained the East Wicklow seat in the general election of 1895, replacing the anti-Parnellite Edward Peter O'Kelly, who had won Sweetman's seat just three months previously. Corbet retired from parliament at the general election of 1900, aged 76.[3]

Fr James Dunphy (1828–1914)

Fr Dunphy remained as parish priest of Arklow until his death in 1914. Although his health declined slowly and he became increasingly reliant on representation at meetings and assemblies rather than attending himself, he never let loose the reins. He had an infant boys' school built on Harbour Road, appropriately named after St Peter the fisherman, and was an ardent supporter of the County Wicklow Vocational Education Committee attempts to establish Arklow as the location of one of the five pilot vocational schools established in Ireland in 1905.[4] It had humble beginnings, housed in various locations around the town, and its purpose-built home (beside the house

in which Dr Molony had lived) was not built until 1914. It was officially opened just days after Fr Dunphy's death.

Dunphy's funeral was one of the largest ever seen in Arklow. His monument, a Celtic cross decorated in the icons of his profession, is in the town cemetery. It is less than 100 yards from where Dr Molony's remains lie, near neighbours in death as they had been in life. We can only hope that they tolerate each other now. It is not known if he and his godson Thomas Troy reconciled their differences.

Fr William Dunphy (1832-1911)

Fr James Dunphy's brother William continued to remain prominent in County Wicklow as both a Catholic parish priest and as
a United League figurehead and speaker. Not surprisingly, when
he died his obituary in the *Wicklow People* was fulsome in its
praise of this 'ideal priest', 'zealous priest', and 'true patriot'.[5]
After serving in both Rathdrum and Ovoca parishes, he was
appointed parish priest of Naul in north County Dublin in
1887, a position he held for twelve years. He became parish
priest of Barndarrig in 1899 and held that post until his death.
The issue of the *Wicklow People*, 4 March 1911, carried a report
of his large funeral, recalling how he had been a stalwart of tenants, standing against 'landlord tyranny, rapacity and eviction'.
It reminded its readers how he had saved the day at Redcross
when the police were massed against the people. He was, in
short, 'a nationalist of the first rank'.

Fr Laurence Farrelly (?-1911)

Coincidentally, in the column beside the eulogy to Fr William
Dunphy was news of the death of Fr Laurence Farrelly.[6] Farrelly
had died on 25 February, within days of William Dunphy's
death, by which time he had become parish priest of Ashford.
He had been in poor health for the final two years. Like
William Dunphy, the *Wicklow People* regarded him as 'a strong
patriot and a useful worker in the sacred ministry'. The death of
these two colleagues in religion and politics prompted a vote of
sympathy by the Rathdrum Poor Law Guardians when John
Barry lamented the passing of 'two distinguished and devoted
churchmen, and ardent and lifelong supporters of our country's
claim to nationhood.'

Revd Richard Hallowes (1848-1915)

Revd Hallowes, like Fr Dunphy, remained in Arklow until his
death in 1915. He continued street-preaching into the 1890s,
but it no longer inflamed passions as it had done during the

period covered in this book. The remainder of his rectorship was more measured, partly perhaps because of the disapproval of many of the Church of Ireland community.

Fr John Manning (1862-1933)

Fr John Manning started his curacy in Arklow in August 1888. From the beginning, he became close with Fr James Dunphy and their relationship deepened as Dunphy aged. References to him in the newspapers of the time show that, although he shared Laurence Farrelly's political beliefs, he was more measured in his utterances. He displayed a coolness under pressure and was rational in his approach to events. Ironically, it was perhaps these qualities which retarded his promotion to parish priest. For twenty-six years he served under Fr James Dunphy and particularly in the latter years he was effectively running the parish. It was only after Fr Dunphy's death in 1914 that Manning was finally given his own parish at Aughrim, eight miles west of Arklow.

Not only was the church grateful to him for his service to his mentor, but so were Dunphy's family and, in one twist of fate in this story, their debt to him was repaid. As Manning himself began to age, a new curate was assigned to him, Fr Paul Phelan. Phelan took on more responsibilities for the parish just as Manning had done in Arklow, and when Manning died in 1933, Fr Phelan replaced him as Aughrim's parish priest. Paul Phelan was James Dunphy's nephew.

'Mrs Dr' Molony

I find the lack of information about Michael Molony's widow frustrating and offensive to her memory. Like 'Shakespeare's Sister', she has been obliterated because of the newspapers not once referring to her by her name. After she put the contents of the house up for auction just weeks after her husband's death, she disappeared from Arklow. The only reference to her thereafter was the mention made by the *Wicklow News-Letter* in the report of the unveiling of the monument to her husband in August 1893, when she is listed 134th out of the named 160 of the estimated 2,000 present. She remains an enigma.

John Sweetman (1844-1936)

Sweetman was the federationist candidate who took William Corbet's seat in the general election of 1892. Ironically, he became a Parnellite in 1895 and resigned the seat on 8 April that year. At the resulting by-election held eighteen days later, he stood as a Parnellite candidate but was defeated by Edward Peter O'Kelly, the anti-Parnellite candidate in a closely fought three-way contest. At the general election in July 1895 Sweetman stood in North Meath, where he narrowly failed to unseat the sitting anti-Parnellite M.P. James Gibney.[7]

He became more radicalised as the new century dawned and he was one of the founders of Sinn Féin in 1905, succeeding Edward Martyn to be the second president of the party three years later in 1908. He was arrested and detained briefly after the 1916 Easter Rising. He turned down a Sinn Fein nomination for the 1918 general election on the grounds that he was too old, then being seventy-four. His son Roger Sweetman was elected T.D. for North Wexford from 1918 to 1921. Sweetman supported the pro-treaty faction in the civil war period but later denounced the government of W T Cosgrave for its abandonment of Griffith's protectionist economic policies, and supported Fianna Fáil after 1927. Throughout his life he wrote many letters to Irish newspapers, and in the late 1920s and early 1930s he was a contributor to the *Leader* edited by D P Moran. He was fiercely opposed to the Blueshirts, comparing Eoin O'Duffy to Hitler. He also opposed plans to build a Catholic cathedral in Merrion Square, Dublin where he himself lived, on the grounds that this would cause great trouble and inconvenience to the residents. He died in Dublin in 1936. His papers were acquired by the National Library of Ireland c.2008 and are currently being catalogued.

Thomas J Troy (1860-1904)

Thomas Troy served as chairman of the Arklow town commissioners several times throughout the 1890s, and was constantly trying to get businesses to invest in Arklow. In fact, he concentrated so much on the well-being of the town that his personal finances failed. He and his brother lost property to the local bank because of their inability to service loans. He was particularly vociferous in urging the re-instigation of the once very lucrative oyster dredging in Arklow.[8] If self-interest was a motivating factor, it was no more so than any other businessman's, and in general his schemes would have had wide-reaching benefits. Despite his innovative thinking, he was no businessman when it came to his own well-being. His family fortunes had been in decline,[9] and by 1904 his business interests were in tatters. His sole income was from seafaring, and even there his luck was about to run out. By 1904 his only means of income was as master of a steam ship *Fitzwilliam*, which disappeared without trace in the North Sea in 1904. His twenty-year-old son Michael was with him. He was bound from Liverpool to Gothenberg in Sweden, with a cargo of naphtha, a highly explosive substance, at a time when war was in the air. The explosion, if that was the cause of the disappearance, may have been accidental, but there was a strong rumour that she was sunk as an act of war.[10] His widow and their children left the town soon afterwards and the family became dispersed, settling in England, the United States and Australia. Nothing remains in Arklow of this remarkable man. One consolation is that sometime in the 1890s at least a degree of reconciliation between him and the local clergy had been reached, if the eulogies of Fr Manning are to be accepted. No record was made of Fr Dunphy's reaction to the loss of his godson.

CONCLUSION

This study of Arklow in the 1880s and early 1890s was suggested to me by the late Mae Greene, founder member, secretary, chairperson and eventually president of the Arklow Historical Society. She had heard the story of the rivalry between Fr James Dunphy and Dr Michael Molony from her mother who was born at the time of, or very shortly after, the events recounted in the preceding pages. It must be twenty years since she first asked me to look into it. It took several years for the idea to simmer and nine years' work on-and-off to bring it to fruition. Sadly, far too late for Mae to see what my investigation turned up.

So, what did come to light? For a start, as is usually the case, it proved to be far more complex than a straightforward clash of personalities. There were understandable reasons – perhaps not amounting to justifications, but valid reasons nonetheless – for their mutual animosity, and these reasons went far beyond simple personal like or dislike. To each, the other represented an unacceptable mindset, personifying social, cultural and political divisions within the town. Every community is composed of smaller sub-groupings, each with its own aims and concerns. Such internal groupings are described as 'communities of interest', overlapping and confusing the main 'lines of cleavage', to use Molony's own words. In doing this, they show the complexities of everyday life in even the smallest of towns. They exist in even the calmest of times; they thrive in the most unsettled. And the 1880s and early 1890s were very unsettled times throughout Ireland.

The main division had been immediately recognisable, that of nationalist and unionist; but what sort of nationalist? Home ruler with land reform as a secondary target after political self-determination had been achieved? Land reformer who believed that tenant rights was the primary aim with home rule a logical next step? A nationalist who believed in the central power of the Dublin–based branch of the National League, or one who advocated the authority of the local branch? Did a nationalist have to be a Roman Catholic to be 'truly Irish'? Did the clergy have an automatic right to leading positions in local branches of the league? Were all Protestants unionist or more hard-line loyalist? Did the local branch of the National League support women's suffrage for its own sake, or simply when the numbers made it attractive? Were the unionists really opposed to women's suffrage in principle, or again was it simply a matter of the tallies being 'right' or 'wrong'? Could Catholic national-ist and Protestant unionist ever find common ground?

This last question is the pivotal one in this story. Michael Molony believed they could and in forming, or at least helping to form, the Arklow Independent Ratepayers' Association he showed that commonality and compromise were possible. In this he advocated nothing new.

The entire basis of the home rule movement, as envisaged by its founder Isaac Butt, was such identification of shared interests. In the words of Michael MacDonagh, he managed to get concensus among 'Liberal and Conservative with a tang of Fenianism and Orangeism'. In the Commons, Irish liberal and conservative M.Ps. agreed to act as a united party when it came to matters affecting Ireland, but in all other matters they were free to act according to their opinions or party whether liberal or conservative.

This is exactly what Molony tried to do at local level a dozen years later, but a great deal had happened in Ireland dur-ing those dozen crucial years – the Land League had been formed and suppressed, the National League had taken its place, the Irish Party under Parnell had advanced the cause of Irish independence to a degree never achieved before – and positions had hardened. Anyone who didn't toe the line or who consorted with the perceived enemy for any reason was deemed a traitor to that cause. Worse, as the leaders of the local branch of the National League were the parish priest and his most vocal curate, refusal to follow the demands of the league was to fly in the face of Catholicism.

What made Molony's defiance more reprehensible in the eyes of Dunphy's supporters was the fact – and *fact* it was whether Molony cared to admit it or not – was that his candidacy for the position of medical officer in April 1885 was successful only because of Dunphy's power in the community and his new-found control over the majority of the dispensary committee members. Without that control, no Catholic doctor would have been successful, irrespective of how well qualified the applicant may have been. Molony denied this reality, but even if he did reluctantly accept it in his most private thoughts he would never have considered himself indebted to Dunphy for pulling the strings on his behalf. He would be beholden to no one and, in the eyes of the local league, that refusal was a direct affront to Dunphy as recognised leader of the nationalist movement in the area and as the spiritual leader of all Catholics in the parish. Molony's unapologetic cavorting with strongly unionist elements on committees with which the Catholic clergy would have no truck confirmed him, again in the eyes of Dunphy's adherents, as a political apostate.

The inextricable merging of religion and politics was exacerbated by the street preaching of the Revd Richard Hallowes. Evangelical Protestantism was regarded as being as closely aligned with conservative unionism as Roman Catholicism was aligned with nationalism (whose emblem, according to one cleric in west Wicklow 'should be the <u>Cross and the Shamrock intertwined'</u>). Yet, many local Protestants disapproved of Hallowes' antics, as did Dublin castle, the local magistrates, and Dr Molony.

Mention has already been made of women's right to vote. No doubt there was division within the various communities of interest over whether women should be allowed to take part in the public sphere. There were even those who questioned whether women could be regarded as 'persons' under the act which established the qualifications of voters in municipal elections. Those for or against women's suffrage did not base their belief on either Catholic nationalism or Protestant unionism, it was based on the conservative (social rather than political conservatism) belief that the woman's place was in the private sphere of the home and not in the 'man's world' of politics. This social conservatism was as strong in the minds and hearts of many Catholics as Protestants, whether middle class merchants or unskilled labourers. It will be remembered that the question of whether the women should vote in the municipal election was based not on whether they had an intrinsic right as adults to take part in the democratic (severely restrictive though it was) process, but which way their votes would go.

Another community of interest was the beginning of organised labour for unskilled workers. In Arklow in the 1880s about one-third of the population was Protestant. While a disproportionate number of these Protestants belonged to the middle class, many were working class. Unskilled Protestant labourers lived and worked beside unskilled Catholic labourers. They came together to form unions in a bid to protect themselves from exploitation by middle class Protestant and Catholic employers. This leaving aside religious and possibly political differences for the sake of common good was exactly what Dr Molony advocated among his middle-class colleagues in the Independent Ratepayers' Association, yet there is nothing to say if he approved or disapproved of such alliances among the working class. Even the term 'working class' must be divided into areas of community interest, because craft workers, for the most part, were as opposed to the formation of unskilled labourers' unions as the employers were, fearing the move was a threat to their perceived social superiority.

All these factors – nationalist/unionist, home rule/land reform, Catholic/Protestant, male/female, employer/employee, skilled/unskilled and general class division – must be taken into consideration when looking at the personal relationship between Fr James Dunphy and Dr Michael Molony. Their mutual antipathy stemmed from the conflicting aims of the various communities of interest then prevalent not only in Arklow and the surrounding district, but throughout the entire island of Ireland. Their early hopes of mutual friendship and respect were quickly dashed as they each recognised something in the other that was opposed to their fundamental outlook. Under different political and social circumstances, they might well have become close friends and confidants. As it was, the initial promise gave way to vitriolic name-calling, back-biting, accusation and counter-accusation.

How long would it have gone on? Who can say? Molony's untimely death at the age of thirty-one took place when the divisions which polarised the two men were at their greatest. Had he lived another twenty years would they have reconciled, as Tom Troy seems to have at least been partially reconciled with the clergy at the time of his death in 1904? Would Dunphy and Molony have set aside their mutual dislike for the sake of the common good as the National League and the National Federation did in the opening years of the 1900s to form the United Irish League? If that had happened, would Dunphy and his curates have attended Molony's funeral as reconciled colleagues if not as friends? Who can tell? As with Parnell's untimely death, Molony's demise in 1892 is one of the great 'what ifs' in the history of the locality.

Molony's headstone and that of Fr Dunphy stand within 100 yards of each other in Arklow cemetery, yet one cannot be seen from the other, each obscured by other monuments, trees and bushes that stand between them. As in life, they are geographically close but there are simply too many things in the way.

BIBLIOGRAPHY

ABBREVIATIONS:

AHSJ   *Arklow Historical Society Journal*
DDA   Dublin Diocesan Archives
NAI   National Archives of Ireland
NLI   National Library of Ireland
PRAI   *Proceedings of the Royal Irish Academy*
RBG   Rathdrum Board of Guardians
RBGM   Minute books of the Rathdrum Board of Guardians
RCBL   Representative Church Body Library
TAB   Tithe Applotment Books
WHSJ   *Wicklow Historical Society Journal*

ARCHIVES:
Arklow Maritime Museum
Blackrock College
Carlow College
County Wicklow Archives, Minutes of the Rathdrum Board of Guardians
DDA, Cullen Papers, Walsh Papers
NAI, TAB
NLI, Townsend-Trench, John, *Valuation of the town of Arklow* 1877
Pat Power Collection, Arklow.
Pontifico Collegio Irlandese, Rome
RCBL
Registry of Deeds
Rockwell College, Tipperary
Royal College of Physicians, Edinburgh
Royal College of Surgeons, Edinburgh
St Saviour's, Church of Ireland, Arklow – Preacher Books
University College Cork
Valuation Office, Irish Life Centre, Dublin

NEWSPAPERS & JOURNALS:
Daily Express
Dublin Evening Mail

Freeman's Journal
Lancet
The medical press circular
Nationalist & Tipperary Advertiser
Times (London)
Wicklow News-Letter
Wicklow People
Wicklow Star

ACTS OF PARLIAMENT & GOVERNMENT PUBLICATIONS
10 Geo. IV, c. 7 (Roman Catholic Relief Act, 13 April 1829)
32 Geo. III, c.24 [Ireland] (18 June 1792)
48 & 49 Vic. c.3
33 & 34 Vic. c.46
45 & 46 Vic. c.13, (19 June 1882)
Land Law (Ireland) Act (1881)
10 & 11Vic. c.34. Towns Improvement Clauses Act (1847),
Census of Ireland 1871, 1881, 1891
Registration of births and deaths (Ireland) Act, 1863
*Memorandum giving the facts as to the STREET PREACHING IN
ARKLOW* (London, 1892)

GENEALOGICAL RECORDS
Ancestry.co.uk
Irish Midlands Ancestry
Tipperary Family History Research
Wicklow Family History Research

ARTICLES, PAMPHLETS & BOOKS:
Arklow Parish Magazine vol. VIII, no.96, December 1895
Boylan, Henry (ed.), *A dictionary of Irish biography* (3rd
    edition, Dublin, 1998)
Butt, Isaac, *Irish federalism; its meaning, its objects, and its hopes*
    (Dublin, 1870)
Byrne, Joseph, *Byrne's dictionary of Irish Local History* (Cork, 2004)
Byrne, Michael, 'St Michael's Terrace – a legacy of the Carysforts' in
    AHSJ 2001-2002.
Carrigan, Rev William, *History and antiquities of the diocese of Ossory*
    (Dublin, 1905 in three vols.)
Connolly, S.J., *Priests and people in pre-Famine Ireland* (Dublin, 2001).

'County Wicklow farmers' club and tenants' defence association circular', dated Feb 1873.

Cruise O'Brien, Conor, *Parnell and his party 1880-90* (Oxford, 1957)

Donnelly, Brian, *For the betterment of the people; a history of Wicklow County Council* (Wicklow, 1999)

Doyle, Peggy, *The Coolgreany evictions 1887* (Coolgreaney, 1986)

Forde, Frank, *Maritime Arklow* (Dun Laoghaire, 1988)

Foster, Roy, 'Parnell and his neighbours' in Hannigan, Ken and Nolan, William (eds.)*Wicklow history and society* (Dublin, 1994)

Foster, Roy, *Charles Stewart Parnell: the man and his family* (Harvester Press, 1976)

Geary, L.M., *The plan of campaign, 1886-91* (Cork, 1986)

Hannigan, Ken and Nolan, William (eds.)*Wicklow history and society* (Dublin, 1994)

Holmes, Janice, 'The role of open-air preaching in the Belfast riots of 1857' in *PRIA*, 102C, no.3 (Dublin, 2002)

Hurlbert ,William Henry, *Ireland under coercion, the diary of an American* (?, 1888), see electronic sources

Kee, Robert, *Ireland, a history* (London, 1980)

Leslie, Canon J.B. and revised, edited and updated by Wallace, W.J.R.,*Clergy of Dublin and Glendalough, biographical succession lists,* (Dublin, 2001)

Lewis, Samuel (ed.), *A topographical dictionary of Ireland,* (London, 1837 in two volumes)

Lyons, F.S.L. *Charles Stewart Parnell* (London, 1978).

MacDonagh, Michael, *The home rule movement* (Dublin, 1920)

Marshall, M. 'The Three Schools at Carysfort' in *AHSJ* 1996/97

Medical directory 1886, 1893

Medical register, 1883

Micks, W.L. *An Account of the Constitution, Administration and Dissolution of the Congested Districts Board for Ireland from 1891 to 1923* (Dublin 1925)

Molony, M.J., 'Aural reservoir' in*The medical press circular*

Morrison, John, 'Arklow Chemical Works Limited', in *Journal of the* *Tyne Social Chemical Society, 1872*

Murphy, Hilary, *The Kynoch era in Arklow 1895-1918* (Wexford, no date but c.1975).

Murray, P.J., 'The Glenart estate' in *AHSJ 1982*

Nairn, Richard & Crowley, Miriam, *Wild Wicklow, nature in the garden of Ireland,* (Dublin, 1998),

Ó Cathaoir, Eva, 'Revoluntionary undercurrents in Wicklow and south Dublin' in *Bray Historical Record no.5 the journal of the Old Bray Society 1991*

O'Cleirigh, Noel, *All Our Yesterdays, Arklow Community College 1905-2005; Centenary Year- Book* (Arklow, 2005).

O'Donnell, Ruán, *Aftermath, post-rebellion insurgency in Wicklow, 1799-1803*, (Dublin, 2000)

Ó Lionán, Fíachra, *Croghan to the sea*, (Castletown Development Group, no date but c.2000)

Parnell, Katherine, *Charles Stewart Parnell, his love story and political life* (London, 1914)

Power, Pat, 'Arklow Rock quarries thrived under Parnell' in *Wicklow People*

Power, P.J., *The Arklow calendar* (Arklow, 1981).

Rees, Jim, *Arklow, the story of a town*, (Arklow, 2004)

Rees, Jim, 'The cholera epidemic in Arklow, 1866' in *AHSJ 1982*

Rees, Jim, *The fishery of Arklow 1800-1950* (Dublin, 2008)

Rees, Jim, *The life of Captain Robert Halpin* (Arklow, 1992)

Rees, Jim, 'The Storm of 1886' in *AHSJ 1987*

Rees, Jim, 'Captain Thomas Troy, 1860-1904' in *AHSJ 2009/2010*

Rees, Jim & Charlton, Liam, *Arklow – last stronghold of sail* (Arklow, 1985)

Shepherd, E. & Beasley, G., *The Dublin and south eastern railway* (Leicester, 1998)

Spellissy, S. *Window on Aran* (Ennis, 2003)

Sr. Magdalena, 'A sketch of the history of the Arklow convent' in *AHSJ 1983*

Stenton , M. & Lees, S.(eds.) *Who's Who of British Members of Parliament*: Vol. II 1886-1918, (The Harvester Press 1978).

Stewart, Colin & Costelloe, Jean, *Old Ironside*, (Rathdrum, 2001).

Sullivan, S.J., Priests and people in pre-Famine Ireland, 1780 1845 (Dublin, 2001)

Thom's directory 1884

Townsend-Trench, John, *Valuation of the town of Arklow 1877*, (NLI MS)

Walker Brian M., (ed.) *Parliamentary election results in Ireland 1801–1922* (Dublin, 1978).

ELECTRONIC:

http://griffiths.askaboutireland.ie/gv4/gv_start.php

http://www.libraryireland.com/topog/d5.php

http://www.unc.edu/celtic/catalogue/manuscripts/durrow.html

http://en.wkipedia.org/wiki/Wicklow_(UK_Parliament_constituency)

http://www.Gutenberg.org/files/14511/14511-8.txt   [William Henry

Hurlbert, *Ireland under coercion, the diary of an American* (?, 1888), e-book]

http://www.tfhr.org

http://multitext.ucc.ie/d/Home_RuleThe_Elections_of_1885_1886

http://en.wikipedia.org/wiki/index.html?curid=443211

http://www.clarelibrary.ie/eolas/coclare/genealogy/delahunty/chap5_francis_hynes_execution_1882.ht also /delahunty/chap6_murder_near_ennis.htm

http://www.failteromhat.com/book/mcdonnell-homerule.htlm p. 108

http://www.vatican.va/holy_father/leo_xiii/encyclicals/documents/hf_lxiii_enc_24061888_saepe-nos_en.html

http://hansard.millbanksystems.com/people/mr-william-corbet/1889

http://hansard.millbanksystems.com/commons/1890/jun/19/open-air-preaching-at-arklow

www.wikipeadia.org/wiki/Wicklow_(UK_Parliament_constituency)

http://archive.org/stream/landlawirelanda00healgoog#page/n12/mode/2up.

www.arts-humanities.net/.../eppi_enhanced_british_parliamentary_papers. EPPI: Enhanced British Parliamentary Papers on Ireland, 1801 – 1922

Library@RoyalNavalMuseum.org

FOOTNOTES

Chapter 1: Fr James Dunphy, P.P.

1 For a description of the fishermen's calendar and other aspects of their lives see Jim Rees, *The Fishery of Arklow 1800-1950*, (Dublin, 2008), pp.14-24.

2 Also referred to as Ballybooden and Ballyboden. For the sake of clarity I will use Ballyboodin throughout as this is the form used in Griffith's *Valuations*.

3 Letter from Margaret White Mulligan, head research officer with Irish Midlands Ancestry to me dated 24 Aug 2009, quoting register entries for the Roman Catholic parish of Durrow

4 Ibid.

5 *Wicklow People*, 25 Feb 1911.

6 Headstone to Very Revd Joseph Dunphy, parish priest, in the grounds of Mooncoin parish church, County Kilkenny.

7 NAI, TAB 24/31 film 85

8 Samuel Lewis (ed.) *A topographical dictionary of Ireland*, (London, 1837 in two volumes), ii, pp.494-5

9 Ibid. http://www.libraryireland.com/topog/d5.php accessed 27 Aug 2009.

10 Now housed in Trinity College, ms a.4.15(57). See http://www.unc.edu/celtic/catalogue/manuscripts/durrow.html

11 *Wicklow People*, 25 Feb 1911

12 *Wicklow People*, 28 Nov 1914

13 Rev William Carrigan, CC, *History and antiquities of the diocese of Ossory* (Dublin, 1905 in three vols.), iii, p.452.

14 Headstone in Mooncoin church grounds.

15 Ibid.

16 Roman Catholic Relief Act, 13 April 1829 (10 Geo. IV, c. 7).

17 For a concise history of tithes in Ireland see Joseph Byrne, *Byrne's dictionary of Irish Local History* (Cork, 2004), pp.303-6.

18 S.J. Connolly, *Priests and people in pre-Famine Ireland, 1780-1845* (Dublin, 2001), p.219.

19 Byrne, *Byrne's dictionary* ... p.305.

20 In accordance with these wishes, when he died in Genoa, Italy on a pilgrimage to Rome in May 1847, O'Connell's heart was embalmed and taken to the Irish College in Rome and his body was returned to Ireland and buried in Glasnevin.

21 Connolly, *Priest and people* ... p.89.

22 Carrigan, *History and antiquities* ... *Ossory*, iii, p.452.

23 E-mail from Vera Orschel, *archivista, Pontifico Collegio Irlandese, Roma* to Jim Rees, 24 Sept 2007.

24 E-mail from Fr John McEvoy, Carlow College, to Jim Rees, 16 Aug 2007.

25 DDA, Cullen Papers, Redmond to Cullen, file II 3339/7, 19 Aug 1857.

26 Ibid, dated 30 Oct 1857; dated 15 Nov 1857; and dated 20 Dec 1857

27 Ibid, dated 30 Oct 1857

28 Ibid. dated 12 Nov 1857

29 Ibid, dated 30 Oct 1857
30 DDA, Redmond to Cullen, file II 339/4 dated 27 Mar 1856; dated 16 May 1857
31 ibid, dated 27 Mar 1856
32 DDA, Redmond to Cullen, file II 339/4 dated 18 Jan 1856
33 DDA, Redmond to Cullen, file II 320/5 dated 20 Jan 1864
34 DDA, Redmond to Cullen, file II 339/4 dated 22 June 1856
35 See for example, DDA, Redmond to Cullen, file II 339/4, dated 27 March 1856; ibid, dated 20 May 1856; ibid, dated 6 July 1856; ibid dated 6 July 1856
36 DDA, Redmond to Cullen, file II 339/4 dated 20 May 1856
37 ibid. dated 27 Sept 1856
38 ibid. dated 7 Oct 1856
39 DDA, Redmond to Cullen, file II 339/4, dated 18 Jan 1856
40 ibid, dated 12 Feb 1856
41 Rees, *The Fishery of Arklow*, pp.29-31
42 DDA Cullen Papers, File II section 339/4, Redmond to Cullen dated 16 Oct 1856, and File II section 339/7, Redmond to Cullen dated 2 Mar 1857.
43 See, for example, DDA, Walsh papers.
44 Inscription on the altar in Ss Mary and Peter parish church, Arklow.
45 Unpublished brief history of Ss Mary and Peter's Church, Arklow, circulated in 1961 as part of the church's centenary celebrations. Copy in author's possession. Also plaques inside the church.
46 DDA, Walsh papers, File II section 339/4 dated 25 Feb 1856 et al throughout the 1850s and 1860s.
47 Jim Rees, 'The Cholera epidemic in Arklow, 1866' in *Arklow Historical Society Journal 1982*. No page numbers; Sr Magdalena 'A sketch of the history of the Arklow convent' in *Arklow Historical Society Journal 1983*. No page numbers.
48 *Wicklow People*, 28 Nov 1914
49 P. J.Murray, 'The Glenart estate' in *Arklow Historical Society Journal 1982*. No page numbers.
50 *The Address of the Roman Catholic Clergy residing on his Lordship's estate in the Parish of Arklow* dated 1872 in the possession of Mr Allen Proby, Inch, County Wexford, reproduced in full in Jim Rees, *Arklow – the story of a town* (Arklow, 2004), pp.181-2
51 Michael Byrne, 'St Michael's Terrace – a legacy of the Carysforts' in *Arklow Historical Society Journal 2001-2002*, pp.57-60.
52 For a general overview of these developments see Rees, *Arklow Fishery* and Frank Forde, *Maritime Arklow* (Dun Laoghaire, 1988).
53 32 Geo. III, c.24 [Ireland] (18 June 1792)
54 *Wicklow News-Letter* 17 Apr 1869
55 ibid. 22 July 1876
56 Forde, *Maritime Arklow*, p.280-1.
57 *Wicklow News-Letter* 22 July 1876
58 *Wicklow News-Letter* Dec 1877
59 ibid. 6 Jan 1878
60 45 & 46 Vic. c.13, 19 June 1882.

Chapter 2: Home Rule, Land League and the National League

1   33 & 34 Vict., c.46
2   *County Wicklow farmers' club and tenants' defence association* circular, dated Feb 1873. Copy in author's possession
3   The variant spellings Molony and Moloney were used interchangeably in regard to this man and his family in a wide range of sources. I have opted for the former for consistency.
4   *County Wicklow farmers' club and tenants' defence association* circular.
5   The following summary is based on several sources including Michael MacDonagh, *The home rule movement* (Dublin, 1920); Isaac Butt, *Irish federalism; its meaning, its objects, and its hopes* (Dublin, 1870).
6   MacDonagh, *The home rule movement*, p.7.
7   Ibid, p.18.
8   Ibid, p.33.
9   Ibid, pp.38 & 39.
10 http://en.wkipedia.org/wiki/Wicklow_(UK_Parliament_constituency) accessed 2 Sept 2009
11 Roy Foster, 'Parnell and his neighbours' in Hannigan, Ken and Nolan, William (eds) *Wicklow history and society* (Dublin, 1994), p.900.
12 See Colin Stewart & Jean Costelloe, , *Old Ironside,* (Rathdrum, 2001).
13 Henry Boylan (ed), *A dictionary of Irish biography* (3rd edition, Dublin, 1998), p.361.
14 Foster, 'Parnell and his neighbours', p.899.
15 MacDonagh, *Home Rule movement,* p.72.
16 *Freeman's Journal,* 24, 26, 28 May 1877.
17 Boylan (ed), *Dictionary of Irish biography*, p.96.
18 Quoted in Robert Kee, *Ireland, a history* (London, 1980), p.120.
19 Ibid, p.123
20 Robert Kee, *Ireland, a history*, p.126.
21 Eva Ó Cathaoir, 'Revolutionary undercurrents in Wicklow and south Dublin' in *Bray Historical Record no.5 the journal of the Old Bray Society 1991*, pp.20-21
22 *Wicklow News-Letter*, 26 Mar 1881.
23 http://archive.org/stream/landlawirelanda00healgoog#page/n12/mode/2up. Accessed 16 June 2012
24 MacDonagh, *Home rule movement*, p.162
25 *Wicklow News-Letter*, 21 Jan 1882.

Chapter 3 Fr Dunphy's Fiefdom

1   I am grateful to historian Pat Power, among whose treasure trove of documents relating to County Wicklow history is a typescript copy of a note on the boundaries of the parish of Arklow as marked on an OS map in the parochial house in Arklow. Apart from the delineated boundaries, pasted to the map (presumably on the back – the map itself is no longer available) was a written list titled 'Boundary of Arklow parish' which describes the townlands on its fringes.
2   *Census of Ireland 1881*
3   Castletown became a separate parish in 1974. Scarcity of priests in the diocese

of Dublin in 2008 necessitated that the separate parishes of Castletown and Arklow should share the same parish priest. Source – Arklow parish office, 12 Nov 2009.

4   Ruán O'Donnell, *Aftermath, post-rebellion insurgency in Wicklow, 1799-1803,* (Dublin, 2000), p.26.

5   *Wicklow People,* 28 Nov 1914.

6   Fíachra Ó Lionán, *Croghan to the sea,* (Castletown Development Group, no date but c.2000), p.85)

7   There are several letters in the DDA giving such figures, for example Dunphy to Walsh, 20 April 1890, and even the unionist *Wicklow News-Letter,* 14 Mar 1885 stated 'two thousand' at the mission in 1885 and also referred to the abstinence from alcohol.

8   Some of the roll books from this pre-1900 school are kept in the Arklow Maritime Museum. See Jim Rees, *Arklow, the story of a town,* (Arklow, 2004), p.229-30.

9   *Freeman's Journal,* 26 Aug 1885 includes these men as curates of Arklow who attended the appointment of Dr William Walsh as archbishop of Dublin.

10 Unpublished and unattributed short biography circulated as part of the centenary celebrations of the consecration of Arklow Catholic parish church, Sts Mary and Peter, in 1961. The author is generally believed to have been respected local historian P J Murray, who died in 1985.

11 For example, his letter to the editor of *Freeman's Journal,* reprinted in *Wicklow News-Letter,* 17 Jan 1891.

12 *Wicklow People,* 4 Mar 1911.

13 Ibid.

14 Ibid.

15 DDA, Walsh papers, Dunphy to Walsh 350/8/-, dated 26 May 1885.

16 William Henry Hurlbert, *Ireland under coercion, the diary of an American* (?, 1888), e-book http://www.Gutenberg.org/files/14511/14511-8.txt accessed 6 Oct 2009, endnote K, no page number but vol.ii, p.216 in the original printed edition. This incident will be dealt with fully in Chapter 7.

17 DDA, Walsh papers, Farrelly to Walsh, dated 4 June 1891.

18 This often appeared as Hanagan, and both variants are used in this book as they appeared in the sources. Condren could sometimes appear as Condron.

19 *Wicklow People,* 28 Nov 1914.

20 John Morrison, 'Arklow Chemical Works Limited', in *Journal of the Tyne Social Chemical Society, 1872,* pp.42-3.

21 *Wicklow News-Letter,* 18 Mar 1882.

22 This was probably Owen Fogarty, a leading Home Rule supporter in the town.

23 *Wicklow News-Letter,* 18 Mar 1882.

24 *Wicklow News-Letter,* 14 Mar 1885.

25 Ibid. 30 May 1885.

26 *Wicklow News-Letter,* 7 Feb 1885.

27 For handiness, further references to this will be simply 'dispensary committee'.

28 The following outline is based on Brian Donnelly, *For the betterment of the people; a history of Wicklow County Council* (Wicklow, 1999).

29 1 & 2 Vict., C.56

30 Donnelly, ... *betterment of the people* ...,, p.7.
31 EPPI 1883-1883, vol. 53, 230. See *Thom's directory 1884*, p.1190 for a comparison with the other eight dispensary districts in the Rathdrum Union.
32 County Wicklow Archives, Minutes of the Rathdrum Board of Guardians, 25 February 1885.
33 Ibid. 11 March 1885.

Chapter 4: Dr Michael J Molony

1   Headstone inscription, Arklow Cemetery.
2   All Moloney/Molony family history details, except that of Michael born 1812, supplied by the Tipperary Family History Research, www.tfhr.org in two blocks, one dated 16 Jan 2008 and the second on 29 Feb 2008.
3   *Wicklow People*, 22 Feb 1890.
4   Tipperary Family History Research, www.tfhr.org, report to author dated 29 Feb 2008.
5   E-mail to author from the librarian of the Royal College of Physicians of Ireland, 17 Oct 2005. See also *Medical directory 1886*, p.1250.
6   *Medical directory 1893*, p.1453. E-mail to the author from Paul Raven, library assistant, Library@RoyalNavalMuseum.org dated 21 Aug 2007.
7   Tipperary Family History Research, www.tfhr.org report to the author dated 16 Jan 2008.
8   The baptismal record lists him simply as Michael, but in later documents he is repeatedly given his full name of Michael Joseph Molony.
9   It is likely that James Street should read John Street as I could find no James Street in Cashel maps or directories for the period.
10 Letter to the author from Edward J. Stirling C.S.Sp., archivist of Rockwell College dated 3 Aug 2004; e-mail to the author from Catríona Mulcahy, College Archivist, UCC, 11 Aug 2004.
11 *Wicklow News-Letter* 29 Oct 1892; *Wicklow Star*, 26 Dec 1896. The Blackrock College archivist informed the author by telephone that despite a very good archive, she could find no record of his having attended there. 28 July 2004.
12 Obituary, *Nationalist & Tipperary Advertiser*, 1 Dec 1894.
13 http://www.rockwellcollege.ie accessed 5 July 2009
14 Obituary, *Wicklow News-Letter*, 29 Oct 1892.
15 E-mail to me from Catríona Mulcahy, College Archivist, UCC, 11 Aug 2004.
16 E-mail to me from Steve Kerr, Asst Librarian, RCS Edinburgh, 3 Aug 2004.
17 Ibid.
18 *Medical Directory*, 1886, p.1250.
19 Obituary, *Wicklow News-Letter*, 29 Oct 1892; *The Medical Directory 1893*, p1453.
20 *The Lancet*, 22 Nov 1884, p.910.
21 Obituary, *Nationalist & Tipperary Advertiser*, 1 Dec 1894.
22 A random selection of entries in the various *Medical Registers* attests to medical officers also having private practices and lucrative contracts.
23 Rathdrum Board of Guardian Minutes, 1 Apr 1885.
24 Cardinal McCabe had died on 11 Feb 1885, just two months previously, and Bishop Walsh was acting until a new appointment was made.
25 DDA, Dunphy to Walsh, Easter Sunday (5 Apr) 1885, ref. 350/8/355.

26   *Freeman's Journal*, 13 Jan 1891.
27   *Wicklow People*, 19 Oct 1889.

Chapter 5: Molony settles in

1   This will become more apparent as the chapter progresses. Also see Rees, *The Fishery* ... pp.10-24

2   Ibid, passim.

3   Census of Ireland, 1871, 1881 and 1891.

4   Frank Forde, *Maritime Arklow* (Dun Laoghaire, 1988), chapters 1, 5, and 6.

5   *Wicklow News-Letter*, 30 May 1885.

6   John Morrison, 'Arklow Chemical Works Limited', (Tyne Chemical Society, 1872). This pamphlet gives a comprehensive description of the factory, but does not give a date of establishment, but from the text it was obviously a relatively recent development.

7   Richard Nairn & Miriam Crowley, *Wild Wicklow, nature in the garden of Ireland*, (Dublin, 1998), p.123.

8   Pat Power, 'Arklow Rock quarries thrived under Parnell' in *Wicklow People*, 13 May 1988.

9   E. Shepherd & G. Beasley, *The Dublin and south eastern railway* (Leicester, 1998), p.154.

10   John Townsend-Trench, *Valuation of the town of Arklow 1877*. This manuscript is now in the National Library of Ireland. A transparency copy is in the author's possession. The terrace and road were re-named St Mary's Terrace and St Mary's Road soon after independence in 1922, but the Church of Ireland-owned Marlborough Hall retained its unionist associations and is still called Marlborough Hall today.

11   It was later renamed St Mary's Terrace.

12   Molony was to be one such resident, see several of his letters to the *Wicklow News-Letter* in August 1890.

13   This is the current number, in the 1880s and 1890s numbering was more fluid and this also appears as No.1 in Valuation Office, Irish Life Centre, Dublin, property number 651851, book 1885-1891.

14   *Wicklow News-Letter*, 19 Nov 1892.

15   Valuation Office, property number 651851, book 1885-1891.

16   The market house was where The Loft pub and restaurant now stand, i.e. 56 Main Street.

17   The site is now occupied by Church Buildings.

18   This graveyard and its Catholic counterpart at Castlepark were closed because of the interment of cholera victims in 1866, and a new graveyard was opened about a mile outside the town. The 'New' Cemetery, sometimes called St Gabriel's, is still in use. Both St Mary's (Protestant) and the Old Abbey Graveyard (Catholic) are now public parks.

19   The village, parish and river of Avoca were more usually spelt Ovoca in the 1880s. Both spellings will appear in this book.

20   John Townsend-Trench, *Valuation of the town of Arklow 1877*. This manuscript is now in the National Library of Ireland. A transparency copy is in the author's possession.

21 Rathdrum Board of Guardians Minutes, 24 Apr 1885.
22 Ibid. 12 May 1885.
23 Ibid. 1 July 1885 and 8 July 1885.
24 Ibid. 15 July 1885.
25 RBG 17/1885
26 Little had changed since the *Wicklow News-Letter*'s scathing report of 9 Dec 1866 in the aftermath of the cholera epidemic in the Fishery.
27 Molony to the RBG 16 Sept 1885.
28 Valuation Office.
28 Ibid, 31 Oct 1885.
30 Ibid, 16 Sept 1885.
31 'Mr M J Molony's "Aural reservoir"', *The Medical Press Circular*, 12 May 1886, p.440.
32 *Wicklow News-Letter*, 22 Aug 1885.
33 DDA, Walsh papers, Dunphy to Walsh dated 30 June 1885.
34 DDA, Dunphy to Walsh, Easter Sunday (5 Apr) 1885.
35 *Wicklow People*, 19 Oct 1889.
36 The series of four letters ranging in date from 9 July 1885 to 22 July 1885 was published in *Wicklow News-Letter* 5 Sept 1885.

Chapter 6: National politics and local division

1   48 & 49 Vic. c.3
2   For useful analyses of these and other developments at national level see Conor Cruise O'Brien, *Parnell and his party 1880-90* (Oxford,1957) and F.S.L. Lyons, *Charles Stewart Parnell* (London, 1978).
3   http://multitext.ucc.ie/d/Home_RuleThe_Elections_of_1885_1886 accessed 26 Sept 2009.
4   *Wicklow News-Letter*, 21 Mar 1885.
5   *Wicklow News-Letter*, 7 Feb 1885.
6   See Town Commissioner election returns in various issues of *Wicklow News-Letter* and *Wicklow People* for a political complexion of Arklow.
7   Forde, *Maritime Arklow*, (pp.56-60). *Wicklow News-Letter*, 5 Dec 1885.
8   *Wicklow News-Letter*, 24 Oct 1885.
9   The full text of this was published in *Wicklow News-Letter*, 7 Nov 1885.
10 *Wicklow News-Letter*, 30 Jan 1886.
11 *Wicklow News-Letter*, 28 Nov 1885.
12 *Wicklow News-Letter*, 5 Dec 1885.
13 *Wicklow News-Letter*, 16 Jan 1886.
14 Ibid., 27 Mar 1886 and 3 Apr 1886 (supplement).
15 Ibid., 10 Apr 1886.
16 http://en.wikipedia.org/wiki/index.html?curid=443211 accessed 2 Oct 2009.
17 *Wicklow News-Letter*, 28 Nov 1885.
18 Ó Lionáin, *Croghan to the sea*, pp.84-86.
19 Boylan, *A dictionary of Irish biography*, p.235.
20 Quoted in Ó Lionáin, pp.84-86.
21 DDA, Walsh papers, Dunphy to Walsh 5 Dec 1885; Taylor to Dunphy, 10 Aug 1886.

22 *Wicklow People*, 19 Oct 1890.

23 *Freeman's Journal*, 13 Jan 1891.

24 *Wicklow People*, 19 Oct 1890. Also, the leader in the *Wicklow News-Letter*, 13 Oct 1888 cites Molony as a member of the central branch of the National League.

25 *Wicklow News-Letter*, 5 Oct 1889.

26 RBG Minutes, 3 Mar 1886.

27 Ibid, 21 April 1886.

28 Ibid, 8 May 1886; 12 May 1886; 16 June, 1886; 23 June 1886; 7 July 1886; 24 July 1886.

29 Ibid, 4 Oct 1886.

30 Ibid, 3 Nov 1886.

31 Registration of births and deaths (Ireland) Act, 1863.

32 For a full account see Jim Rees, 'The Storm of 1886' in *AHSJ* 1987, pp.52-56.

33 *Wicklow News-Letter*, Oct 1886.

34 Marshall, M. 'The Three Schools at Carysfort' in *AHSJ* 1996/97, p.34

35 *Wicklow News-Letter*, Jan 1887

36 *Wicklow News-letter*, 9 Jan 1886.

37 *Wicklow News-Letter*, 16 Jan 1886.

Chapter 7: The Coolgreaney evictions

1   This is also spelt Coolgreany, and the spelling on roadsigns and other official items falls roughly 50/50. I have heard discussions as to which is the 'correct' form, but it can be argued that neither is as both are corruptions of *Cúil Ghréine*, the original Irish name meaning 'the sunny corner', because of its hillside south-facing aspect.

2   Most of this synopsis is based on Peggy Doyle, *The Coolgreany evictions 1887* (Coolgreaney, 1986), augmented chiefly by William Henry Hurlbert, *Ireland under coercion, the diary of an American* (?, 1888), e-book http://www.Gutenberg.org/files/14511/14511-8.txt accessed 6 Oct 2009.

3   Peggy Doyle, *The Coolgreaney evictions 1887*, (1986), p.10. See also www.libraryireland.co/Thom1862/Doan.php accessed 23 Jan 2010; and www.askaboutireland.ie/Griffith valuations accessed 23 Jan 2010.

4   Rental Book, Brooke Estate1889, in the possession of the author. Note the slight difference in spelling from the modern versions.

5   Boylan, *A dictionary of Irish biography*, p.300.

6   Hurlbert, *Ireland under coercion*, no page number.

7   *Wicklow People*, 12 Apr 1890.

8   Hurlbert, endnote K, no page number, but vol.ii, p.216 in the original printed edition.

9   Ibid.

10 http://www.clarelibrary.ie/eolas/coclare/genealogy/delahunty/chap5 francis hynes execution 1882.htalso.../delahunty/chap6 murder near ennis. htm accessed 6 Oct 2009.

11 Hurlbert, no page number.

12 Doyle, *Coolgreany evictions*, p.57.

13 Quoted in Doyle, *Coolgreaney evictions*, pp.5-6.

14 Ibid, p.7.
15 Ibid. p.9
c16 Ibid. p.16
17 MacDonagh, *Home Rule*, p.177.
18 Doyle, *Coolgreany evictions*, p.27.
19 Hurlbert, *Ireland under coercion*, no page number
20 Doyle, *Coolgreany evictions*, p.43
21 *Wicklow News-Letter*, 22 October 1887.

Chapter 8: Extremists and moderates

1   http://www.failteromhat.com/book/mcdonnell-homerule.htlm p. 108, accessed 20 Oct 2009

2   http://www.vatican.va/holy_father/leo_xiii/encyclicals/documents/hf_l-xiii_enc_24061888_saepe-nos_en.hhtml Accessed 18 Nov 2009.

3   Cruise O'Brien, *Parnell and his party, 1880-90*, pp.213-16

4   http://www.failteromhat.com/book/mcdonnell-homerule.htlm p. 108, accessed 20 Oct 2009

5   Cruise O'Brien, *Parnell*, p.214

6   The townland is incorrectly identified in the *Wicklow News-Letter*, 8 Sept 1888, as Coolroe, a townland two miles south of Arklow. The *Wicklow People*, 10 Aug 1889 correctly records it as Coolmore. The correct location has been identified by referring to http://www.askaboutireland.ie/griffithvaluation/index.xml?action=doNameSearch&PlaceID=1436231&county=Wicklow&barony=Arklow&parish=Ennereilly&townland=Coolmore accessed 23 Jan 2010.

7   The following account of the meeting and subsequent trial is taken from *Wicklow News-Letter*, 22 Sept 1888.

8   *Wicklow News-Letter*, 8 Sept 1888 quoting *Daily Express*, 5 Sept 1888.

9   50 & 51 Vict., cap.20.

10 *Wicklow News-Letter*, 24 Dec 1885

11 *Wicklow News-Letter*, Oct 1888.

12 *Wicklow News-Letter*, Oct 1886

13 Doyle, *Coolgreany evictions*, p.23

14 Ibid.

15 See Jim Rees, 'Captain Thomas Troy, 1860-1904' in *AHSJ 2009/2010*, pp.6-19.

16 Details relating to the Troy family are taken from the baptismal and marriage registers of the Roman Catholic parish of Arklow; a 'Birthday Scripture Textbook' and other family papers in the possession of Keith Troy, a grandson of Thomas Troy, living in New South Wales, Australia; and Griffith's Valuation for the Town of Arklow, 1854.

17 Various *Lloyd's Registers*, but the distilled information can be had in Jim Rees & Liam Charlton's *Arklow – last stronghold of sail* (Arklow, 1985) and Frank Forde's *Maritime Arklow* (Dun Laoghaire, 1988)

18 *Wicklow News-Letter*, 31 Dec 1887.

19 Unfortunately, despite a great deal of research, I can find no version of this song extant which might suggest the content.

20   *Wicklow News-Letter*, 24 Nov 1888 and 15 Dec 1888. Hurlbert, *Ireland under coercion*, no page number.bid. endnote K, no page number but vol.ii, p.216 in the original printed edition

21   *Wicklow News-Letter*, 24 Nov 1888.

22   Hurlbert, *Ireland under coercion*, no page number, endnote K, no page number but vol.ii, p.216 in the original printed edition.

23   *Wicklow News-Letter*, 24 Nov 1888.

24   *Wicklow People*, 15 March 1890.

25   *Wicklow People*, 24 Nov 1888; *Wicklow News-Letter*, 1 Dec 1888.

Chapter 9: Widening the divide

1   *Wicklow News-Letter*, 2 Feb 1889, 16 Feb 1889, 30 Mar 1889.

2   In the House of Commons, William Corbet was later to contest the police assertion that a barricade had been erected, or that Fr Farrelly had been expecting the police to arrest him in the middle of the night. Aspects of the subsequent arrest were discussed in the Commons on 27, 28, and 29 March and 1 and 4 April, 1889. http://hansard.millbanksystems.com/people/mr-william-corbet/1889 accessed 13 Feb 2010.

3   Ibid.

4   *Wicklow News-Letter*, 13 Apr 1889.

5   The following account is taken from *Wicklow News-Letter*, 11 May 1889.

6   *Wicklow News-Letter*, 15 Feb 1890, *Wicklow People*, 22 Feb 1890.

7   This is the field in which Áras Lorcháin and St Peter's Boys's School now stand.

8   *Wicklow News-Letter*, 16 Mar 1889.

9   See, for example, *Wicklow News-Letter*, 20 July 1889.

10   *Wicklow News-Letter*, 20 July 1889.

11   Ibid.

12   Ibid.

13   *Wicklow People*, 10 May 1890.

14   Ibid, 6 July 1889.

15   Ibid. 6 July 1889, 12 Oct 189, 15 Mar 1890.

16   Ibid. 9 Nov 1889.

Chapter 10: Another zealous cleric

1   The following biographical details are taken from Canon J.B. Leslie and revised, edited and updated by W.J.R. Wallace, *Clergy of Dublin and Glendalough, biographical succession lists*, (Dublin, 2001).

2   The RCBL have only two documents, neither of which is relevant, and relevant records held by the local rector, Revd Nigel Sherwood, are Preachers' Books from the late 1860s.

3   Petition of support from the parishioners to the rector, W.G. Ormsby, 1871, Representative Church Body Library, MS P24.

4   Preacher's Books, 1886-1914, St Saviour's Church, Arklow

5   Circular dated January 1859 as part of the fundraising campaign for the construction of the new parish church. Copy in author's possession.

6   Geary, L.M., *The plan of campaign, 1886-91* (Cork, 1986), p.104, quoting *Freeman's Journal* 4 Dec 1889, letter from Hamilton to the editor.

7   See Janice Holmes, 'The role of open-air preaching in the Belfast riots of 1857' in *Proceedings of the Royal Irish Academy*, 102C, no.3 (Dublin, 2002), p.60 for a convincing argument showing this connection.

8   Unless otherwise stated the events recorded in this chapter are taken from *Memorandum giving the facts as to the STREET PREACHING IN ARKLOW* (London, 1892)

9   *Wicklow News-Letter*, 12 July 1890

10 *Street preaching in Arklow*, p.3.

11 Ibid.

12 Ibid. p.4.

13 *Wicklow People*, 14 and 21 June 1890.

14 Ibid.

15 *Dublin Evening Mail*, 27 May 1890.

16 *Freeman's Journal*, 28 May 1890

17 This was the sandy area in Lower Tinahask, now occupied by the harbour dock and Arklow Golf Club.

18 *Wicklow News-Letter*, 14 June 1890

19 *Wicklow People*, 21 June 1890.

20 http://hansard.millbanksystems.com/commons/1890/jun/19/open-air-preaching-at-arklow accessed 28 Nov 2009. HC Deb 19 June 1890 vol 345 cc1332-4.

21 *Street preaching in Arklow*, p.4

22 Ibid pp.4-5.

23 DDA, Walsh papers, Dunphy to Walsh, 3 Aug 1890.

24 *Wicklow News-Letter*, 16 Aug 1890.

25 *Street preaching ...*, p.12, section F

26 *Wicklow News-Letter*, 30 Aug 1890.

27 Ibid, 6 Sept 1890.

28 The persistent use of 2,000 as the numbers in large gatherings might be accurate enough, but it does seem to be a default figure for any large assembly.

29 DDA, Walsh papers, Dunphy to Walsh, dated 29 Nov 1890.

30 *Street preaching ...*, p.6.

31 DDA, Walsh papers, Dunphy to Walsh, dated 23 Feb 1891.

32 A court order compelling a person or body to perform a public duty which they are obliged to do. I am grateful to Pauric Hyland, solicitor, for this definition.

33 *Wicklow News-Letter*, 7 Mar 1891.

34 *Street preaching ...*, p.7.

35 Ibid, p.9.

36 Ibid. It is not possible to give a direct correlation between monetary values the and now, but various models suggest that this figure would be worth in excess of €200,000 in 2010 terms.

37 DDA, Walsh papers, Dunphy to Walsh, dated 29 Nov 1890

38 This book is now in the possession of the National Library of Ireland.

39 This account is taken from *Street preaching ...* pp.10-15, which also carries annotations indicating that police records of the event verify its accuracy.

40   *Street preaching ...* p.17.

41　Ibid, p.20.
42　He spent the rest of the year either at his Lincolnshire estate or at his London residence.
43　Ibid, p.22.
44　Ibid. No page number but forms part of an appendix.
45　*Arklow Parish Magazine* vol. VIII, no.96, December 1895, p.2. The author has a copy of this publication in his possession.
46　Power, P.J., *Arklow Calendar*, (Arklow, 1981), p.103.

Chapter 11: Parnell's fall

1　*Wicklow News-Letter*, 20 July 1889.
2　Boylan (ed), *Dictionary of Irish Biography*, pp.365-6.
3　Ibid, p.384.
4　MacDonagh, *Home Rule* p.185.
5　Ibid, p.186. The priest referred to was probably Fr Dunphy.
6　Boylan, p.352
7　MacDonagh, *Home Rule* p.188.
8　Katherine Parnell, *Charles Stewart Parnell, his love story and political life*, (London, 1914), vol i, p.247.
9　Quoted in MacDonagh, *Home Rule* p.190.
10　Ibid.
11　Cruise O'Brien, *Parnell and his party*, pp.166 sqq. O'Brien gives a useful summary of who did know.
12　MacDonagh, p.191.
13　Boylan, *Dictionary of Irish Biography*, pp.352-3.
14　MacDonagh, p.191 and O'Brien as in footnote 11 above.
15　Quoted in MacDonagh, *Home rule*, p.196.
16　Ibid, p.199.
17　Ibid, p.201.
18　Quoted in ibid, pp.201-2.
19　Ibid. p.206.
20　Ibid. pp.222-3.
21　Ibid. p.225.
22　*Wicklow News-Letter*, 22 Nov 1890.
23　Ibid, 27 Dec 1890, giving a lengthy account of his visit home.
24　Ibid, 17 Jan 1891.
25　DDA, Walsh papers, 30 Jan 1891.
26　Ibid, 4 June 1891.

Chapter 12: Division within division

1　Davitt, *The fall of feudalism*, pp. 59-60.
2　*Wicklow People*, 16 and 23 Aug 1890.
3　Ibid. 13 Sept 1890.
4　Ibid. 27 Sept 1890.
5　Ibid. 25 Oct and 1 Nov 1890

6   Rees & Charlton, *Arklow – last stronghold of sail*, p.133; Forde, *Maritime Arklow*, p.91.
7   Forde, *Maritime Arklow*, p.59.
8   Rees & Charlton, *... last stronghold ...*, p.120; Forde, *Maritime Arklow*, p.73.
9   *Wicklow News-Letter*, 29 Nov 1890.
10   *Wicklow People*, 14 Feb 1891.
11   Ibid, 13 and 27 June, 4 July 1891.
12   Towns Improvement Clauses Act (1847) Ch.34, 10 & 11Vict. See *Wicklow People*, 12 Oct 1889 for an outline of this.
13   *Wicklow People*, 12 Oct 1889.
14   Ibid.
15   Ibid.
16   *Freeman's Journal*, 17 Oct 1889.
17   *Wicklow People*, 19 Oct 1889
18   *Wicklow News-Letter*, 18 Oct 1890.
19   The official census figure for 1891 was 4,172. Despite Fr Farrelly's assertion from time to time that the town had 6,000 inhabitants in the late 1880s, it was not until 1966 that the 6,000 mark was reached.
20   *Wicklow News-Letter*, 18 Oct 1890.
21   *Wicklow People*, 27 Sept 1890.
22   *Wicklow News-Letter*, 28 Mar 1891.
23   *Wicklow News-Letter*, 20 Dec 1890.
24   Ibid. 16 and 23 Aug 1890; *Street preaching in Arklow ...*, p.21.
25   *Wicklow News-Letter*, 7 Mar 1891.
26   Census of Ireland 1891.
27   *Wicklow News-Letter*, 15 and 22 Nov 1890.
28   Census of Ireland 1901.
29   *Wicklow News-Letter*, 20 Dec 1890.

Chapter 13: '... no divroce between religion and politics ...'
1   *Wicklow People*, 3 Jan 1891.
2   Ibid. 17 Jan 1891.
3   Cruise O'Brien, *Parnell and his party*, p.335
4   *Wicklow People*, 17 Jan 1891.
5   Ibid. 31 Jan 1891.
6   Ibid. 14 Mar 1891.
7   Ibid. 25 Apr 1891
8   Ibid. 2 May 1891.
9   Ibid.
10   Ibid, 23 May 1891.
11   *Wicklow News-Letter*, 6 June 1891
12   *Wicklow People*, 4 July 1891.
13   MacDonough, *... Home rule ...* p.234
14   Ibid, p.239
15   Ibid.
16   *Wicklow People*, 24 Oct 1891

17 Ibid.14 Nov 1891.
18 *Wicklow People*, 7 Nov 1891.

Chapter 14: Two elections, two outcomes
1   Rathdrum board of guardian minutes, 9 Aug 1892.
2   Ibid. 16 Aug 1892.
3   *Wicklow People*, 20 Feb 1892.
4   Ibid. 16 April 1892
5   Ibid. 30 Jan and 30 April, 1892.
6   Ibid. 19 Dec 1891
7   Spellissy, S. *Window on Aran* (Ennis, 2003), p.43
8   Micks, W.L. *An Account of the Constitution, Administration and Dissolution of the Congested Districts Board for Ireland from 1891 to 1923* Dublin 1925. See also Jim Rees *Arklow – the story of a town* (Arklow, 2004), pp.216-7.
8   *Wicklow People*, 2 April 1892.
10 www.wikipeadia.org/wiki/Wicklow_(UK_Parliament_constituency) accessed 23 Dec 2009.
11 For Halpin's career see Jim Rees, *The Life of Captain Robert Halpin* (Arklow, 1992)
12 *Wicklow News-Letter*, 26 June 1892.
13 Local lore, attested by various crew lists housed in the PRO, Kew, London.
14 Roy Foster, *Charles Stewart Parnell: the man and his family*, p.210.
15 *Wicklow People*, 11 and 25 June 1892.
16 *Wicklow News-Letter*, 2 July 1892.
17 *Wicklow People*, 2 July 1892.
18 Ibid.
19 Ibid.
20 Poor attendance in the Commons had been a major cause of concern for some time, and Corbet was not alone in his lax ways. See Cruise O'Brien, *Parnell*, p.264, footnote 1.
21 *Wicklow News-Letter*, 9 July 1892.
22 *Wicklow News-Letter*, 17 Oct 1891.
23 *Wicklow People*, 9 July 1892.
24 *Wicklow People*, 16 July 1892.
25 It has often been brought to the author's attention in a semi-jocular fashion.
26 *Wicklow People*, 6 Aug 1892.
27 Ibid, 27 Aug 1892.
28 Ibid. 15 Oct 1892

Chapter 15: The death of Dr Molony.
1   *Thom's directory 1884*, p.1190.
2   *The medical directory 1893*, p.1453
3   *Wicklow News-Letter*, 29 Oct 1892.
4   One of several epidemics and threatened epidemics he had dealt with in his six years in Arklow.
5   *Wicklow News-Letter*, 6 February 1892

6   On-line research through avenues such as Ancestry.co.uk did turn up a few pos-
     sibilities – particularly in Scotland and Liverpool – but these were to prove red
     herrings.
7   Personal knowledge.
8   *Wicklow People*, 29 Oct 1892.
9   *Wicklow News-Letter*, 19 Nov 1892.
10   *Wicklow People*, 5 Nov 1892.
11   Rathdrum board of guardian minutes, 3 Nov 1892.
12   Ibid., 12 Dec 1982.
13   Ibid., 12 Dec 1892.
14   *Wicklow News-Letter*, 19 Nov 1892.
15   *Wicklow News-Letter* and *Wicklow People*, both 12 Nov 1892.
16   *Wicklow News-Letter* and *Wicklow People*, both 19 Nov 1892.
17   *Wicklow News-Letter*, 26 Nov 1892. This should read, 'beside of the Catholic
     church' where all such meetings were held, it later became the GAA pitch at
     Castlepark and is now the site of Árus Lorcáin and St Peter's School and possi-
     bly the parish priest's house, the old house then being much nearer the road.
18   A copy of the December 1895 issue is in the author's possession.
19   Quoted in *Wicklow News-Letter*, 28 Jan 1893.
20   *Wicklow News-Letter*, 4 Feb 1893.
21   *Wicklow News-Letter* 5 Aug 1893; *Wicklow People* 12 Aug 1893.

Chapter 16: A slow healing

1   For a brief history of this company see Hilary Murphy, *The Kynoch era in Arklow*,
     1895-1918 (Arklow, c.1975) and chapters elevn and twelve of Rees, *Arklow, the
     story of a town*.
2   Ibid. p.10
3   *Who was who, 1897-1916*
4   Noel O'Cleirigh, *All Our Yesterdays, Arklow Community College 1905-2005,
     Centenary Year-Book* (Arklow, 2005).
5   *Wicklow People*, 25 Feb 1911.
6   Ibid. 4 Mar 1911.
7   Brian M. Walker, (ed) *Parliamentary election results in Ireland 1801–1922*
     (Dublin, 1978), pp. 151, 155.. See also *Who's Who of British Members of
     Parliament*: Vol. II 1886-1918, edited by M. Stenton and S. Lees (The Harvester
     Press 1978). *Times* (of London), 27 Dec 1881, 5 Apr 1889, 3 June 1892, 5 July
     1892, 10 Apr 1895, 17 Sept 1895, 13 Oct 1905 and 10 Sept 1936.
8   For more on this industry see Rees, *The Fishery of Arklow*.
9   See Registry of Deeds records of transactions1893-28-101, 1893-65-203, 1900-
     8-223, 1901-5-47, 1901-37-247, 1901-46-5, 1902-84-253.
10   See Jim Rees 'Captain Thomas Troy 1860-1904', Arklow Historical Society
     Journal 2010

INDEX

Annacurra, 123, 210, 259.
Anderson, Revd Thomas, 32.
Arklow
– Dispensary and Sanitary Committee (and office), 51, 54, 55, 56-8, 64, 69, 74-6, 78, 80, 94-5, 188, 222, 236, 241-2, 269.
– extent of Catholic parish, 46-7.
– fever hospital, 56, 69, 74, 75, 77, 78, 95-6, 222.
– general description of, 69-74.
– harbour board, 29, 143, 219.
– Land League branch formed, 41.
– port development, 27-9, 41, 52, 55, 68, 87, 145, 170, 183, 214, 229.
– town commissioners, 69, 71, 87, 91, 95, 123, 143, 148, 180, 181, 182, 189-190, 195-6, 205-6, 212, 220, 234-5, 242-8, 252, 258, 265.
Arklow Independent Ratepayers Association, 128, 133, 134, 144, 189-198, 209, 215, 218-9, 224, 234-5, 268, 270.
Arklow Amateur Aquatic & Athletic Sports, 79, 99.
Ashford, 41, 92, 123, 259, 263.
Aughrim, 88, 100, 143, 208, 234, 259, 264.
Avoca (Ovoca), 27, 49, 73, 87, 122, 123, 136, 137, 141-3, 234, 248, 259, 263.

Balfour, Arthur, 112-3, 123, 156, 163.
Ballot Act (1872), 35.
Ballyfad, 99-121, 180.
Ballygarrett, 47.
Ballykillageer, 95.
Baltinglass, 41.
Barraniskey, *see Barniskey*
Barndarrig, 32, 41, 49, 58, 59, 60, 64, 79, 88, 123, 142, 143, 147, 239, 259, 263.
Barniskey, 136.
Barrack Croghan, 102, 114.
Biggar, Joseph, 35, 37, 40, 174.
Birthistle, Thomas, 146, 196, 207, 215, 217, 220.
Blunt, Wilfred, 117, 119.
Boycotting, 40, 44, 54, 106, 109, 111, 116, 119, 120, 122, 124, 125, 126, 129, 131-2, 136, 147, 158, 160, 180, 217, 233.
Brabazon, William, 44, 100.
Bradford, David, 215, 217, 220.
Bradford, John, 190-2, 234-5.
Bradford, Patrick, 206.
Bray, 32, 41, 44, 88, 89, 92, 136, 210, 228, 259.
Brooke, George, 101, 103, 108.
Butt, Isaac, 32-3, 36-9, 268.
Byrne, Hugh, 133, 209, 215, 220, 240.
Byrne, William, 42. .
Byrne, William, 161.

Caldwell, James B, 91.

Carlow College, 20.
Carnew, 41, 259.
Carysfort, earls of. *Also see Proby family,* 24, 26-7, 51, 55, 66-9, 78, 81-2, 88, 93, 145, 148, 160, 164, 167, 170, 190, 193, 219, 241.
Castletown, 46, 49, 81, 83, 92-3, 108, 123, 143, 208.
Catholic emancipation, 17, 18, 20, 30, 91.
Clarke, James, 208.
Clarke, Fr Michael (Avoca), 122-6, 136, 141-2, 156, 200.
Clarke, Michael, 208, 215, 217, 220.
Coercion Acts, 41-3, 86, 103, 112, 194.
Condren, Daniel, 51, 144, 190, 195-8, 207, 215-7, 220, 241, 244.
Coolgreaney, 101-18, 119, 128, 132, 143, 151,   170, 207. .
Coolmore, 122.
Corbet, William M.P., 28, 42-3, 55, 68, 89-90, 92, 117, 140, 155, 227-32, 251-3, 261, 265.
County Wicklow Farmers' Club and Tenants' Defence Association, 32, 36, 49.
County Wicklow Property Defence Association, 44, 109.
Criminal Law and Procedure (Ireland) Act (1887), 123, 124.
Culleton, John, 134-5.

Dalton, Fr B, 48.
Davitt, Michael, 38-9, 114-5, 176, 181, 185, 231.
Delahunt, Henry, 190-2, 196, 234-5.
Delgany, 90, 227, 259.
Dillon, John, M.P., 99, 111, 112, 116.
Dillon, Fr Patrick J, 104-5, 107, 114-6, 117, 132-4.
Dixon, S, 160.
Donnelly, John, 133, 240.
Doyle, James, 146, 196, 207.
Doyle, Joseph, 190-2, 234-5.
Doyle, Fr P, 32,
Dunphy family, 13-17.
Dunphy, Fr. James,
– Arklow appointment, 20-22
– becomes parish priest, 25
– death and funeral, 262.
– early life, 13-20.
– political stance, *passim*
Dunphy, Fr. William, 13-4, 49, 55, 116, 263.
Durrow, 13, 15-6.

Electoral system (and franchise), 84, 148, 189-92, 196-8, 215, 216, 234, 268-70.
English, Andrew, 161, 162.
Esmonde, Sir Thomas, 104, 107.
Evans, John, 96, 240.

Farrelly, Fr Laurence, 48-9, 55, 104-8, 116, 121-6, 136-44, 146-8, 159, 183-5, 199, 203, 205, 207, 208, 229-31, 244, 248-9, 263, 264.
Flavin, Fr James, 48, 55, 79-80, 142, 143.
fishing fleet, 97.
fishermen, in support of tenants, 110.

Fitzhenry, W H, 190, 215.
Fitzwilliam, Lord, 100.
Fogarty, Owen, 52, 66, 144, 188.
Ford, William, 111.
Furlong, Anna, 129.
Furlong, Fr J L (Gorey), 108.
Freeman, George, 104, 107, 111, 115. .
French, Dr, 58, 75.

Galvin, Fr Richard, 32, 35.
Garvey, Peter, 183, 198.
Gladstone, William, 31, 32, 34, 40-5, 85-6, 90-2, 117, 173, 175, 177-9, 256.
Gordon Highlanders, 162.
Gorey, 93, 98, 104, 108, 110, 114, 144.   .
Gray, Sir John, 34.

Hallowes, Revd Richard, 123, 149-69, 182, 200-203, 220, 231, 239, 245, 246, 249,
    252, 263, 269.
Halpin, Dr Richard, 58, 66, 67, 75-6, 78, 133, 223, 240, 241, 252, 253.
Halpin, Captain Robert, 226-9, 231,232.
Halpin, Dr Stopford William, 57, 70.
Hamilton, Edward, 104-7, 109-13,121.
Hanagan, Laurence, 207.
Hannigan/Hanagan, James, 51, 57, 74, 75.
Hannigan/Hanagan, John, 195-7, 208, 235, 244.
Harpur, Revd, 151, 153, 155.
Harrington, Timothy, 103, 124, 170,178, 207.
Harrison, Revd, 151, 153, 160-2, 164-9, 200-1, 239, 245-6, 249-52, 258.
Hibernian Mining Company, 27.
Hoffe, Revd, 151, 155, 201.
Home Rule, 31-8, *passim.*
Howard, Dr Richard, 133, 195, 197, 209, 221, 223, 235, 241, 242, 244-5.
Hudson, Richard, 128, 134-5, 194, 219, 235.
Hudson, Robert, 82.
Hurlbert, Henry, 107, 114, 132.

Inch, 46, 55.
Irish College, Rome, 20.
Irish Loyal and Patriotic Union, 89, 91, 100, 171.
Irish National Federation, 206, 207-9, 210, 212-3, 215-7, 218-9, 225, 227-9, 231,
    235, 260, 265, 271.
Irish National Land League, 41, 109.
Irish National League, 31, 44-5, 67, 81, 86-88, 93, 94, 103, 104, 108, 109, 113,
    116, 120, 121-2, 124, 127-9, 136, 142-3, 146, 147-8, 175, 180, 190-5, 204-9,
    243, 256, 260, 268.

Johnstown, 46-7, 101, 116, 143.

Kavanagh, D, 160.
Kavanagh, Denis, 234-5, 240.
Kavanagh, John, 128.

O'Brien, William, M.P., 103, 116, 170, 181.
Obstructionism, 35, 37.
O'Byrne, William Richard, 35.
O'Connor, James, 229, 234.
O'Connor, John, 122, 124-6.
O'Donnell, Fr Pierce, 55, 101, 104, 105, 116, 141, 142, 207, 223.
O'Neill, James, 161.
O'Neill, John, 111.
O'Neill, Fr William, 101ff, 142.
Orange Order/Orangemen, 34, 91, 109, 169.
Ormsby, Revd William, 22, 23, 150.
O'Shea, Katherine, 172-7, 210, 225.
O'Shea, Captain William, 172-6, 179.

Parnell, Charles Stewart, 29, 35—45, 55, 68, 84-87, 90-1, 103, 108, 131, 145, 147-8, 170-185, 186, 187, 189, 204-215, 217, 225, 230, 251, 259.
Parnell family, 35, 225.
Perpetual Crimes Act, 111.
Persico, Archbishop, 116, 118,119, 121.
Pigott, Richard, 171.
Plan of Campaign, 103ff, 145, 151, 170.
'Priestcraft' (ram), 87-8.
Port development, *see under Arklow*
Proby family, 24.
Proby's Row *see St. Michael's Terrace*
Proby, William (5th earl of Carysfort), 26-7, 29, 69, 145, 167, 200.
Public health, 56-7, 76-7, 95. .

Quarries, 87, 131, 145, 170, 182, 186, 189, 205, 214, 236.
Queen's College, Cork (now NUI Cork), 61, 62.

Rathdowney, 13, 15, 16.
Rathdrum, 25, 32, 35, 41, 47, 49, 86, 88, 142, 259, 263.
Rathdrum Board of Guardians, 54, 56-7, 75-7, 87, 94-6, 222, 225, 263.
Redcross, 49, 136, 263.
Redmond, Archdeacon James, 21-30, 31-2, 35, 42, 49, 51, 69, 129, 142, 145, 150.
Redmond, John M.P., 42, 175, 231, 243, 251, 260.
Reform Act (1884), 84, 86.
Reynolds, John, 144, 190, 191, 192, 196, 207, 223, 234, 235.
Riverchapel, 108.
Rockwell College, 61.
Roundwood, 41, 210, 259.
Royal College of Physicians, Edinburgh, 63.
Royal College of Surgeons, Edinburgh, 63.
Royal Irish Constabulary (R.I.C.), 71, 111, 122-3, 136, 138-40, 156, 205, 232.
Ryan, Dr James, 76.

Scarlatina, 95-6.
Shaw, William, 38.
Sisters of Mercy convent, 25, 69, 142.
St Kieran's College, Kilkenny, 20.

St Mary's (Church of Ireland), 26,73.
Sts Mary and Peter's (R.C.), 69, 71.
St Michael's Terrace (Proby's Row), 27.
Storey, John, 133, 144, 223, 235, 240, 254.
Synod of Thurles, 20, 141.

Taylor/Taylour/Tailyour, Alexander, 81-2, 144, 157, 160, 169, 190-1, 193-4, 219, 223.
Tinahely, 41, 259.
Thomastown, 137.
Tottenham, Col. Charles George, 90, 232.
Townsend Trench, John, 164-5.
Trade unionism, 186-9, 206, 270.
Troy family, 129-130, 133, 201-2, 223, 252.
Troy, Thomas, 129-130, 133, 180, 190-2, 194, 209, 214, 215, 217, 219-20, 223, 234-5, 240, 242-8, 253-4, 258, 262, 265-6, 271.
Twomey, Harry, 130.
Twomey, J.K., 90, 130-1.
Tyrrell, James, 128, 215, 234, 235
Tyrrell, John, 128, 190-2, 194, 197, 198, 215, 219-20, 224, 234, 235, 240.

Walsh, Archbishop William, 66, 79-80, 92-3, 116, 160, 184-5, 243.
Waldron, Thomas, 122, 125, 126.
Wexford Gaol, 140-2.
Wicklow grand jury, 56-8, 222-3.
Wicklow Mining Company, 27, 29.
Wicklow town, 32, 41, 42, 47,91, 92, 98, 123, 136, 142, 143, 154, 180, 181, 189, 204, 206, 208, 209, 229, 232, 233, 234, 236, 259.
Women's suffrage, see also electoral system and franchise, 189.
Woodenbridge, 46, 137.